A Very Political Economy

A Very Political Economy

Peacebuilding and Foreign Aid
in the West Bank and Gaza

REX BRYNEN

UNITED STATES INSTITUTE OF PEACE PRESS
Washington, D.C.

United States Institute of Peace
1200 17th Street NW
Washington, DC 20036

First published 2000

Printed in the United States of America

The paper used in this publication meets the minimum requirements of American National Standards for Information Sciences—Permanence of Paper for Printed Library Materials, ANSI Z39.48-1984.

Library of Congress Cataloging-in-Publication Data
Brynen, Rex.
    A very political economy : peacebuilding and foreign aid in the West Bank and Gaza / Rex Brynen.
      p. cm.
    Includes bibliographical references and index.
    ISBN 1-929223-04-8 (pbk.)
    1. Economic assistance—West Bank. 2. Economic assistance—Gaza Strip. 3. Peace.
I. Title

HC415.254 .B79 2000
338.91'095695'3—dc21

                                  00-020541

Contents

Tables, Figures, Boxes, and Maps

Tables

Figures

Boxes

Maps

Foreword

In *A Very Political Economy*, Rex Brynen addresses a set of controversial subjects. First, there is the subject of foreign aid, a contentious issue for many donor and recipient nations and a hotly debated topic in the United States for at least the past twenty years. Second, there is the subject of the Israeli-Palestinian conflict, a conflict whose history is as long as the passions it arouses are high.

In this thought-provoking volume, Professor Brynen investigates the nature, extent, and impact of foreign aid dispatched to the West Bank and Gaza since Israel and the Palestine Liberation Organization signed the Oslo Agreement in September 1993. Brynen has sifted through all kinds of evidence, listened to dozens of key figures, surveyed a broad array of explanatory factors, and assessed the merits of competing claims and interpretations. As a consequence, the analytical course he has charted is well chosen and the conclusions he has reached are well supported. Whether readers agree with all of it or not, his frank assessment certainly offers major insight into the complex politics of peacebuilding, with lessons that extend well beyond the Middle East.

In researching this volume, the author interviewed numerous officials within donor governments, the Palestinian Authority, and international organizations, many of whom offered surprisingly frank opinions on the motives and ambitions of both donors and recipients and on the strengths and shortcomings of the machinery for raising and distributing foreign aid. Brynen has repaid these officials for their candor with a wealth of analysis that is not only astute and objective but also distinctly useful. Indeed, this volume's observations and conclusions seem virtually certain to influence the future making and implementation of aid policy in the West Bank and Gaza. The conclusions are also likely to be of value to those who must decide if and how to raise and disburse assistance in other parts of the world that are struggling to make the transition from long-term violence to enduring peace. With politicians, diplomats, and scholars now paying increasing attention to peacebuilding, rather than limiting their efforts more narrowly to peacemaking and peacekeeping, Brynen's criticisms and recommendations should find a large and attentive audience.

Mandated by Congress to promote and disseminate research into the causes of international conflict and the means by which it can be peacefully managed or resolved, the United States Institute of Peace puts a high premium on the kind of sophisticated and pragmatic analysis contained in *A Very Political Economy*. The Institute helped to support Brynen's research with funding from our Grant Program, and we are pleased to publish the results of his work. Aside from contributing to informed debate on the value of foreign aid as a tool for building peace and advancing the national interests of donor nations, *A Very Political Economy* enlarges the Institute's already substantial list of books concerned with conflicts in the Middle East. That body of research and analysis, we trust, reflects the breadth of opinion on how best to build peace in that volatile region. In just the past year, for instance, the Institute has published *The Enemy Has a Face*, John Wallach's account of how his Seeds of Peace program builds understanding and trust between Arab and Israeli youngsters; a revealing look at *Jordanians, Palestinians, and the Hashemite Kingdom* by Adnan Abu-Odeh, political adviser to both King Hussein and King Abdullah II; Helena Cobban's in-depth examination of *The Israeli-Syrian Peace Talks, 1991–96 and Beyond;* and two accounts—one by James A. Baker III and the other by Jan Egeland—of behind-the-scenes diplomacy that spurred the peace process in the 1990s, both of which appear in the edited volume *Herding Cats: Multiparty Mediation in a Complex World*. Other Institute books have included *In Pursuit of Peace: A History of the Israeli Peace Movement,* by Mordechai Bar-On; *Reluctant Neighbor: Turkey's Role in the Middle East,* edited by Henri J. Barkey; *Islamic Activism and U.S. Foreign Policy,* by Scott W. Hibbard and David Little; *The Arab World after Desert Storm,* by Muhammad Faour; and *Islam and Democracy,* by Timothy D. Sisk.

Whether written by individuals who have participated directly in the events they describe or by scholars from outside the region, these books all contribute to the Institute's effort to encourage well-informed and constructive consideration of the prospects for peace in the Middle East and how best to enhance those prospects. Professor Brynen's well-researched, insightful, and engaging book is very much at home among such company.

Richard H. Solomon, President
United States Institute of Peace

Acknowledgments

The intellectual journey upon which this book is based began in a very specific time and place: shortly after 10:25 A.M. on Monday, September 6, 1993, on a flight from Washington, D.C., to Montreal. There, on my trusty Apple Powerbook 170 laptop, I jotted down some initial thoughts on the economic challenges of the impending Palestinian-Israeli Declaration of Principles. A few days later, a brainstorming meeting of Canadian officials and academics met in Ottawa to discuss precisely that subject.

Six years later, much has changed. My indestructible old Mac, having faithfully traversed well over a hundred thousand miles, has been replaced by a much more powerful and stylish Powerbook G3. Well over $2 billion in donor assistance has flowed to the West Bank and Gaza. The Palestinian-Israeli peace process has shifted from optimism to stalemate and back again. And economic conditions in Palestine have faltered.

This book explores donor assistance in Palestine, the difficulties it has encountered, and the extent to which it has affected the prospects for peace. Despite the disappointments of the post-Oslo period, and the particular difficulties encountered by the aid effort, it is not a story of failure. For all its shortcomings, international assistance to the West Bank and Gaza has played an important and valuable role. It has also undergone an instructive process of evolution, generating a number of lessons relevant to other countries in war-to-peace transitions and other cases of international peacebuilding assistance.

My research would not have been possible without the encouragement of many. Friends and colleagues at the Canadian Department of Foreign Affairs (in which I briefly served as a member of the Policy Staff in 1994–95), the Canadian International Development Agency, the International Development Research Centre, the Palestinian Ministry of Planning and International Cooperation (MOPIC), the Palestinian Economic Council for Development and Reconstruction (PECDAR), the World Bank, the United Nations Relief and Works Agency (UNRWA), and the Office of the United Nations Special Coordinator in the Occupied Territories (UNSCO) were extremely helpful and supportive throughout my research. I would also like to thank those who assisted this project from other ministries of the Palestinian Authority or departments of the Palestine Liberation Organization, other foreign ministries and aid agencies, the International Monetary Fund (IMF), other agencies of the United Nations, and Palestinian and international nongovernmental organizations (NGOs).

In the course of my work, I have had the good fortune to cooperate with a number of overlapping research projects that have considerably benefited this study. One of these is the Pledges of Aid project, organized by Shep Foreman and Stewart Patrick at the Center on International Cooperation at New York University. The Palestinian case study for that project—coauthored with Hisham Awartani (Center for Palestine Studies and Research) and Clare Woodcraft (first at *Palestine Economic Pulse* and now at *Middle East Economic Survey*)—overlapped with portions of the present analysis. I am pleased to have had a chance to work with Hisham and Clare, and very grateful for their permission to publish some of the results of our joint research herein. I am also very grateful to the Center for Palestine Research and Studies for providing me with special polling data on Palestinian attitudes, and to Sari Hanafi and the Welfare Association for allowing me access to their draft report on funding for Palestinian NGOs.

In the category of general research projects that have enhanced this work are those by Nicole Ball at the Overseas Development Council (Washington, D.C.) and Jim Boyce at the University of Massachusetts; and the work on peace implementation undertaken by Terje Larsen, Mark Taylor, Rick Hooper, and their colleagues at Fafo (Oslo). I have shared ideas with a broad group of people, including colleagues at McGill University and a wide variety of contributors to the *Palestinian Development InfoNet*/PALDEV and *Palestinian Refugee ResearchNet*/*FOFOGNET* Internet networks. None of them, of course, bears any responsibility for the analyses presented herein.

Financial support for this project has been received from the United States Institute of Peace, the Social Science and Humanities Research Council, the Fonds FCAR, the Pledges of Aid project, McGill University, and the Interuniversity Consortium for Arab Studies (Montreal). Without such support this research would not have been possible. It certainly would not have been possible to pay the excellent research assistants who have worked with me during the course of this project: Mira Sucharov (Jerusalem); Michelle Kjorlien (Washington, D.C.); Joelle Zahar, José Hamra, and Maren Zerriffi (Montreal); and Manal Jamal (everywhere). Their hard work and good cheer have been much appreciated. Helen Wilicka was a wonder in fixing up many of the tables and charts. Equally appreciated has been the constant support of Nigel Quinney at the United States Institute of Peace, who oversaw the transformation of my manuscript into this final printed product.

For readers who have made it thus far through the acknowledgments, I offer a final and most important one to my wife, Alex, and to our children, David and Chloe. Alex assisted with innumerable aspects of this project, read multiple drafts of the manuscript, and proved (as ever) to be my most valuable critic. David and Chloe, on the other hand, will be enormously pleased that the book is now finished and that my computer is now free for more entertaining uses.

Acronyms

AFESD	Arab Fund for Economic and Social Development
AHLC	Ad-Hoc Liaison Committee
CFSP	Common Foreign and Security Policy (of the European Union)
CG	Consultative Group
CIDA	Canadian International Development Agency
COPP	Committee on the Palestinian Police
CPRS	Center for Palestine Research and Studies
DAC	Development Assistance Committee (of the OECD)
DFLP	Democratic Front for the Liberation of Palestine
EAP	Emergency Assistance Program
EC	European Commission
EGS	employment generation schemes
EHRP	Education and Health Rehabilitation Project
EIB	European Investment Bank
EPD	Environmental Planning Directorate (of MOPIC)
ERP	Emergency Rehabilitation Project
EU	European Union
FCO	Foreign and Commonwealth Office (of the United Kingdom)
FIDA	Palestinian Democratic Union
GAO	General Accounting Office (of the U.S. Congress)
IDF	Israeli Defense Forces
IFC	International Finance Corporation
IFI	international financial institution
IMF	International Monetary Fund
INGO	international NGO
JLC	Joint Liaison Committee

JMCC	Jerusalem Media and Communications Center
LACC	Local Aid Coordination Committee
MAS	Palestine Economic Policy Research Institute
MIDP	Municipal Infrastructure Development Project
MIGA	Multilateral Investment Guarantee Agency
MOPIC	Ministry of Planning and International Cooperation (of the PA)
NGO	nongovernmental organization
OECD	Organization for Economic Cooperation and Development
OPIC	Overseas Private Investment Corporation
PA	Palestinian Authority (also Palestinian National Authority)
PCBS	Palestinian Central Bureau of Statistics
PCHR	Palestinian Center for Human Rights
PDP	Palestinian Development Plan
PECDAR	Palestinian Economic Council for Development and Reconstruction
PENA	Palestinian Environmental Authority
PFLP	Popular Front for the Liberation of Palestine
PHC	Palestinian Housing Council
PIP	Peace Implementation Program (of UNRWA)
PLC	Palestinian Legislative Council
PLO	Palestine Liberation Organization
PMD	Public Monitoring Department (of the PA)
PMO	Prime Minister's Office (Israel)
PNGO	Palestinian NGO
PPIP	Palestinian Public Investment Program
PPP	Palestinian People's Party
REDWG	Regional Economic Development Working Group
RWG	Refugee Working Group
SIDA	Swedish International Development Agency
SWG	Sectoral Working Group
TAP	Tripartite Action Plan
TATF	Technical Assistance Trust Fund
UNDP	United Nations Development Program
UNHCR	United Nations High Commissioner for Refugees
UNICEF	United Nations Children's Fund

UNRWA	United Nations Relief and Works Agency
UNSCO	Office of the United Nations Special Coordinator in the Occupied Territories
USAID	U.S. Agency for International Development
WFP	World Food Program

Chronology

1993

September 13   Israeli-Palestinian Declaration of Principles (Oslo Agreement)

October 1   Conference to Support Middle East Peace, Washington, D.C.
— first pledging conference (1994–98) for West Bank and Gaza

November 5   first formal meeting of Ad-Hoc Liaison Committee (AHLC), Paris

December 16   first Consultative Group meeting, Paris

December 20   police donors conference, Oslo

1994

January 27–28   special donors meeting on Palestinian start-up and transitional budgetary expenditures, Paris
— establishment of Holst Fund

March 24   police donors conference, Cairo
— formation of Coordinating Committee for International Assistance to the Palestinian Police Force (COPP)

April 29   Protocol on Economic Relations

May 4   Agreement on the Gaza Strip and Jericho Area

May 23   informal meeting of the AHLC, Washington, D.C.

June 9–10   formal AHLC meeting, Paris

August 24	Agreement on the Preparatory Transfer of Powers and Responsibilities
September 1–2	informal AHLC meeting, Washington, D.C.
September 9	Consultative Group meeting, Paris — postponed due to dispute over Jerusalem projects
September 13	Oslo declaration — parties agree not to bring contentious issues before donors
October 26	Israeli-Jordanian Peace Treaty
November 29–30	formal AHLC meeting, Brussels — formation of Joint Liaison Committee (JLC) — formation of Local Aid Coordination Committee (LACC) — Understanding on Revenues, Expenditures and Donor Funding for the Palestinian Authority

1995

January 11	informal AHLC meeting, Washington, D.C.
January 30–31	first meeting (of many) of the LACC, Gaza — formation of Sectoral Working Groups
April 3	informal AHLC meeting, Washington, D.C.
April 27–28	formal AHLC meeting, Paris — first Tripartite Action Plan on Revenues, Expenditures and Donor Funding
August 27	Protocol on Further Transfer of Powers and Responsibilities
September 27	AHLC "experts" meeting, Washington, D.C.
September 28	Palestinian-Israeli Interim Agreement AHLC ministerial meeting, Washington, D.C.
October–December	Israeli redeployment in West Bank
October 18–19	Consultative Group meeting, Paris — focus on requirements of Interim Agreement
November 4	assassination of Israeli prime minister Yitzhak Rabin

November 30   informal AHLC meeting, Washington, D.C.

1996

January 9   ministerial Conference on Economic Assistance to the
                     Palestinian People, Paris
                     — high-profile mobilization of aid before Palestinian
                        elections

January 20   Palestinian elections

February–March   four suicide bombings in Jerusalem and Tel Aviv

April 12   informal emergency AHLC meeting, Brussels
                     — focus on impact of closure

May 29   Israeli elections
                     — election of Benjamin Netanyahu as prime minister

September 5   informal AHLC meeting, Washington, D.C.

November 19–20   Consultative Group meeting, Paris

December 10   informal AHLC meeting, Brussels

1997

January 15   Protocol Concerning the Redeployment in Hebron

June 5   informal AHLC meeting, Washington, D.C.

November 6   informal AHLC meeting, Washington, D.C.

December 14–15   Consultative Group meeting, Paris

1998

May 13   informal AHLC meeting, Oslo

October 23   Wye River Memorandum

November 30   Conference to Support Peace and Development in the
                     Middle East, Washington, D.C.
                     — second pledging conference (1999–2003) for West
                        Bank and Gaza

1999

February 4	AHLC meeting, Frankfurt
February 4–5	Consultative Group meeting, Frankfurt — presentation of Palestinian Development Plan for 1999–2003
May 4	expiry of Oslo Agreement
May 17	Israeli elections — election of Ehud Barak as prime minister
September 4	Sharm el-Sheikh Memorandum on Implementation Timeline of Outstanding Commitments of Agreements Signed and the Resumption of Permanent Status Negotiations
October 15	AHLC meeting, Tokyo

A Very Political Economy

1

Introduction

The Political Economy of Peacebuilding

IN JUNE 1967 ISRAELI FORCES OCCUPIED East Jerusalem, the West Bank, and the Gaza Strip—the only portions of Palestine that had remained under Arab control following the establishment of Israel in 1948. More than a quarter century of military occupation followed.

On September 13, 1993, after months of secret, Norwegian-mediated negotiations, Palestine Liberation Organization (PLO) leader Yasir Arafat, Israeli prime minister Yitzhak Rabin, and U.S. president Bill Clinton met in Washington, D.C., to sign the Oslo Agreement—or, as it was formally known, the Israeli-Palestinian Declaration of Principles. In it, the two core parties in the Arab-Israeli conflict agreed that "it is time to put an end to decades of confrontation and conflict, recognize their mutual legitimate and political rights, and strive to live in peaceful coexistence and mutual dignity and security to achieve a just, lasting and comprehensive peace settlement." To do so, they committed themselves to a series of principles, to various interim measures (including partial Israeli territorial withdrawal and limited Palestinian self-government), and to eventual negotiations on the so-called permanent status issues: Jerusalem, refugees, settlements, security arrangements, and borders.[1] A few weeks later, on October 1, representatives of some forty-three countries met in Washington and pledged over $2 billion in aid to support the anticipated five-year interim period, an amount that would eventually grow to over $4 billion.

This first Washington donors conference was intended, its organizers announced, "to support the historic political breakthrough in the Middle East through a broad-based multilateral effort to mobilize resources to promote reconstruction and development in the West Bank and Gaza."[2] The level of aid promised by the international community reflected the strategic importance of the

3

Palestinian-Israeli peace process, as well as the widespread view that economic development had a key supporting role to play. It represented, as the president of the World Bank remarked, an "unprecedented opportunity: to open the door to development—and to invest in peace."[3] "[It] is very important," noted another World Bank spokesperson, "for the people to see very early that their situation will improve under peace."[4] Certainly, there was much anticipation of such a peace dividend within the territories themselves: one opinion survey in June 1994 found that more than a third of Palestinians felt that the peace process would improve their economic situation, while only one in seven expressed fear that conditions would worsen.[5]

Five years later, the outcome of the aid effort appeared rather uneven, measured against the standards of a healthy peace process or sustainable development. In November 1995 Prime Minister Yitzhak Rabin was assassinated by an Israeli extremist opposed to the peace process. Six months later, his successor, Labor Party leader Shimon Peres, was defeated in elections by a hard-line Likud coalition headed by Benjamin Netanyahu—defeated in part because of a series of terrorist bombings in Jerusalem and Tel Aviv by Palestinian rejectionists. The new government was openly critical of the Oslo process and reluctant to withdraw from additional Palestinian territories as its predecessor had undertaken to do. Instead, the government intensified Israeli settlement activity in the occupied territories despite widespread international condemnation. Palestinian-Israeli cooperation, and implementation of previously signed agreements, effectively ground to a halt. On May 4, 1999, the Oslo Agreement itself expired without resolution of permanent status issues. Later that same month, on May 17, a pivotal election in Israel saw the defeat of Netanyahu and the return to power of a Labor government, led now by Ehud Barak. With this, the prospects for diplomatic progress became much brighter.

The economic picture has also been mixed—or worse. The resolution of key issues (notably regarding Gaza port and safe passage between Gaza and the West Bank) was delayed. By mid-1997, and despite the disbursement of some $1.5 billion in international aid, more than two-thirds of Palestinians expressed the view that the peace process had harmed the economy.[6] Periodic Israeli closure of the West Bank and Gaza prevented movement in or out of these areas, cost millions of dollars in lost employment and exports, deterred investment, and undercut development efforts. As a result, Palestinian per capita incomes actually *declined* in each year following the Oslo Agreement, dropping by almost one-quarter before stabilizing in 1998. In addition to the costs of closure, the Palestinian Authority (PA) and local nongovernmental organizations (NGOs) frequently complained about the tardiness or inappropriateness of much donor assistance. Problems of inefficiency and corruption in the PA itself further clouded the picture.

This combination of political setbacks and economic restrictions combined to create a situation very different from the one donors had initially imagined. At a donor meeting in December 1997, the World Bank noted:

> Many of you were here at the first [Consultative Group] for the West Bank and Gaza in December 1993. The atmosphere then was very different. There was a sense of anticipation. We were quite confident that Palestinian economic skills would at last flourish; that sustained growth was feasible; and that a sound economy would make a major contribution to peace.
>
> That was almost exactly four years ago. Where do we find ourselves today?
>
> Clearly, not where we expected to be. Far from witnessing a renaissance of the Palestinian economy, we have lived through an extended crisis —punctuated by terrorist acts and severe economic decline. Palestinian real per capita incomes have fallen by a quarter. Unemployment has risen from less than ten percent to over twenty percent today, with peaks of fifty percent in Gaza in times of tight border closure. The number of Palestinians living in poverty, using a benchmark of $650 per annum, has risen to more than twenty-five percent of the population, and over a third in Gaza.
>
> Private investment, far from increasing, has collapsed. Estimates suggest that about $1 billion was invested in 1993, and that this fell to a mere $250 million by 1996—truly sobering when you recall that Palestinian economic strategy has always been based on vigorous private sector growth.
>
> To put it bluntly: we expected the economic program to succeed, and to strengthen the political process. Instead, political conflict has undermined the Palestinian economy and blunted the efforts of donors.[7]

This volume examines the history and assesses the impact of external assistance to the West Bank and Gaza during the Oslo period, beginning with the 1993 Washington donors conference and extending through to the election of the Barak government in May 1999. There are several reasons to undertake such a task. Perhaps most important, the donor effort in Palestine is not yet over: on the contrary, donors met again in Washington in November 1998 to pledge some $3 billion in additional support for the territories over the next several years. If continuing assistance is to have greatest effect, it is essential that the lessons of the past be identified and understood. As this study will also show, the process of economic assistance has been intimately bound up with both the political consolidation of the Palestinian Authority and the dynamics of Palestinian-Israeli negotiation. Understanding either of these important processes, therefore, requires a recognition of how they have been shaped by the flow of external resources.

The experience of foreign aid in Palestine, moreover, has implications not only for the future of Palestinians but also for a great many other cases where the international community has sought to promote peacebuilding through development assistance. To what extent did the deterioration in the peace process and the decline of the Palestinian economy cast doubt on the efficacy of donors' efforts? What were the shortcomings of aid, whether in terms of resource mobilization, donor-donor and donor-PA coordination, or project selection and implementation? To what extent were these shortcomings unavoidable—that is, structurally and largely unalterably embedded in the social, economic, and political context of the territories—and to what extent might more effective models and mechanisms be found? Indeed, what evolutions occurred in donor assistance over the years, and to what effect? Where could and should assistance be most effectively targeted? What trade-offs have been involved? And what are the social and political—as well as economic and developmental—implications of all of this?

This volume addresses all of these questions. Chapter 2 sketches the context of the Palestinian effort: the legacies of Israeli occupation, the contours of the Palestinian economy, patterns of prior international aid, and the course of the Middle East peace process. While much of this information may be already known to some readers, it provides essential background to those who are less familiar with the region. Chapters 3 through 6 explore different aspects of the aid process: the mobilization of resources, coordination among donors, the factors shaping the timely delivery of assistance, and the sectoral allocation of such aid. Finally, chapter 7 summarizes findings from the Palestinian experience. It recounts some of the issues raised at the outset of this study and draws lessons relevant not only to the West Bank and Gaza but also to other comparable peacebuilding efforts.

It is useful first to set the Palestinian case against a larger backdrop: the general challenges involved in using international donor assistance to support war-to-peace transitions, as well as the particular ways in which donor assistance is bound up with local political processes. The remainder of this chapter seeks not only to illuminate some of the operational dilemmas and political complexities of the Palestinian case, but also to facilitate the formulation of later, more general conclusions about peacebuilding and foreign aid.

THE POLITICS OF GIVING

Challenges of Peacebuilding and Foreign Aid

Through the 1990s, and more particularly with the end of the Cold War, the international community has increasingly become involved in multilateral efforts to support transitions from civil conflict to peace. Typically, these efforts involve not only the traditional tools of diplomacy (good offices, mediation, and monitoring) and the established mechanisms of military peacekeeping but also a variety of social and economic objectives and instrumentalities, underpinned by substantial commitments of financial support. Consequently, the past decade has seen a substantial and growing share of foreign aid resources devoted to conflict-related programming, whether in the form of humanitarian relief operations in times of conflict, or reconstruction afterward. Bilateral humanitarian and refugee assistance expenditures by Western donors increased from around $1 billion in 1990 to over $3 billion in 1995, while the amount channeled through the major multilateral agencies increased from $1 billion to over $2 billion during the same period.[8] Total aid to war-torn and postconflict countries was still larger, averaging over $11 billion per year from 1993 to 1997. Given the decline in Western aid during this same period, this represents an increase from 20 percent to 28 percent of all official development assistance (ODA).[9] In the case of the U.S. Agency for International Development (USAID), for example, five of the top ten recipients of assistance (Bosnia, South Africa, El Salvador, Haiti, and Mozambique) are postconflict countries and several others (Israel, Egypt, and Jordan) are linked to regional peace processes.[10] In the case of the World Bank (the more formal name is the International Bank for Reconstruction and Development [IBRD]) some 16 percent of its total lending portfolio in 1998 was with postconflict countries, up from 5–8 percent in the 1980s (figure 1.1).[11] If conflict-prone countries were added, the proportion would be much higher still: Indonesia, Nigeria, and Yugoslavia together account for around $1 billion in annual bilateral donor assistance and some 9 percent of current World Bank lending.[12] In per capita terms, almost all of the top twenty ODA recipients around the developing world are conflict or postconflict cases. Donors, for example, disbursed some $1.4 billion in aid to Cambodia between 1992 and 1995 to support political transition; pledged some $2.0 billion for reconstruction in Haiti (1995– 99); and undertook to support the $5.1 billion Priority Reconstruction Program (1996–99) for Bosnia.

Various terms have been used to define all or part of this process. In his *Agenda for Peace,* then UN secretary-general Boutros Boutros-Ghali defined "postconflict peacebuilding" as "action to identify and support structures which will tend to strengthen and solidify peace in order to avoid a relapse into conflict," and "rebuilding the institutions and infrastructures of nations torn by civil war and strife," involving such specific measures as "disarming the previously warring parties and the restoration of order, the custody and possible destruction of weapons, repatriating refugees, advisory and training support for security personnel, monitoring elections, advancing efforts to protect human rights, reforming or strengthening governmental institutions and promoting formal and informal processes of political participation."[13] Other terminology—"postconflict reconstruction," "transitional assistance," "peace nurturing," "complex humanitarian emergencies," and "peace implementation," among others—has also been used, each term having slightly different connotations. Part of the problem in defining the process arises

Figure 1.1. World Bank Commitments to Postconflict Countries

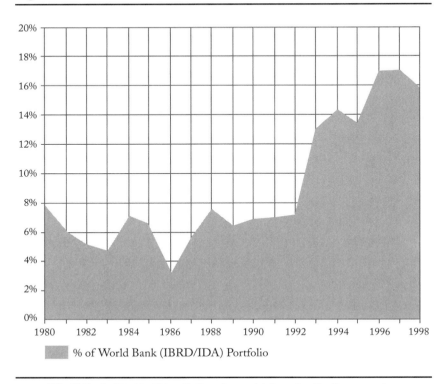

% of World Bank (IBRD/IDA) Portfolio

Source: World Bank, *The World Bank's Experience with Post-Conflict Reconstruction* (Washington, D.C.: World Bank Operations Evaluation Division, 1998), 13.

from its relative novelty: although reconstruction assistance is nothing new (as the post–World War II Marshall Plan demonstrates), both the range of instrumentalities employed and the multilateral character of interventions are. Further complicating the picture is the frequent involvement of so-called second-generation peacekeeping missions, where (as in Bosnia) elements of peace enforcement, humanitarian relief, and reconstruction are added to the picture.[14]

Perhaps most important of all, the challenges of contemporary postwar reconstruction are magnified by the civil character of most of the conflicts concerned. As Steven Holtzman has noted, this severely complicates the tasks at hand: "Aside from damage to physical infrastructure, the state apparatus and economic potential (such as in natural disasters and external warfare), it is the fabric of societies which has been torn and in many ways transformed. Conflict alters societies, creating incentives, patterns of behavior and institutional legacies which influence the reconstruction process."[15]

Indeed, the very concept of "peace" has a far more ambiguous character in the context of civil conflict than it does in the context of interstate war. In the latter case, the identity of the combatants is clear and their formal status established by principles of state sovereignty. Demarcation lines can be set between armies, formal armistices or peace agreements signed, and the disengagement or withdrawal of military forces monitored by the deployment of traditional peacekeeping operations. In the former case, however, societies are literally at war with themselves. Political legitimacy is unclear—indeed, it is the object of the conflict—and hence parties may not recognize each other's right to participate in the peace process. Although in most cases the resolution of civil conflict involves some form of formal peace agreement between the parties, these agreements are often transitional in nature, leaving key issues unresolved. Indeed, it may be during the "in-between" period, when some negotiations are being finalized, transitional agreements are being implemented, and contending parties are jockeying for the best possible political positions, that outcomes are most uncertain and international engagement is most critical. One useful way of thinking about this is offered by Michael W. Doyle, who notes that "peace" itself should be thought of as a spectrum or process rather than as a single discrete good. Consequently, "peacebuilding" involves fostering a political and societal shift from anarchy and civil violence to increasingly effective, widely accepted, and nonviolent mechanisms of conflict resolution.[16] Inherent in this conception is the uncertainty of the process and the constant and very real danger of a return to violence. As Canadian foreign minister Lloyd Axworthy has noted:

> I see peacebuilding as casting a life line to foundering societies struggling to end the cycle of violence, restore civility, and get back on their feet. After the fighting has stopped and the immediate humanitarian needs have been addressed, there exists a brief critical period when a country sits balanced on a fulcrum. Tilted the wrong way, it retreats into conflict. But with the right help, delivered during that brief, critical window of opportunity, it will move toward peace and stability.
>
> This is not, of course, an easy thing to do. These are highly volatile situations, where the needs are many and the time to respond is short. An effective response often requires co-ordination among organizations— non-governmental organizations, the military, and civilian experts—that usually work independently. It requires horizontal thinking that cuts across military, diplomatic, and aid-based solutions. And it has become clear from the events in Bosnia, Rwanda, and now Zaire that, while its thinking may have evolved, the international community does not yet have the tools it needs for the task of peacebuilding.[17]

Donor Responsiveness

Does the international community indeed lack, as Axworthy suggests, "the tools it needs for the task of peacebuilding"? One way of exploring such issues of urgency, uncertainty, and appropriate mechanisms is by examining *donor responsiveness* to war-to-peace transitions. Such responsiveness can be assessed along four inter-related dimensions:

- *Mobilizing assistance.* A first step in any peacebuilding effort is the generation of the required resources. How much have donors pledged in support of peace-building? What forms have these pledges taken, and how have they been expressed? What factors shape the relative and absolute size of the pledges? Are donor pledges adequate for the tasks at hand? What accounts for varia-tion (among donors and across conflicts) in donor mobilization?

- *Coordinating assistance.* Whatever the level of resources generated by the international community, these are likely to be most effective when there is a greater degree of multilateral coordination among donors, agencies, and recipients. How can such coordination be fostered, at both the headquarters and the field levels? What particular roles might be assumed by the United Nations and by the international financial institutions (IFIs)? To what extent might donors be able to use their collective resources to encourage or discourage certain behaviors on the part of local actors, whether through donor conditionality or otherwise?

- *Delivering assistance.* In some cases, there appears to be a significant gap between the level of resources promised by donors and the amounts that actually find their way to the ground. How quickly, and to what extent, are pledges of support translated into actual peacebuilding programs on the ground? What obstacles impede the timely delivery of assistance, and what actions can be taken to overcome these?

- *Allocating assistance.* Spending donor money is one thing—and spending it in the right places is quite another. To what extent are international assistance programs responsive to local social and economic needs and at the same time supportive of the political objectives of peacebuilding? To what extent do the parties (donors, agencies, recipient governments, and NGOs) agree on priorities? What are these? What factors shape the agenda for assistance?

Mobilizing Assistance

The level of donor mobilization in support of peacebuilding can be seen from several perspectives: first, in absolute terms of the total amount pledged; second, relative to local needs; and third, relative to the amounts generated by other donors and in support of other war-to-peace transitions. The first two indicators measure the adequacy of international mobilization. The third, however, provides an interesting window into donor motives.

A quick glance shows that levels of donor financial support for peacebuilding vary across cases and countries. Some donors appear more generous than others in any given case; some conflicts attract more peacebuilding aid than others. It can be argued, of course—as neorealist international relations theory would predict—that this variation is primarily shaped by strategic relevance, measured in such terms as geographic distance from the donor and the perceived threats to donor interests that might arise from unresolved regional conflict. Such an approach would underscore that development assistance has always been a mechanism of foreign policy and hence has reflected the strategic and economic priorities of donors. It would also underscore the importance of examining interdonor politics and, in particular, any jockeying for international profile and regional leverage that might accompany donor pledges. Certainly, the Palestinian case provides any number of significant examples of such rivalry among donors, as will be seen later.

In fact, donor mobilization for reconstruction *does* tend to be greatest among the most affected donors and in respect to more strategically important areas, and least among distant donors and in respect of strategically marginal areas. However, realpolitik fails to fully explain why, in a time of scarce donor resources, substantial amounts are still mobilized for some African conflicts (Angola, Mozambique, and Rwanda) despite the apparent strategic marginality of these areas. Part of the answer to this puzzle may lie in the rise of liberal institutionalism and the emergence of international humanitarian norms. Media coverage (the "CNN factor") and other domestic factors may also play an important role in foreign policy formation regarding peace and conflict.[18]

In addition to the question of the level of donor mobilization, related questions can be raised about how sustained this mobilization is. The World Bank highlights this as a key shortcoming: while "sustainable transitions out of conflict take several years," there is a "tendency for donors to disengage once the conflict has receded from public attention."[19] Thus, any analysis of donor support should also address the potential for donor fatigue.

Coordinating Assistance

As peace processes develop and donor programs expand, peacebuilding frequently faces severe problems of coordination. According to the World Bank, "There are serious shortcomings in the present arrangements for aid coordination in reconstruction, as evidenced by fragmentation of assistance and large administrative burdens. The overlaps and gaps in mandates and sheer number of actors . . . can exacerbate confusion and induce delays."[20] Alvaro de Soto, former UN special representative in El Salvador, writing of the weak communications between UN agencies and the IFIs, likened the situation to a patient on an operating table "with the left and right sides of his body separated by a curtain and unrelated surgery being performed on each side."[21] Such lack of coordination prevents synergy from emerging between donor efforts, increases the possibility that agencies will support contradictory or incompatible initiatives, and makes it difficult for actors to learn critical lessons from the experiences of others. A multiplicity of uncoordinated donor programs can (in the short term) overwhelm the weak institutions of a recipient country and (in the medium and longer term) inhibit strategic planning, thus diminishing a recipient's longer-term ability to set its own developmental agenda.

Frequently, the signing of a peace agreement is followed by formal pledges of transitional aid by donors, often in multilateral pledging conferences. At this time, donors may begin to establish new architecture for aid mobilization and coordination, or they may rely on other mechanisms, such as an existing World Bank consultative group. For effective coordination to occur, those institutions or fora charged with the task require a clear mandate (usually defined in functional terms) and the authority (both legal and moral) to perform the task. Transparent information flows are central to effective coordination. Finally it is important to stress that coordination is not merely a technocratic exercise, but, as Mark Taylor notes, a fundamentally political exercise, both in its donor-recipient and donor-donor dimensions.[22] Coordination may be inhibited by the fact that donors are simultaneously peacebuilding partners and political-economic competitors. The result may be an excess of support for certain types of projects (such as infrastructure or technical assistance projects that might be serviced by private-sector suppliers in the donor country) and a shortage of support for other equally critical areas (such as security-sector reform).

Within the UN system, the largely autonomous character of the major humanitarian and development actors—the United Nations High Commissioner for Refugees (UNHCR), the World Food Program (WFP), the United Nations Children's Fund (UNICEF), the United Nations Development Program (UNDP), and, in the Palestinian case, the United Nations Relief and Works Agency (UNRWA)—has tended to inhibit optimal interagency cooperation, although the reform package announced by UN secretary-general Kofi Annan seeks in part to address this problem.[23] Coordination problems are further compounded when peacekeeping missions are also involved, thereby involving both the Department of Peacekeeping Operations and the national authorities of the various military contingents.

Effective coordination is also problematic between NGOs and international organizations. This is due in part to their very different organizational cultures.[24] NGOs may vigorously guard their operational terrain, whether to shield themselves from undue (donor or host) government influence, to protect their ability to raise funds, or because of simple organizational jealousy. The multiplicity of NGOs further aggravates the picture. Although donors, UN agencies, and IFIs alike have increasingly recognized the critical role of nongovernmental organizations, accommodating disparate NGOs within formal coordinating structures has proved an extremely difficult task.

Delivering Assistance

In some cases of international peacebuilding there often appears to be a significant gap or lag between aid pledges and actual aid disbursements. In Cambodia, only $200 million of $880 million of support pledged in June 1992 for the transitional period had been disbursed by the time an elected government was formed in June 1993. In Bosnia, only $1 billion of the $1.85 billion promised in 1995–96 had been spent by April 1997. In other cases, little or no gap appears to exist: in El Salvador, for example, most donors seem to have actually exceeded the levels of aid pledged.[25] Apart from the obvious fact that undisbursed funds can hardly contribute to the urgent task of peacebuilding, any gap between large amounts of aid committed by donors at highly publicized international pledging conferences and the apparent trickle of projects on the ground can, in and of itself, undermine political reconciliation by creating a local crisis of unmet expectations.

Theoretically, the problem of unfulfilled pledges may be seen as a problem of cooperation under conditions of international anarchy and more specifically as "free rider" problems inherent in multilateral collective action. In this view, donors fail to deliver on promises because they hope to reap the benefits of regional peace without footing the bill for peacebuilding. Gaps may also arise from confusion over who has promised what. Cases of higher or lower rates of aggregate disbursement across different conflicts may therefore be explained by the adoption of different sets of donor coordination or monitoring mechanisms, and hence the incentive structures and degree of transparency that these sustain.

Delayed implementation, on the other hand, may be due to local factors, such as the degree of devastation wrought by the conflict, the limited absorptive capacity of the local economy, and the weakness of local government. Unforeseen political developments can also derail donor plans, slowing the flow of assistance.

However, this is only part of the picture. Although both the problems of collective international action and the constraints imposed by local conditions may reduce the rate at which resources arrive on the ground, neither set of factors fully explains the very substantial variation *across* donors *within* the context of a particular transition. In Cambodia, for example, disbursement rates (1992–95) have apparently varied from over 90 percent (Japan, the Netherlands) to less than 30 percent (Belgium, Norway, the World Bank).[26]

Explaining this requires attention to the particular aid strategies adopted by different donors, as well as to an array of institutional factors within agencies. To what extent do institutional procedures within some donor agencies—including the risk of budgetary "raiding," the career interests of project officers, and the danger of losing unspent funds at the end of the financial year—motivate programs to expend funds expeditiously? What role do domestic political pressures play, whether from political elites, interest groups, or mass publics? What role do key individuals play in the process? The latter question of idiosyncratic factors in peacebuilding is a particularly interesting one, given the number of accounts wherein substantial weight is placed on the leadership abilities (or lack thereof) of particular officials.[27]

Central among the dilemmas facing donors in this regard is the inherent tension between the *need to act* and the *tendency to be careful.* This dilemma is evident, for example, in the World Bank's guidelines on involvement in postconflict reconstruction (table 1.1), which attempt to balance both sets of concerns.[28] On the one hand, the uncertain nature of transitional assistance and the high-stakes character of peacebuilding naturally demand considerable innovation in program design and create considerable uncertainty in program operations—in short, require a substantial degree of risk taking. Development agencies, however, may be naturally risk averse. This stems in part from the career consequences to professionals arising from association with failed projects, as well as the growing pressures on scarce staff resources at a time of budgetary retrenchment. Organizations may be particularly sensitive to public or political criticism of waste and inefficiency, a sensitivity heightened still further by strong domestic watchdog institutions (such as a national auditor or controller's office), the domestic politicization of some international conflict (the Arab-Israeli conflict being a prime example), and the substantial media attention often given to peace operations.[29] Such caution in donor assistance programs has been further reinforced by a decade of budgetary retrenchment in most donor agencies. Between 1990 and 1996 Western aid budgets collectively shrank some 13 percent in real terms.[30] In response to all of these pressures, agencies have typically developed even more careful financial oversight, procurement, accounting, reporting, and project assessment requirements.

Allocating Assistance

The final element of donor responsiveness is the relevance of donor allocations: to what extent do assistance programs address needs and support the objectives of peacebuilding? Although hugely important, this is perhaps the most difficult aspect

Table 1.1. Phases of World Bank Involvement in Postconflict Reconstruction

Phase	
Watching Brief	"A watching brief has four main objectives: to develop an understanding of context, dynamics, and needs so that the Bank is well positioned to support an appropriate investment portfolio when conditions permit; to evaluate the comparative advantages of institutions, including NGOs, operating in the relief phase . . . ; to consult with humanitarian agencies on the long-term implications of short-term relief strategies; and to counter the adverse economic and environmental problems resulting from refugee and other spillover effects on neighboring countries."
Transitional Support Strategy	The World Bank would develop a transitional support strategy that includes "a clear statement of risks as well as strategies for entry and exit and recommendations . . . on how envisaged activities would be financed. Approval of a transitional support strategy would depend on the fulfillment of three basic preconditions: sufficient indication that a sustainable cease-fire has been or will be achieved shortly; presence of an effective counterpart for the Bank; and strong international cooperation with a well-defined role for the Bank."
Early Reconstruction Activities	"Early reconstruction activities would be initiated as opportunities arise. They would be small-scale activities that can be undertaken relatively quickly—in many cases by or in partnership with UN agencies and NGOs—and would not be dependent on normal Bank preparation procedures. Small-scale activities during this phase, in addition to representing a response to urgent needs, can function as pilot activities that enhance learning for the design of later, larger-scale programs."
Postconflict Reconstruction	"As soon as large-scale operations are possible . . . they may be carried out under either normal or emergency procedures. Where security conditions and government commitment allow, support would include physical reconstruction, economic recovery, institution building, and social reintegration."
Return to Normal Operations	The bank returns to normal lending operations, although cognizant of "the effects of the conflict and the sometimes permanent transformation of society that may make the return to the status quo *ex ante* impossible and even undesirable."

Source: World Bank, *Post-Conflict Resolution: The Role of the World Bank* (Washington, D.C.: World Bank, 1998), 6–9.

of the concept to assess, in part because what may (or may not) contribute to long-term political stability is not always self-evident.

One possible measure is the extent to which donor programs respond to the needs of recipient countries, as defined by recipient countries themselves. Often there has been a substantial mismatch between these assessments and what donors have actually supported. In El Salvador, for example, many projects deemed "low priority" by the government were funded by donors, while "high-priority" projects were not.[31]

Yet this measure is not perfectly satisfactory in and of itself: local governments may not be driven by peacemaking but by a host of other considerations, such as improving their position against internal opponents or personal enrichment. Indeed—as argued later in this chapter—examining the interrelationship between external assistance and local political dynamics "from the ground up" is as essential as exploring the factors that shape donor responsiveness "from the top down."

Other possible criteria for evaluating the allocation of peacebuilding assistance are the assessments of international financial institutions such as the World Bank and the International Monetary Fund (IMF). Although these institutions are usually analytically rigorous, they have sometimes been criticized on the grounds of both excessive adherence to neoliberal orthodoxy and an uncritical insistence on structural adjustment policies. Such policies may sap central government capacity (through budgetary retrenchment) at a critical period, inhibit the demobilization of former combatants through restrictions on public-sector employment, and produce disruptive socioeconomic effects that can destabilize a fragile social peace.[32] In such cases, the efforts of IFIs to promote economic stabilization may actually imperil donor efforts to support political stabilization and vice versa.

Another way of approaching the issue of donor relevance is to look at program design. Here it soon becomes apparent that a host of considerations exogenous to peacebuilding may all play a role in determining what donors do. John Prendergast, for example, has highlighted the "law of the tool"—that is, that what agencies do is determined by the means at their disposal, rather than by needs on the ground.[33] Donors are often driven by the desire to promote exports and by the effort to enhance their regional political profile. Similarly, the imperatives of publicity and fund-raising can loom large in NGO decision making. Even personal or cliental relations between agency staff and local actors can play a role in determining what does or does not get funded.

There are also diffuse but important ideological factors at work. Most Western donors, for example, have long tended to emphasize liberal, capitalist models of economic development, both out of ideological conviction and because such a development model best suits their own interests in promoting trade and investment opportunities. As a consequence, greater emphasis has been placed on private-sector development, and donors (and even more so international financial institutions such as the World Bank and the IMF) have tended to frown on any public-sector expansion. As donor agencies have come under increased political scrutiny and have faced increasingly desperate battles to protect their budgets from cutbacks, many have placed renewed emphasis on the promotion of national interests, whether through tied aid, consultancies, or other forms of export promotion. This defensiveness is particularly apparent in the case of the United States, where total official donor assistance has fallen to a level comparable to that of France, Germany, and Japan, and where conservative lobby groups and congressional critics have called for the elimination of USAID ("an independent federal government agency that conducts foreign assistance and humanitarian aid to advance the political and economic interests of the United States") altogether.[34]

Within agencies, program design is also profoundly shaped by the norms and criteria of two long-established functions: humanitarian relief and development assistance. These two functions of organizational culture may be reinforced by the institutional division of agencies (and budgets) into differing branches responsible for each. Donald Brandt, for example, argues that

> practitioners assume that discrete subsets of activities are associated with each phase. Certain interventions are done in the relief stage but not in rehabilitation or relief. Likewise, rehabilitation or development are associated with their own set of strategies and operations. This classification of activities into relief, rehabilitation, and development interventions is often arbitrary. Requirements of donors are partially responsible: government grants usually mandate discrete activities because program boundaries simplify financial accountability.
>
> This specialization of activities associated with relief, rehabilitation, and development produces a double-edged sword. On the positive side, professionalism is encouraged. Negative aspects include a separation that arises between relief (or relief and rehabilitation) and development staffs. Separation in function and expertise lead to a division in programs and even personality types. Relief professionals see staff in developmental programs as ill trained generalists, while developmentalists view relief personnel as anti-developmental technicians. Often chasms evolve that lead to departmental "tribalism" and a "we-they" attitude.[35]

In the case of humanitarian relief, operations are directed at immediate consequences of disaster, whether natural (such as flood, famine, or earthquake) or man-made (most notably war). Humanitarian relief typically involves the urgent provision of food, shelter, and medical assistance to refugees and other affected populations. Organizationally, humanitarian NGOs and agencies are designed to provide rapid response and are frequently forced to improvise planning in the midst of complex and changing circumstances. The ten-point code of conduct adopted by the world's largest humanitarian organizations stresses (among other items) that "the humanitarian imperative comes first," so that "aid is given regardless of the race, creed or nationality of the recipients and without adverse distinction of any kind," and "aid priorities are calculated on the basis of need alone." Moreover, aid should not be given "to further a particular political or religious standpoint," while relief organizations "shall endeavor not to act as instruments of government foreign policy."[36]

By contrast, traditional development assistance has focused its attention on the issue of long-term sustainability. The Development Assistance Committee (DAC) of the Organization for Economic Cooperation and Development (OECD), for example, emphasizes that donors should seek to "improve the capacity of developing countries to carry forward their own development, by integrating social, economic and ecological perspectives in a sustainable way . . . establish sound principles and effective donor frameworks, promoting flexible approaches, longer time frames and innovative funding mechanisms, to encourage growth and reduce poverty, while protecting the environment, and to foster widespread capacity development—in particular for environment, technological capability, good governance and conflict management."[37] Operationally, ensuring sustainability requires a substantial degree of project planning, feasibility analysis, and environmental and social impact assessment. While the result of these efforts is more effective long-term programming, they also tend to involve a greater degree of complexity, greater interagency and stakeholder cooperation, and longer project cycles, particularly with integrated and multisectoral programs.

In the context of countries emerging from conflict, peacebuilding assistance is faced with the immediate tasks of addressing substantial human needs (a humanitarian relief role) and rebuilding the basis for future social and economic development (the task of conventional developmental assistance). Certainly, the imperatives of both immediate *need* and socioeconomic *sustainability* are relevant in such cases, although they are potentially in conflict with each other. For this reason, the past decade has sustained an apparently endless debate among practitioners as to the appropriate relationship between the two. Early discussion of a "relief-to-development continuum" (in which humanitarian operations would give way to longer-term developmental projects as conditions stabilized) was criticized for falsely implying linearity in operations, failing to recognize how many activities had consequences spanning both categories, and obscuring the extent to which activities of one sort had profound implications for the other. Subsequent concepts—of "transitions," of "linking relief and development," and even of a "contiguum"—were put forward in an attempt to address this.[38]

Collectively, Western donor agencies now express the view that such tensions can be overcome through appropriate program design:

In situations of open conflict, other policy instruments such as humanitarian assistance, diplomatic initiatives and political or economic measures tend to move to the forefront of the international response. Contrary to many past assumptions, we have found that a sharp distinction between short-term emergency relief and longer-term development aid is rarely useful in planning support for countries in open conflict. Development co-operation agencies operating in conflict zones, respecting security concerns and the feasibility of operations, can continue to identify the scope for supporting development processes even in the midst of crisis, be prepared to seize upon opportunities to contribute to conflict resolution, and continue to plan and prepare for post-conflict reconstruction.[39]

Similarly, Mats Karlsson, Swedish secretary of state for development cooperation, argued that these institutional constraints can, under suitable circumstances, be overcome: "The gap between relief, rehabilitation and development is not only a result of stereotypical administrative or budgetary structures. More important is the policy that guides the manner in which existing resources are used." Thus, a clear policy can manage within a variety of administrative-budgetary contexts. A weak policy, however, "easily becomes the prey of bureaucratic rules and procedures."[40]

In attempting to develop such a policy, however, peacebuilding adds other complications. Put simply, not one of these models—not humanitarian relief, nor the sustainable development model, nor some integration of the two—necessarily addresses the fundamentally *political* imperatives of peacebuilding.

Unlike humanitarian operations in particular, peacebuilding assistance may be —and indeed often should be—deliberately *discriminatory*, intended to strengthen parties supportive of the peace process and marginalize (or perhaps co-opt) those who oppose it. It is certainly true, as Kenneth D. Bush has suggested, that "rebuilding wartorn societies is not about the impositions of 'solutions,' it is about the creation of opportunities."[41] However, the opportunities created by international aid can be designed to encourage certain types of behavior, discourage others, and generally produce incentives for cooperation. In Bosnia, for example, aid was largely withheld from Serb areas in 1996–97 in an effort by donors to force greater compliance with the terms of the Dayton Peace Accords. As a more moderate Bosnian Serb leadership emerged, aid began to flow. At a microlevel, aid was also used to encourage municipal leaders to cooperate with international efforts to return refugees to their homes. Here and in other cases, politics—and not simply need— is a primary determinant for programming, and conditionality a key element of delivery. More broadly, the very process of rebuilding state institutions, allocating scarce state resources, fostering improved local security conditions, reducing excessive military expenditures, modifying the taxation system, and extending the state's territorial control (among many other possible examples) all have profoundly political implications.

Such tasks, however, may sit uncomfortably with development agencies. As James Boyce has noted, "in development circles, conditionality often is regarded as something of a dirty word."[42] This problem is even more severe in international financial institutions such as the World Bank and IMF, which "historically have sought to distance themselves from such political issues, straying as little as possible from their familiar economic terrain in which they can claim technocratic expertise."[43] One Western aid official—responsible for a sizable peacebuilding budget envelope—expressed the view that aid agencies don't do politics well and ought to focus on such developmental issues as "capacity building, democratization, generally working on the people side of the equation."[44] Yet it seems self-evident that democratization is a fundamentally political, and politically sensitive, exercise. Similarly, a recent World Bank review of postconflict reconstruction devotes around one page to the importance of contextual political factors and largely ducks the important issue of linking assistance to the implementation of peace agreements.[45] In short, the required paradigm shift from more traditional models of assistance has not yet fully occurred.

The resulting tensions are evident in many forms. Security service reform, for example, is generally regarded as critical to successful peacebuilding. However, many aid agencies are legally prohibited from directly engaging in projects involving security agencies; others prefer to focus on less controversial areas. Similarly, the broader expansion of state power may be a necessary aspect of enhancing political stability but may also be seen by donors (and especially by IFIs) as a developmental drawback, given their ideological preference to support private- over public-sector development. In this regard, the financing of central government budgets may be a particularly troublesome issue. On the one hand, wartime destruction and weak bureaucratic institutions make domestic tax collection difficult at a time when both reconstruction and political consolidation require growing state spending. On the other hand, donors are reluctant to commit support to recurrent government expenditures. There are several reasons for this: budget support tends to be seen as nonproductive; such support lacks the local political visibility and export-promotion possibilities of project funding; and support for recurrent government expenditures tends to be seen as a potentially never-ending burden on donor resources. A lack of clear mechanisms of accountability and transparency on the part of recipient governments further aggravates these effects.

The operational difficulties created by differing imperatives is heightened, ironically, when aid programming fails to recognize the unavoidable trade-offs among them. It is not necessarily the case, for example, that donor concern with environmental issues can be easily squared with the need for rapid project implementation; that the fundamentally important issue of gender equality is easily reconciled with the political imperative to address the needs of armed, and potentially politically destabilizing, young men; that human rights protection and the necessity of suppressing terrorism are easily accomplished in tandem; or that vibrant civil society and rapid democratization are the best ways of promoting a smooth transition toward lasting peace.[46] In short—and despite the public rhetoric of NGOs and donor agencies—it is far from clear that "all good things go together," or that regular social priorities of development assistance can invariably retain their pride of place in the context of peacebuilding initiatives. As Pauline Baker has suggested, "experience thus far should serve as a cautionary tale. The pursuit of peace in the post–Cold War period will be an infinitely more complex and morally ambiguous process than anyone ever imagined it would be."[47]

Yet, despite all of these complications, it is possible to identify some broad sets of priorities that should shape the allocation of donor assistance during war-to-peace transitions. The *DAC Guidelines on Conflict, Peace, and Development Cooperation* drawn up by the DAC—that is to say, the collected wisdom of Western development agencies—suggest a number of operational priorities (box 1.1), as well as the key importance of donor coordination in pursuing these.[48]

Box 1.1. DAC Priorities in Peacebuilding

Foundations for Peacebuilding
- Respect for human rights
- Participatory political processes
- Strengthening public institutions
- Strengthening systems of security and justice
- Reinforcing civil society

Supporting Postconflict Recovery
- Restoring economic management capacity
- Restoring internal security and rule of law
- Legitimizing state institutions
- Fostering the reemergence of civil society
- Improving food security and social services
- Building administrative capacity
- Reintegrating uprooted populations
- Demobilization/reintegration of former combatants
- Land mine clearance

Source: DAC, *DAC Guidelines on Conflict, Peace, and Development Cooperation* (Paris: Organization for Economic Cooperation and Development, 1997).

Nicole Ball and Tammy Halevy suggest that these sorts of tasks should be seen in relation to a dynamic process of conflict resolution and peacemaking. In particular, they identify a stage of "conflict resolution," characterized first by *negotiations* and then by a *cessation of hostilities;* and subsequently a stage of peacebuilding, characterized by a *transition* followed by an extended period of *consolidation* (table 1.2).[49] Of course, not all countries progress through precisely the same sequence. The Palestinian case—characterized by a series of successive interim arrangements, a state of no war/no peace between the parties, substantial changes in Israeli government policy, and an indeterminate final outcome—especially defies categorization in this way. Nevertheless, the schema highlights how different periods involve different challenges and how the allocation of assistance must be shaped by changing political and economic realities on the ground.

During *negotiations,* the "carrot" of international assistance (or the "stick" of it being withheld or provided to rivals) may be an important tool for international mediators. The promise of a future economic "peace dividend" may also be an important factor in encouraging parties to sit down at the table and reach agreement. The subsequent *cessation of hostilities* is particularly vulnerable to disruption —a point illustrated in Angola by the inadequacy of demobilization, resulting in renewed fighting after the September 1992 presidential elections, or by the April 1994 genocide in Rwanda, less than a year after the Arusha peace agreement had called for demobilization and transitional elections. Given this vulnerability and the scarcity of local resources (both financial and human), donors must play a key role in supporting such initiatives. During the *transition,* a new government must often be elected so as to confirm the new, postpeace distribution of political power and legitimize the reconstructed state. The international community typically supports this through aid for voter registration, technical assistance in the design of electoral systems, and the provision of election monitors. As before, external mediators may find foreign aid to be a useful incentive in encouraging the formerly warring parties to maintain their commitment to the nascent political process.[50] In some cases—such as was the case with UNTAG in Namibia or UNTAC in Cambodia (1992–93)—the international community may even acquire a degree of political and administrative authority for the duration of the transitional period.[51]

Choices also have to be made about what channels might best be utilized for the delivery of assistance. During wartime, local and international NGOs may have come to occupy a key role in the provision of assistance, in part because of their flexibility, responsiveness, and perceived neutrality. Moreover, official donors, unwilling to provide government-to-government aid during a civil conflict or unable to establish a bilateral development program amid conditions of local strife, may have heavily depended on NGOs and UN agencies (such as UNHCR or WFP) as the primary channel of assistance. As peace processes develop,

Table 1.2. Phases in Peacebuilding

Phase	
Conflict Resolution: Negotiations	"[T]he main objective is to reach a political agreement on key issues so that fighting can stop. The donors need to devote only a relatively modest amount of resources at this point. They should focus on planning for post-conflict rebuilding and on developing collaborative relationships with the parties to the conflict as well as with civil society. Donors can also provide mediators and the parties with advice on issues under negotiation in their areas of institutional expertise."
Conflict Resolution: Cessation of Hostilities	"[D]onors can begin to match assumptions made during planning with realities on the ground. They can also provide assistance for activities that will begin once the peace agreement has been signed, such as equipping assembly areas for troops to be demobilized or clearing mines from critical areas. The possibility always exists that the peace process will break down and hostilities will resume. Donors are, therefore, typically cautious about what can be accomplished during this period."
Peacebuilding: Transition	"The major objectives of the transition phase are to establish a government with sufficient domestic and international legitimacy to operate effectively and to assist the parties to comply with the terms of the peace accords. However, peace accords vary considerably in their comprehensiveness. Some cover only a small portion of the many activities required to strengthen the institutional base of war-torn countries, consolidate internal and external security, and promote economic and social revitalization. It is thus important that the international community assist the parties to prioritize the tasks of peacebuilding."
Peacebuilding: Consolidation	"The major objective of this phase is to continue implementing reforms in the peace accords that take longer to execute than the one to two years that the transition phase typically lasts. In addition, although the provisions of the peace accords may constitute necessary steps toward consolidating peace, they rarely deal adequately with the problems that led to the war or create an environment conducive to resolving future conflicts peacefully. The reform process must be deepened during the consolidation phase so that issues such as significant economic imbalances among social groups and the lack of mechanisms to prevent human-rights abuses can be addressed."

Source: Nicole Ball with Tammy Halevy, *Making Peace Work: The Role of the International Development Community,* ODC Policy Essay no. 18 (Washington, D.C.: Overseas Development Council, 1996).

donors may, in the absence of effective government capacity or amid local political factionalization, continue to use such channels. To do so, however, risks com-
promising the state's ability to assume its governmental functions, thus undercutting the processes of both state and legitimacy building. As Doyle suggests,
"NGOs and other development agencies, however well-motivated, should resist
the temptation to become the *de facto* government."[52]

Donors face other dangers in shifting their support from earlier NGO channels to the (re)emerging state structure. As Ball and Halevy note in the case of El
Salvador, "assistance may be used to gain electoral advantage at the expense of the
most war-affected groups, fostering a political environment inimical to reconciliation."[53] A sudden shift of donor support from the indigenous NGO community
to bilateral assistance programs can weaken civil society, facilitating the centralizing
and perhaps authoritarian inclinations of state authorities. The frequent politicization of individual NGOs adds a further level of complexity, especially when
local groups are aligned with political factions. None of this, of course, obviates the
essential work that both local and international NGOs perform in peacebuilding. It does, however, point out the potential complications of that role.

If formerly war-torn countries survive the transitional period with peace
intact, *consolidation* involves a shift of donor efforts to the support of longer-term
objectives: revitalizing the economy in a way that promotes greater social equity;
strengthening governmental capacities so as to reinforce political legitimacy and
foster a productive synergy between state and civil society; encouraging the rule
of law and reforming the security sector; promoting principles and institutions of
participation and accountability, so as to open up effective, nonviolent mechanisms
for social conflict resolution. At the same time, continued donor vigilance (and
some degree of aid conditionality) may be necessary to ensure that parties continue
to abide by existing agreements and do not resort to force to resolve disputes.[54]

Whether donors have the will and/or leverage to do so is not always clear,
however. In Cambodia, for example, Hun Sen was clearly not deterred from his
1997 quasi coup by the threat of aid suspension. Nor, tellingly, did all donors subsequently suspend aid. In Bosnia, aid conditionality certainly contributed to the
emergence of Serb moderates, but it also had a backlash effect that served to
strengthen Serb hard-liners.

In fact, the Cambodian and Bosnian examples underscore an important
caveat: although donor support for peacebuilding is an important (and, in some
cases, perhaps necessary) component of fostering a war-to-peace transition, it is
far from a sufficient condition. A whole range of other factors shape domestic politics in war-torn societies, and these powerful and complex dynamics can easily
overwhelm whatever positive effects are achieved by even hundreds of millions
of dollars of donor assistance.

Indeed, it is perhaps telling that some of the most notable cases of war-to-peace transition in the post–Cold War period did not rest heavily on donor assistance or have involved actions by the international community that were substantially more confrontational. South Africa, for example, has often been cited as an example of successful peacebuilding through support for civil society and dialogue. Yet, in practice, it was quite stark political pressures that played the key role in the old regime's decision to negotiate an end to apartheid: the ultimately unwinnable position of apartheid against the majority nonwhite population, continuing and potentially escalating violence, and sanctions and others forms of pressure against the white minority government. Aid funds were channeled to those segments of "civil society" that were actively involved in political conflict with the authorities, and indeed to groups in open or tacit alliance with an armed liberation movement, the African National Congress. The policy of diplomatic dialogue ("constructive engagement"), initially favored by the Reagan administration, was ultimately abandoned by the United States under congressional pressure; instead, external sanctions weakened and isolated the regime. True, donor assistance did play a modest role in promoting dialogue and thereby helped to support a "soft landing" despite the high potential for political violence during the transitional period. Its more important effect, however, was probably to strengthen one of the combatants in the conflict. Today it plays a still lesser role, to the point that a significant portion of donor assistance to South Africa has not been spent. Lebanon—another striking example of the termination of civil war in recent years—is also an interesting case. Here, donor support for peacebuilding played absolutely no significant role. Instead, external coercion and internal exhaustion ended fifteen years of bitter domestic strife.[55]

The point here is not, of course, to diminish the importance of economic instrumentalities in the search for peace, or to recommend the South African or Lebanese model. It is to suggest the need for a constant, self-critical review of the presumptions, accepted wisdom, and achievements of peacebuilding.

THE POLITICS OF GETTING

The preceding discussion generates a number of observations relevant to the Palestinian case, ranging from the need to explore the presumptions and objectives of donor programs through to the importance of institutional and other factors in shaping program design. In particular, it points to the "very political" economy of peacebuilding, underscoring the extent to which assessment of transitional assistance cannot and should not be measured solely against narrow economic and social criteria.

Examining the "politics of giving," however, illuminates only part of the picture. Attention must also be directed toward the "politics of getting." Recipients of peacebuilding assistance are not passive, but rather active agents in their own right, pursuing their own political and other agendas. In this, external assistance represents a potentially potent resource. Understanding the dynamics of peacebuilding assistance thus requires attention to how donor programs actually impact on local societies and polities—and how local political actors seek to shape assistance to serve their own purposes.

Winners and Losers

Within the literature, considerable attention has been paid to how peacebuilding should reshape polities by fostering shared interests and incentives for peacemaking, resurrecting state authority, promoting nonviolent mechanisms for conflict resolution, and encouraging social reconciliation. All of these are obviously fundamentally political aspects of a fundamentally political process. Consequently, it is important to recognize that they create losers as well as winners, and that—whatever the good motives of donors and NGOs—they may be resisted in whole or part by local actors. To the extent that peacebuilding measures seek to reform or break down some of the old structures of conflict—strong ethnic or sectarian loyalties, militias, heavily politicized militaries, entrenched elites—they may engender considerable local resistance among those who are stakeholders in the status quo. If donor assistance goes beyond this, to address the social grievances and economic inequalities that generate civil strife, the stakes are even higher. Traditionally dominant classes and communal groups will likely resist the erosion of their power and wealth; newly mobilized groups may press their demands beyond the capacity of political system to adapt. In this sense, change intended to promote longer-term harmony may itself be the cause of more immediate conflict.

Such resistance, moreover, is likely to be felt not only at the level of political leaders, but also at other levels and in a variety of ways. Former militia leaders may seek to delay demobilization, fearing that a loss of military assets will weaken their political power. Field commanders may fear for their own social influence, or may be concerned that their hard-fought cause is being sold out by politically ambitious elites. Rank-and-file combatants may fear insertion (perhaps with few skills) into an uncertain labor market. Similarly, revitalization of the state bureaucracy may be resisted both by self-serving entrepreneurs who have flourished amid the collapse of state authority and by NGOs that have sought to cope with the collapse of state services but that now face marginalization as the state reassumes its responsibilities. Even within the state, revitalization of state services and the bureaucratic needs of reconstruction create the scope for empire building and intense turf wars both horizontally (between different government agencies) and vertically (between senior management and field personnel). The wartime "capture" of parts of the state apparatus by political factions, or the division of administrative responsibilities that may accompany any postconflict power-sharing agreement, further aggravates this. Here, it become vital to look at the fragmented character of social power and authority, to disaggregate the "state," and to examine the complex conflicts and accommodations among leaders, bureaucrats, and social elites.[56]

Local politics and the fragile peace process also impact on donor agendas in a variety of other ways, many of them alluded to earlier: possible tensions between democratization, power sharing, and the consolidation of central political control; competing postconflict demands for justice and reconciliation; the trade-offs between addressing social needs and addressing political priorities. Volumes can —and have—been written on some of these issues, and so they will not be examined in detail here.[57] However, what is important to reiterate is that how local actors orient themselves will depend very much on who they are. Democratization may be the favored device not only of democrats but also of those advancing a majoritarian agenda; power sharing may not be so much a signal for reconciliation as a mechanism for co-opting or exercising veto; calls for "justice" may be thinly veiled calls for revenge, or "reconciliation" a byword for sweeping past atrocities under the carpet; social priorities may be determined by constituency interests rather than by objective need. The point of such observations is not to promote universal cynicism; on the contrary—the experience of peacebuilding is one rich with sacrifice, dedication, altruism, and vision. However, it is to underscore— once again—the profoundly messy political issues at stake.

The Political Importance of Donor Resources

After suffering years of economic devastation, war-torn states obviously look to the international community to provide needed resources and rebuild critical infrastructures. In the struggles that accompany war-to-peace transitions, however, external donor assistance also represents a potent *political* resource—the external goose laying domestic golden eggs. For this reason, a variety of actors are likely to seek to use assistance to further their own political agendas.

NGOs, faced with both the possibly authoritarian inclinations of the new state and the (re)extension of the state into areas of social policy, will likely also see donor funding and external linkages as critical assets in the struggle to retain their position. In the highly politicized environment of war-torn countries, local NGOs may be closely aligned to one faction or another, lending an even sharper edge to such conflicts.

Similarly, for state elites, external support is about more than simply state building; it is also about regime consolidation. External development initiatives can be used to reward loyal constituencies, co-opt potential opponents, and alter the domestic balance of power. From their perspective, such assistance ideally flows directly to state coffers in the form of budgetary support, where it can be used to finance political patronage through state grants and employment. If donors are unwilling to finance such expenditures directly, planning processes and needs assessments can be biased so as to encourage donors to finance certain types of projects in certain areas of the country.

In addition to this, parts of the state may see donor support as a critical element in internal bureaucratic and political battles over jurisdiction. Donors are thus inevitably implicated in local turf battles and empire building. As Holtzman notes, this problem is aggravated by the coalition basis of most postconflict governments: "Sectorally-targeted donor funds may become the property of specific ministries within the government. Where ministries have been distributed among former combatants, the provision of development funds to one particular sector may consequently have far-reaching implications by increasing the power of one former combatant or another."[58]

The dependence of local governments on donor resources can also have other political effects. To the extent that external resources reduce the need for regimes to rely on domestic taxation, political elites are less reliant on and more autonomous from the society they govern and hence less vulnerable to *domestic* pressures. Such "rentierism" may thus encourage both authoritarianism and neopatrimonial, patronage-based politics. Conversely, use of donor support to service political constituencies creates a certain vulnerability to *external* pressures. For this reason, recipient countries may, at times, prefer weaker rather than stronger mechanisms of donor coordination. Weak donor solidarity and poor coordination can be exploited by recipients so as to lessen the threat of imposed conditionality. Incompatibilities between competing donor objectives can similarly be used to offset international leverage.[59]

Patronage and Corruption

Widespread corruption is a frequent characteristic of reconstruction programs. In large part, this is a legacy of the conflict itself, during which illegality may have thrived in a variety of forms amid collapsing public institutions. In the particular context of wartime, moreover, humanitarian relief may have also generated an array of parasitic actors sustaining themselves from the "aid economy."[60] To the extent that such endemic corruption represents a manifestation of both economic entrepreneurship and local survival skills, its eradication is difficult despite the gradual reassertion of state authority. One IMF public expenditure review in Cambodia, for example, found that up to $79 million per year in potential government revenue (equal to around one-third of all government income) was lost due to leakage and illegal timber cutting.[61] Similar tales could be told of other sectors and other cases.

Corruption is also linked with the process of economic transition. The huge disparities between foreign aid and local poverty create myriad opportunities

and incentives for corrupt behavior, whether grand (embezzlement, extortion, contracting irregularities) or petty (thefts, small bribes to and from officials). Such "developmental" corruption may create flexibility in otherwise inflexible processes, although in general it tends to generate inefficiency, undercut planning, and sap needed resources. The propensity to corruption is further increased by the almost inevitable bureaucratic disarray at this stage. Such disorganization obfuscates lines of responsibility while reducing the risk of punishment to those involved in illegal activities.[62]

Corruption becomes even more significant when it is combined with political patronage and the dynamics of regime consolidation—what John Waterbury has termed "planned corruption."[63] Tolerance of corruption by subordinates may become one of the rewards used by political elites to consolidate their support bases. It may also be used as a way of generating funds for "off-the-books" expenditures outside the normal budgetary process (and away from the prying eyes of donors). As a reward for fealty, corruption has the advantage that it is wholly or partly self-financing and renders clients dependent on a leader's continued goodwill and protection. It is easily withdrawn from clients when political circumstances dictate, or leveled as a charge against excessively ambitious or political suspect subordinates—as the leader cloaks himself or herself in the mantle of feigned moral outrage.[64] This type of explicitly political, planned corruption has all the adverse effects of other forms, including resource wastage and policy distortion. It also tends to solidify short-term support at the cost of longer-term legitimacy and political institutionalization.

Donors, of course, typically object to such behavior and may respond to it through technical assistance, good governance programs, aid conditionality, and/ or the redirection of aid flows into nongovernment channels. All of these measures may be effective in promoting reform. However, these often fail to adequately recognize that patronage and the official toleration of corruption may fulfill a certain political rationality—the needs of immediate political survival—even if they have substantial long-term social, economic, and political costs. The IMF review of the Cambodian logging sector described here is a perfect example: it contains no real discussion of who benefits from the illegal trade and what the political consequences might be of moving to end it—despite recognition that much of the "extrabudgetary" charges on logging are a significant source of revenue for provincial authorities, and despite anecdotal evidence that official toleration of smuggling is being used by the government as a mechanism to secure the defection of former Khmer Rouge commanders. To the extent that donors treat corruption as if it were simply a moral or administrative lapse, and fail to take political considerations into account, donor-supported reforms potentially undercut their own effectiveness. They may also invite perverse effects. A cutoff of external support, for example, may not promote reform but rather may force a government into even greater reliance on extralegal mechanisms of revenue generation, thereby achieving the opposite effect to that intended.

Statebuilding and the Primacy of Survival

Statebuilding is, as noted earlier, a central requirement of successful war-to-peace transition. The degree of statebuilding required from case to case may vary. In some cases, such as Somalia or Mozambique, the state has wholly or partially collapsed. Here, as I. William Zartman has noted, the challenge is to reconstitute power structures, restore legitimacy (often through expanded political participation and elections), and find the resources necessary for both administrative functioning and socioeconomic reconstruction.[65] In other conflicts, the institutions of authority may have remained intact, even if the legitimacy of the state has been contested. In such cases—of which El Salvador and Guatemala would be examples—the major problem is one of imbalance, with some parts of the state apparatus (notably the security forces) having become overdeveloped, while other aspects have languished.

Hillel Frisch and Menachem Hofnung have suggested that there are two main issues at stake in the provision of international aid for political (re)construction. The first is the question of sequence: "What should come first—political centralization of power or economic development?" The second issue is that of the "mix"—that is, "the degree of autonomy the state should possess relative to society; the proper ratio between investment in non-governmental developmental tasks on the one hand, and building and maintaining state bureaucratic capacity on the other; the degree of selectivity the state should undertake in promoting economic tasks; and the importance of cultivating civil society and democratic governance as a means of restraining the state."[66] From this, they suggest, four basic elements emerge that must be addressed in building the postconflict state:

> [First,] the accumulation of power sufficient to monopolize violence and ensure a high degree of personal security is more important and prior to anything else. Without state centralization of power there is no reform, and without stability there is little private initiative and investment. Second, containing the accumulation of power cannot be left to the fortuitous emergence of a non-rent-seeking autocrat (however important this emergence may be). It is rather to be achieved by the cultivation of a civil society strong enough to prevent rent-seeking and provide the necessary feedback for evaluating state policies. . . . Third, bureaucratic capacity must be given priority over projects designed to achieve immediate but short-term increases in economic welfare. Fourth, the state must carefully select the tasks it takes upon itself and thus augment bureaucratic capabilities of defining and implementing strategic economic growth policies.[67]

To the extent that statebuilding strengthens regime consolidation, it can be expected that many of these tasks (notably "state centralization of power") will be embraced by transitional governments. Others (for example, strengthening the watchdog functions of civil society) may be less appealing to many political leaders. Finally, those that require immediate sacrifice to attain eventual gains are most likely to be entertained in periods of relative political stability and limited immediate social need—conditions that rarely endure in the context of war-to-peace transitions.

How all this is attempted in the transitional period, and the extent to which it is achieved, is likely to have lasting consequences. In the Palestinian case, as elsewhere, political futures are likely to be heavily shaped by that which went before them. As both Shibley Telhami and Glenn Robinson have suggested, "The preeminent lesson from state-building enterprises throughout the ex-colonial world in the past few decades is . . . 'how you start significantly determines how you finish.' That is, 'many well-meaning officials in emerging states rationalized early excesses as necessary, or emergency, compromises that would be corrected in the future, only to discover that these mistakes often become permanent features' of the new states, with their own bureaucratic defenders."[68] Yet against this long-term logic of path dependency and the virtue of good governance must be set the equally powerful immediate imperatives of political survival—imperatives that local actors are inclined to find both more salient and more pressing.

The British economist John Maynard Keynes once noted that the "*long run* is a misleading guide to current affairs. *In the long run* we are all dead."[69] For political leaderships in weak, unstable, formerly war-torn countries, those words may have a particular (and perhaps quite literal) resonance.

2

The Context

The West Bank and Gaza from Occupation to Peace Process

TO UNDERSTAND THE CHALLENGES of peacebuilding and reconstruction in Palestine, it is necessary first to explore the context within which such initiatives have been undertaken. Of particular importance is the backdrop of social, economic, and political conditions in the West Bank and Gaza before the Oslo Agreement. The impact of post-1967 Israeli rule is an important part of this picture, shaping as it did significant aspects of the Palestinian political economy. Palestinian responses to occupation are also very important, with the evolution of Palestinian economic strategy, nongovernmental organizations, and nationalist mobilization all having important implications for subsequent peacebuilding programs. Finally, it is useful to sketch the pre-Oslo pattern of external assistance to the territories, since it was these activities that provided the initial base upon which donor programs expanded after 1993.

This chapter surveys all of those elements. It also provides an overview of key political and economic developments in Palestine after Oslo, including the provisions of the various interim Palestinian-Israeli agreements, challenges to sustainable growth, and the diplomatic ups and downs in the peace process through the 1994–99 interim period.

THE LEGACIES OF OCCUPATION

The Palestinian-Israeli conflict has a centurylong, complex, and often contentious history, with its fundamental origins in the clash between the Zionist ambition of regathering the Jewish diaspora in the historic land of Israel and the

Palestinians' dream of self-determination on their national soil.[1] With the first Arab-Israeli war in 1948, the state of Israel was established on most of the territory of the former British Mandate of Palestine. Only the Gaza Strip (controlled by Egypt) and the West Bank and East Jerusalem (controlled, and later annexed, by Jordan) remained under Arab control. Furthermore, during the war some three-quarters of a million Palestinians fled, or were driven from, their homes within Israel. These refugees would come to make up approximately one-third of the population of the West Bank and three-quarters of the population of Gaza, in addition to substantial concentrations in Jordan, Syria, Lebanon, the Gulf, and elsewhere.

Further Arab-Israeli wars followed in 1956 and 1967. In the course of the latter, Israeli forces captured both Gaza and the West Bank, resulting in the flight of another 300,000 refugees from these areas. After the war, the territories came under decades of Israeli military occupation.

The occupation of the West Bank and Gaza revitalized Palestinian nationalism, which had been disrupted by *al-nakba* (the disaster) of 1948, and which until 1967 had tended to look for hope to pan-Arabism. The Palestine Liberation Organization (established in 1964) was energized and would by the mid-1970s become the preeminent voice for Palestinian political ambitions. Initially, those ambitions were focused on the liberation of all Palestine through armed struggle. Over time, however, the goals of the mainstream PLO came to be refocused on the establishment of a Palestinian state in the West Bank and Gaza, alongside Israel.

This shift in PLO strategy and goals was due in part to Israel's enduring strategic power. Growing international diplomatic support for the Palestinians also played a role. So too did Arab factors: the weakening of Arab nationalism in the aftermath of the 1967 and 1973 Arab-Israeli wars; confrontations with Jordan (1970–71), Syria (1976, 1983–present), and other Arab countries; entanglement in the Lebanese civil war (1975–90); the 1979 peace treaty between Egypt and Israel; and Israel's 1982 invasion of Lebanon, which destroyed part of the PLO's external infrastructure. Further impetus was provided by the eruption of the Palestinian intifada in 1987. The uprising saw widespread popular mobilization throughout the territories in resistance to Israeli occupation. It also brought, like the 1982 war before it, growing international sympathy for the Palestinian cause. Within Israel, the costs and long-term viability of the occupation began to be questioned. Within the Palestinian movement, the uprising (and the prior destruction of PLO infrastructure in Lebanon) shifted political weight from the diaspora to the West Bank and Gaza, setting the stage for the Palestine National Council's 1988 declaration of Palestinian independence and even clearer endorsement of resolving the conflict through a negotiated "two-state" solution.

A few other factors were added to this context early in the 1990s. One was the gradual weakening of the intifada. A second, related factor was political frustration and the threat posed to the mainstream PLO by the growing Islamic movement in the territories. The 1990–91 Gulf War had important effects, with the perceived pro-Iraqi tilt of the PLO resulting in the suspension of important financial and political support from the conservative Arab Gulf states. The decline and eventual collapse of the Soviet Union, which had been a major supporter of the Palestinian cause, also had an impact. Finally, the regional preeminence of the United States in the Middle East—a preeminence confirmed by both the Gulf War and the collapse of the Soviet Union—set the stage for a new era, an era characterized by the opening of a comprehensive Arab-Israeli peace process in Madrid in October 1991.[2]

The Social and Economic Context

At the start of the peace process in 1991, approximately 2 million Palestinians (out of over 5 million Palestinians worldwide) resided in the West Bank (including East Jerusalem) and Gaza. This population was expanding, moreover, at one of the highest natural growth rates in the world: over 4 percent per year. This rate of population growth also resulted in a relatively young population, with 46 percent of Palestinians aged fourteen years and younger.[3] It has also resulted in growing pressure on land, water, and other natural resources, as well as in a rapidly growing labor force and hence an ever-present threat of accelerating levels of unemployment.

Social conditions in the West Bank and Gaza were, by most indicators, somewhat above regional averages, but somewhat inferior to those in Jordan—the most comparable case, with a large Palestinian population (table 2.1). Within the territories, moreover, a number of significant disparities could be observed. In particular, Gaza was characterized by much higher population density (1,870 persons per square kilometer, almost ten times the density of the West Bank), a higher proportion of refugees (78 percent, with fully 42 percent of the population residing in camps), less physical infrastructure, and a much greater shortage of water and arable land. Substantial differences could also be found among urban, rural, and refugee-camp inhabitants (see figure 2.1). However, overall income disparities appeared comparable to the average for Asia, and more equitable than typically the case in Africa or Latin America.[4]

Although detailed empirical data are not available, it is clear that following the onset of occupation in 1967 Palestinian social structure underwent substantial change. The dispossession and dislocations of 1948 and 1967 undermined the established notable class, although it did not eliminate its power altogether. Traditional, labor-intensive agriculture declined, as evidenced by a one-third decline in the number of persons employed in this sector between 1970 and 1991. This population was largely "proletarianized," in part through urbanization but even

Table 2.1. Social and Economic Indicators in the Middle East and North Africa (1991)

	Occupied Territories		Jordan	Middle East and North Africa
	West Bank	Gaza Strip		
Population (annual rate of natural increase)	1,241,000 (4.1%)	703,000 (5.0%)		
UNRWA–registered Palestinian Refugees (in camps)	430,083 (114,763)	528,684 (288,582)	960,212 (227,719)	2,519,488 (874,014)
GNP per Capita	$2,000	$1,230	$1,050	$1,940
Infant Mortality (per 1,000 live births)	42		29	60
Life Expectancy (years)	66		69	64
Households with Safe Water	90%		96%	83%
Persons per Hospital Bed	658		519	635

Sources: World Bank, *Developing the Occupied Territories: An Investment in Peace,* vol. 1, *Overview* (Washington, D.C.: World Bank, 1993), 6–8; World Bank, *Developing the Occupied Territories: An Investment in Peace,* vol. 6, *Human Resources and Social Policy* (Washington, D.C.: World Bank, 1993), 6, 9.

Note: Population figures are based on Israeli statistics and, according to later PCBS data, undercount the population by approximately 18 percent.

Figure 2.1. Disparities in West Bank and Gaza Living Conditions (1992)

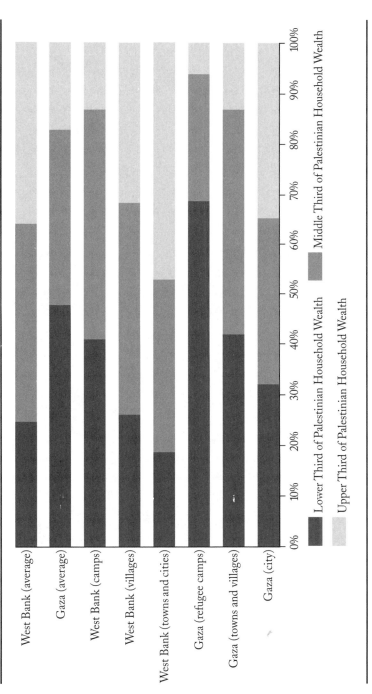

Source: Data drawn from Marianne Heiberg and Geir Øvensen, *Palestinian Society in Gaza, West Bank, and Arab Jerusalem: A Survey of Living Conditions* (Oslo: Fafo, 1993), table 6.3.

more so through incorporation as unskilled and semiskilled laborers in the agricultural or construction sectors of the Israeli economy or local Jewish settlements.
At the same time, the Palestinian middle class grew under the impetus of both
economic growth and the expansion of secondary and postsecondary education.
During the oil boom, substantial emigration of skilled labor to the Gulf and elsewhere occurred, with some 40 percent of Palestinian families reporting one or more
members living abroad.[5] After the boom, however, this option was no longer
available, and highly educated workers were often unable to find commensurate
work in the territories.

Under Jordanian rule, state economic policy had largely been aimed at promoting the development of the poorer East Bank, which was also the primary
power base of the Hashemite monarchy. The Palestinian territories, although ben-
efiting from an expansion of the public sector, continued to be characterized by a
predominant agricultural and large service sector and a relatively small industrial
sector. The imbalance was even greater in Egyptian-administered Gaza.

After Israeli occupation in 1967, the economy of the West Bank and Gaza
experienced periods of very substantial growth. During the first such phase, in the
early 1970s, real per capita gross national product (GNP) grew at an extraordi-
narily high rate of 11.3 percent per year (1970–75). Thereafter, growth continued
at a slower but still impressive rate of 4.1 percent per year in 1976–82, as the Israeli
economy itself slowed. Throughout the 1970s growth was in large part propelled
by external labor earnings, either from Palestinian day laborers and other workers
in Israel or from expatriates whose remittances were fueled by the oil boom in the
Gulf. However, substantial changes in domestic production also occurred, notably
in the modernization of parts of the agricultural sector and the growth of the
service sector.

Thereafter the economy stagnated as the regional oil economy contracted
and the effects of Israeli inflation were felt in the territories. With the Palestinian
uprising in late 1987, the Palestinian economy experienced substantial disruption. This disruption was further compounded by the devaluation of the Jordanian dinar, the severing of Jordan's administrative ties to the West Bank, and the
effects of the 1990–91 Gulf War. During 1987–91, real per capita GNP shrank
at a rate of about 2 percent per year.[6] In 1991, per capita GNP in the West Bank
and Gaza was approximately $1,715. Although this per capita GNP was some-
what higher than in Jordan, it was largely offset by the higher price structure in
the territories.

Aggregate figures, however, tell only part of the story. The experience of the
Palestinian economy under occupation was marked by substantial sectoral imbalances (table 2.2). In particular, the industrial sector in the territories expanded in
relative terms but—unlike in most developing regions—showed little relative

Table 2.2. Structure of Production in the West Bank and Gaza (1992)

Sector	West Bank (% of GDP)	Gaza (% of GDP)
Agriculture	43–45	25–26
Industry	7–8	11
Construction	10–11	21
Public and Community Services	9	16–17
Other Services	29	28

Source: World Bank, *Developing the Occupied Territories,* vol. 2, tables 15, 16.

growth. In 1992 industry in the West Bank represented only around 8 percent of gross domestic product (GDP), a share very much lower than that of Egypt (30 percent), Jordan (28 percent), Syria (23 percent), or most comparable economies. Although the rate of fixed capital formation was quite high and comparable to that of Jordan, the vast bulk of private-sector investment (around 81 percent during 1968–91) was in construction. Only 19 percent of private investment was in the productive sectors of the economy.[7] Between 1967 and 1991 the number of industrial establishments fell by half in the West Bank but almost doubled in Gaza. However, their average size remained very small, with less than 8 percent employing more than ten persons and 43 percent being owner-operated.[8]

By contrast, a large proportion of the Palestinian labor force began to work in Israel. In 1987 the wages of such workers accounted for fully 28 percent of Palestinian GNP and around one-third of all employment. Similarly, Palestinian trade had become heavily dependent on Israel for both imports and exports (table 2.3). These trade flows, moreover, were heavily weighted in Israel's favor, with the Palestinian trade deficit reaching 25 to 30 percent of GDP.[9] The second-largest Palestinian trading partner was Jordan, a continued relationship quietly promoted by Israel under its "open bridges" policy and intended to preserve a residual Jordanian role in the West Bank.

The Impact of Israeli Policies

To some extent, the features described here were a natural consequence of post-1967 economic interaction between the occupied territories and the much wealthier and more powerful Israel. Given the interaction between Israel and the West Bank and Gaza after 1967, the wage and technological differentials between them, and geographical realities, such features were to be expected. Moreover, many of these features might be expected to continue—albeit modified by labor

Table 2.3. Palestinian Dependence on Israel

	From the West Bank	From Gaza
Workers in Israel		
Total (1991)	69,400	41,700
As Percentage of Total Employed	29%	27%
Imports (1992)		
From Israel	89.7%	
From Jordan	7.7%	
From Other Countries	9.5%	
Exports (1992)		
To Israel	85.4%	
To Jordan	12.9%	
To Other Countries	1.8%	

Sources: World Bank, *Developing the Occupied Territories,* vol. 2, tables 26–32; World Bank and MAS, *Development under Adversity?*

policies, trade and customs regimes, and other arrangements—in any postpeace economic relationship.

Other aspects of the relationship, however, derived from the specific contours of Israeli policy during the occupation. Many Palestinians had left or been deported from the territories, quite apart from the refugee flows of 1948 and 1967. Within the territories, many younger Palestinians had forgone education to engage in street confrontations during the intifada or had found their higher education halted by university closures. Moreover, some 70,000 Palestinians (or about one-fifth of the labor force) had been detained by Israel at some point during 1988–93, with the ten thousand or so still in detention scheduled for release following the Oslo Agreement.[10]

Here, seven aspects of Israeli economic policy are discussed: land expropriation, limits on natural resource usage, low levels of public investment, fragmented social services, weak local government, a weak financial-banking sector, and the legal and regulatory system. The legacies of these policies would have important implications for the post-1993 challenges facing donors and the Palestinian Authority alike.

Land expropriation. By the early 1990s approximately 60 percent of the territory of the West Bank and Gaza had been seized by Israel, either by declaring it as state land or by expropriating it for military purposes or settlement construction. By 1992, some 144 Israeli settlements had been established within the territories, with a settler population of around 120,000.[11] These expropriations were in addition to East Jerusalem and its environs, which Israel claimed to have unilaterally annexed (with expanded municipal boundaries) after 1967 and which had been the object of intensive Israeli settlement. Following the eruption of the Palestinian uprising, growing restrictions were placed on the access of non-Jerusalem residents to the city. Given both the cultural and commercial importance of East Jerusalem and its central position in the transportation network of the West Bank, these restrictions had significant economic consequences.

Limits on natural resource usage. Israeli land seizures and settlement activity represented one important limit on natural resource usage. Another important element was severe Israeli restrictions on Palestinian exploitation of local water supplies. Between 1967 and the early 1990s, Palestinian water consumption increased by only 10 percent (from around 200 million cubic meters to around 215–228 million cubic meters), despite a doubling of the Palestinian population. Although Israel justified the water restrictions on grounds of conservation (particularly in Gaza, where the aquifer was threatened by increasing salinity), such concerns did not prevent Jewish settlers from increasing their water usage from zero to around 45 million cubic meters (or about three times Palestinian per capita consumption) over the same period.[12]

Low levels of public investment. The Israeli military government devoted few resources to public-sector investment: during the period 1987–91, public development expenditures accounted for around 3.5 percent of GDP, compared with 4.5 percent in Israel, 9.2 percent in Jordan, 13.3 percent in Egypt, and 7.0 percent in developing countries as a whole.[13] The lack of priority assigned to sustainable development was also evident in the spending of the Israeli Civil Administration in the territories, which through the late 1980s typically allocated only 16–18 percent of its West Bank and Gaza expenditures to its development budget.[14] Similarly, analysis of the outcome of international NGO projects submitted to Israel for approval showed a clear preference for health and social service activities over infrastructure and development.[15]

Palestinian municipal water and electrical enterprises also lacked the necessary funds for expansion and modernization. In the electrical sector, public utilities were almost entirely dependent on power generated by the Israel Electric Corporation. Electrical supply per capita (1991) was around 679 kilowatt-hours, compared with 1,054 kilowatt-hours in Jordan and 815 kilowatt-hours in Egypt. Water utilities were constrained by Israeli restrictions and by substantial loss rates owing to antiquated networks. Daily supply per capita amounted to less than half the amount in Jordan and one-quarter the amount in Israel. The telephone network was fully under Israeli control, and the number of subscribers per 1,000 population (22) was well below the rate in Jordan (64), Syria (39), Egypt (36), and post–civil war Lebanon (111). Some 80 percent of rural villages had no telephone connection whatsoever. According to the World Bank, about 40 percent of the road network in the West Bank was in grave need of repair.[16]

Fragmented social services. Under occupation, the provision of health, education, and welfare services to Palestinians was generally adequate by regional standards but was characterized by substantial fragmentation (table 2.4). In the health sector, the Israeli Civil Administration operated a health insurance scheme covering about one-fifth of Palestinians, as well as fourteen hospitals. However, about half of all primary care facilities were operated by NGOs, and Civil Administration spending accounted for less than a quarter of total health expenditures.[17] In the education sector, Civil Administration schools accounted for about two-thirds of primary and secondary education, with the United Nations Relief and Works Agency (UNRWA) accounting for most of the rest. Government education expenditures were equal to 2.0 percent of local GNP in 1991 (3.8 percent if UNRWA is included), compared with 6.5 percent in Jordan.[18] Postsecondary education was entirely the initiative of nonprofit institutions. Confrontations between the universities and the authorities were commonplace, resulting in the closure of the former during much of the intifada. Social welfare and relief programs were composed of a patchwork of refugee programs operated by UNRWA, the extension of some (but not all) Israel labor benefits to Palestinians working legally in Israel, and an array of local charitable societies. By the 1990s over five hundred of the latter were in operation, almost all of them small (with budgets under $100,000) and geared toward relief rather than development.[19]

Overall, Israeli policy in the social services sector appeared to safeguard social conditions (so as to facilitate political pacification), devolve the associated financial burden to other actors when possible, and refrain from comprehensive reorganization so as to avoid political controversy and retain some of the political advantages of a mixed system. As with other public-sector investments, relatively little modernization was undertaken.

Weak local government. Under military administration, power in the territories rested in Israeli hands, either in military (the Israeli Defense Forces) or civil (the Civil Administration) guise. One consequence of this was a further weakening of the structures of local government, which had already been relatively weak and dependent under previous Egyptian (in Gaza) and Jordanian (in the West Bank) administration. Politically, municipal elections were suspended after 1976 when it became clear that the results reflected widespread support for the PLO. Those

Table 2.4. Provision of Social Services to Palestinians (1991)

	Civil Administration	UNRWA	Nonprofit/ Voluntary	For-Profit/ Private Sector
Health Care Expenditures	$43.8 million 22%	$13.3 million 7%	$38.9 million 20%	$51.2 million 51%
School Enrollments	378,371 67%	144,456 26%	42,671 8%	
Teachers	12,496 67%	4,256 23%	1,842 10%	

Source: World Bank, *Developing the Occupied Territories,* vol. 6, *Human Resources and Social Policy* (Washington, D.C.: World Bank, 1993), 26, 38.

who showed excessive nationalist zeal were fired or deported, and subsequent mayors were thus appointed by Israel.[20] Fiscally, municipalities raised only around 20 percent of revenues from local sources, depending on central administration transfers (or external donors) for the remainder, including virtually all capital investment projects.[21]

It should be noted, however, that the Civil Administration—despite its lack of attention to public investments and sustainable development—did employ some 21,000 Palestinians as teachers, health care and social services workers, and low- and middle-ranking civil servants. This, despite the general legacy of institutional weakness left by the occupation, did offer a substantial nucleus for a future Palestinian civil service.

Israel also permitted Jordan to continue to pay the salaries of Jordanian civil servants in the West Bank as part of its general policy of encouraging a Jordanian role as a counterbalance to the PLO. This policy came to an end in 1988, however, when Jordan announced its disengagement from the West Bank. As a result, the PLO itself assumed much of the former Jordanian payroll.

Weak financial-banking sector. Immediately following occupation of the territories in 1967, Israel suspended the activities of all local, Arab, and foreign banks in the territories. Until 1981 only Israeli banks were permitted to operate. In 1992 some twenty-six bank branches operated in the West Bank and Gaza. Of these, sixteen were Israeli banks (thirteen of these operating in Jewish settlements and hence unavailable to Palestinians), while only ten were Arab bank branches.[22]

The result was a very weak financial services sector, characterized by low deposits and little availability of credit to the private sector. In 1990 domestic credit in the West Bank and Gaza was equivalent to only 0.7 percent of GDP, compared with 108.9 percent in Israel and 120.0 percent in Jordan.[23]

Legal and regulatory system. Under occupation, the legal system in the territories was a complex mix of military regulations, Jordanian law (in the West Bank), British Mandatory regulation, and Ottoman law. With regard to economic development, military orders often appeared to be intended to prevent the emergence of Palestinian competitors to Israeli firms.[24] With the intifada, this policy intensified as a political and economic tug-of-war erupted between Israel (attempting to reestablish social control) and Palestinian popular committees (attempting to promote economic self-reliance). Committees were outlawed; leaders arrested; goods seized; access to outside markets made more expensive and difficult; and bureaucratic processes made more complex and onerous.[25]

Overall, Israeli occupation and interaction between the Palestinian and Israeli economies had mixed effects. Growth rates in the territories were, until the 1980s, very high. Social conditions in the West Bank and Gaza generally mirrored those in comparable countries. However, other, structural aspects of the occupation clearly left the territories with a relatively underdeveloped economic infrastructure, financial sector, and industrial base: in the words of one UN report, "integration into the Israeli economy, in addition to producing higher incomes, also raised the costs, and reduced the availability, of productive inputs needed for the growth and development of the key productive branches of the [Palestinian] economy—agriculture, manufacturing and services. This also impeded the development of coherent and articulated relationships between these branches." Sara Roy has described this process as one of "de-development."[26]

To the extent that this situation was the outcome of deliberate Israeli policy, a future Palestinian administration could be expected to attempt to restructure it—assuming that alternative policy choices existed and political conditions permitted. As will be shown later, however, economic legacies weighed heavily, political realities were often restrictive, and Palestinian integration into and dependency on Israel continued to exert a powerful and entrenched logic—collectively limiting the economic policy options available to post-Oslo Palestinian decision makers.

Patterns of External Assistance

Before the Oslo Agreement, external assistance to the West Bank and Gaza derived from two major sources: from Western donors and from Arab donors (including the PLO). Most Western donor programs were established or grew in the 1970s and further expanded in the 1980s. Reflecting the lack of coordination among donors and the absence of a sovereign Palestinian counterpart, however, little reliable and comparable data exist for the pre-Oslo period. Starting in the early 1990s, some efforts were made to promote greater information sharing. In 1992 the United Nations Development Program (UNDP) published the first *Compendium of Ongoing and Planned Projects,* based on questionnaires sent to donors. The resulting data, however, are not adjusted for financial year and for pledged versus committed versus disbursed funds and likely reflect a double-counting of some assistance pledged in multiple years or disbursed through multi-lateral channels. Furthermore, PLO and many Arab funds are not measured in the UNDP survey. UNDP also initiated monthly "exchange of information" meetings —so called because some donors objected to the label of "coordination" in the view that no external party had the right to "coordinate" them.[27]

The limited data collected by UNDP show aid commitments rising sub-stantially in the early 1990s with the onset of the Madrid peace process, from around $174 million in 1992 to $263 million in 1993 (table 2.5). Aid from Euro-pean countries (including European Union multilateral aid) accounted for the largest share of this growth. Among predominately Western donors, education (30.3 percent) and health (27.6 percent) were the major areas of donor assistance, with industry (8.9 percent) and agriculture (3.2 percent) lagging well behind. According to the Development Assistance Committee of the OECD, however, actual Western aid disbursements in the Palestinian territories were only $182 mil-lion in 1993.[28]

In the absence of a counterpart state, and with donors unwilling to funnel assistance through the occupying authorities, most of this assistance flowed through NGO channels, either directly to Palestinian NGOs (PNGOs) or indirectly through international NGOs (INGOs) based in the donor country. USAID, for example, delivered its entire program through a half-dozen INGOs. This was intended to avoid any official recognition of Israeli occupation and also reduce the domestic political risks for the agency that might arise from bilateral USAID programming in such a sensitive area. Unlike many other donors, however, the United States also required that NGOs obtain Israeli approval for their activities.[29] Approximately two hundred INGOs were said to be active in the territories by the 1990s.[30] Coordination among them was relatively weak, with European and non-European INGOs organized into different networks.

Among the various UN agencies, UNRWA had by far the largest presence in the field, dating back to shortly after the 1948 war.[31] The overwhelming bulk of its expenditures was also devoted to education, health, and social relief. However, the agency—which faced both a rapidly growing refugee population and frequent budgetary difficulties—found itself with a "dramatic shortfall in contributions to its regular budget" from 1993 onward.[32] UNDP's program was very much smaller, having been authorized by the UN General Assembly in 1978 and having

Table 2.5. UNDP Estimates of Donor Assistance to the West Bank and Gaza
(1992–93)

	1992 ($ millions)	1993 ($ millions)
Bilateral Donors	**42.4**	**138.7**
Italy	6.0	23.4
United States	18.6	19.6
Germany	0.3	16.1
Japan	1.1	14.8
Sweden	4.5	12.1
Netherlands	1.5	7.8
France	2.0	6.5
Norway	2.9	5.2
Others (Australia, Austria, Belgium, Canada, Denmark, Finland, Greece, Ireland, Kuwait, Libya, Malaysia, Saudi Arabia, Spain, Switzerland, United Kingdom)	5.5	33.2
Multilateral Donors	**15.3**	**75.5**
European Union	12.0	63.2
Arab Fund for Economic and Social Development	1.4	9.3
Others	1.9	3.0
Multilateral Agencies	**116.2**	**48.6**
UNRWA	109.2	37.4
UNDP	5.2	4.1
Others (FAO, IFAD, ILO, UNCDF, UNCTAD, UNESCO, UNFPA, UNICEF, UNIFEM, WHO)	1.8	7.1
Total	**173.9**	**262.8**

Sources: UNDP, *1993 Compendium of External Assistance to the Occupied Palestinian
Territories* (Jerusalem: UNDP, July 1993); and UNDP, *1994 Compendium of External
Assistance to the Occupied Palestinian Territories* (Jerusalem: UNDP, August 1994).

become active on the ground only in 1986. Other UN agencies had only a limited presence in the territories, if they were present at all.

Much less information is available on Palestinian and other Arab assistance to the territories. Support flowed from Jordan (which retained administrative ties to the West Bank after 1967 and maintained the payroll of its former employees), the PLO (its coffers swelled in the 1970s and early 1980s by Arab petrodollar donations), other Arab states, and wealthy individuals. The level of assistance increased sharply after 1979, when the Baghdad summit meeting of the Arab League agreed to provide up to $150 million per year in support of the territories, allocated through a PLO-Jordanian joint committee. Estimates of the actual flows vary widely. Total PLO aid to the territories between 1979 and 1987 has been pegged at almost half a billion dollars.[33] Another estimate puts Arab steadfastness funds at some $110 million per year in the early 1980s, equal to more than one-third of all funds from abroad (excluding UNRWA).[34] The World Bank has suggested that before administrative disengagement in 1988, Jordan provided some $50 million per year in aid and other Arab governments another $15 million per year.[35] Another World Bank study put Arab support for Palestinian NGOs at between $30 million and $100 million per year, with between $45 million and $50 million from all sources directed toward universities, hospitals, and other semipublic institutions.[36] Although many Arab pledges of assistance to the PLO often went unfulfilled during the intifada, some reports have suggested that the PLO was able to inject up to $10 million *per month* into the territories in 1988–89, with the amounts falling to about a quarter of this level thereafter.[37] Much smaller but growing amounts of external resources also went to various Islamist social groups.

Whatever the actual figures, it is clear that such assistance had important effects. It funded projects in such areas as agriculture, infrastructure, municipal services, housing, and education. The establishment of a Palestinian university system, for example, was largely achieved through external assistance; many Palestinian NGOs also relied heavily on outside aid. One World Bank study suggested that two-thirds of funding for Palestinian charitable societies came from external sources, while for many other PNGOs the proportion was undoubtedly even larger.[38]

External funding also had political effects. PLO funding in particular was closely tied to both nationalist mobilization and factional competition. External assistance was sometimes also associated with patronage and corruption. All of these aspects will be explored in greater detail later.

In the meantime, it is important to note one other characteristic of external assistance: the near collapse of PLO and other Arab transfers in the early 1990s.

In 1988 Jordan announced that it would disengage from its administrative role in the West Bank and in so doing terminated the payment of most former civil service salaries in the territories. The PLO took up paying much of this. In 1989 the Arab pledges of aid made at the 1979 Baghdad summit came to an end. This, coupled with the recession in the regional oil economy, further reduced Arab aid to both Palestine and the PLO, despite periodic pledges of Arab support for the intifada. During the Gulf crisis of 1990–91, PLO policy angered many conservative Arab states, which terminated their direct assistance to the PLO. Saudi Arabia, for example, ended the approximately $85 million per year that it had been paying to the organization, as did Kuwait, which had been providing some $47 million annually.[39] The result was a major financial crisis for the PLO and hence for the institutions that the PLO supported in the West Bank and Gaza. According to one Palestinian economist, PLO funding to the territories fell from $350 million in 1988 to $120 million in 1990 to $40 million in 1993.[40] Certainly, by the summer of 1993 the PLO had been forced to suspend payments to the families of martyrs and reduce financial support for institutions in the territories by some 80 percent.[41] As a consequence, universities were unable to pay staff, nationalist newspapers closed, and many organizations had to trim programs and services. This financial crisis had not only a social and economic impact but also a political one: as noted earlier, the suspension of Arab funding was one of the many factors that convinced the PLO to engage in the Madrid peace process and agree to the Oslo accords.

Palestinian Responses

In addition to the effects of Israeli occupation and donor assistance on the territories, the context for socioeconomic development in the West Bank and Gaza has been shaped by Palestinian responses. Three aspects of this are particularly important in understanding the post-1993 course of peacebuilding and foreign aid in the territories: the PLO-supported strategy of *sumud;* the activities of Palestinian NGOs; and the political economy of nationalist mobilization, factionalism, and control.

Sumud

Through the 1970s and 1980s, the dominant motif of Palestinian economic strategy was that of *sumud* (steadfastness), intended to foster the ability of Palestinian institutions, lands, and infrastructure to resist Israeli pressures. Palestinians often stressed the traditional characteristics of Palestinian culture: village life, peasant attachment to the land, and women as caregivers and mothers-of-the-nation. *Sumud* also tended to be a reactive rather than proactive strategy, reflecting political dependence on the PLO and Arab states for leadership. As Salim Tamari suggests, *sumud* "began as a form of passive resistance to Israeli rule . . . and ended as a form of passive non-resistance. . . . [T]he search for self-sufficiency became a search for autarky—a perspective that was blind to the present economic realities of Israeli domination and market forces."[42] Similarly, Sara Roy notes of Palestinian economic strategy during this period that it was largely directed toward "maintaining, not transforming, economic conditions," seeking to maintain a Palestinian presence on the land rather than proactively restructuring Palestinian production and enterprise.[43]

Alternatives to passive *sumud* were increasingly discussed in the 1980s, particularly with the onset of the intifada. However, despite a number of initiatives emerging from the uprising—greater emphasis on agriculture, home produce, the growth of the cooperative movement, a "buy Palestinian" campaign, and an associated partial boycott of Israeli goods—no fundamental restructuring of Palestinian economic strategy took place. Part of the reason for this was rooted in the power of the traditional nationalist imagery and part in the apparent lack of support by the diaspora PLO leadership for independent and innovative activities by local groups. Equally important was the growing economic crisis that accompanied the intifada, coupled with a lack of Palestinian control over key instruments of economic policy and other constraints imposed by Israeli occupation.

Palestinian Civil Society and the NGO Sector

The second important aspect of Palestinian development in the pre-Oslo period was the critical role played by the NGO sector. Under Israeli occupation Palestinian civil society had grown vibrant and diverse. By the early 1990s, approximately 1,200 to 1,500 PNGOs were in existence, employing perhaps 20,000 to 30,000 persons. Almost half of these organizations were headquartered in the Bethlehem-Jerusalem-Ramallah area.[44] A variety of groups could be discerned: traditional charitable associations and welfare associations, often locally and religiously oriented;[45] professional associations; trade unions; development NGOs; advocacy, research, and human rights groups; popular organizations, such as women's associations, student associations, and grassroots groups; cooperatives;[46] and semipublic institutions such as hospitals and universities.[47] As noted earlier, these organizations provided a substantial share of education, health care, and other social services in the territories.

Several factors accounted for the growth and size of the NGO sector. The expansion of Palestinian incomes and education in the 1970s had led to an expansion of the middle class, of professional groups, and of student and other groups. Whereas the Israeli occupation often sought to weaken Palestinian NGOs, particularly those popular organizations directly linked to Palestinian nationalist groups, Palestinian exposure to the rambunctious pluralism of Israeli politics may

have encouraged efforts at community organization. In the absence of a Palestinian state, and with the Israeli authorities reluctant to engage in public-sector
institution building, the delivery of many key social services depended on Palestinian NGOs. The channeling of Western and Arab donor support through NGOs
was undoubtedly a major factor in their growth, with such funding reaching a
peak of between $140 million and $220 million in the early 1990s.[48]

Many NGOs, as well as Palestinian universities, played an increasingly important role in sustaining critical debate over the future course of Palestinian
development. Their degree of influence on social change, however, was harder to
judge. The Palestinian women's movement offered perhaps the best example: the
intifada energized women's grassroots participation in political protests, and many
women's groups offered articulate social critiques of gender inequity and broader
developmental issues. Counter to this, however, were both the weight of Palestinian nationalist symbolism (with its frequent emphasis on women's maternal roles)
and the pressures to subordinate the "gender agenda" to the imperatives of national
unity and the requirements of nationalist struggle against occupation.[49] Politically, the women's movement was fragmented into rival organizations. Moreover,
the presence of articulate and visible women at the helm of women's groups and
the support offered by donor funds tended to obscure the extent to which women's
groups had—or had not—succeeded in mobilizing a mass social base. Despite
frequent optimism about the liberating effects of the intifada and empowerment
through participation in the nationalist struggle, few if any women penetrated
into the senior decision-making levels of either the uprising or the PLO. Indeed,
Palestinian society seemed at least as patriarchal as—and possibly more so than—
neighboring "conservative" Jordan.[50] All of this raised questions about the extent
to which the movement had made real gains and the extent to which any such
gains would survive the transition from active liberation struggle to a new, post-
Oslo political environment. In many respects, similar sorts of issues would also
confront other sectors of civil society.

Political Mobilization, Factionalism, and Control

As is evident from this discussion, powerful political imperatives were closely
linked with both external assistance to the territories and the evolution of Palestinian NGOs. The foremost of these imperatives was the requirement of nationalist mobilization against Israel.

The PLO's "formal" military-cum-guerrilla apparatus in the territories was
always relatively weak, a function of both geography and Israeli counterinsurgency.
Instead, nationalist leadership tended to be provided in other ways. Through the
1970s this largely took the form of nationalist mayors and other well-known
public personalities, as well as the PLO-affiliated Palestine National Front

(1973–78) and National Guidance Committee (1978–82). The high public visibility of this leadership, however, rendered it vulnerable to arrest, deportation, and other Israeli countermeasures.[51]

In their place, Palestinian nationalist groups placed increasing emphasis on a more diffuse array of groups, popular organizations, and institutions. This meant that, for many NGOs, "development effectiveness was secondary to political solidarity," resulting in "weak systems for evaluation, transparency and quality control."[52] With the growing influence of social and political Islam in the 1980s, parallel growth occurred among religious charitable organizations, clinics, schools, and social institutions—many informally linked with Islamist political groups. It was this rich network of institutions that provided what Salim Tamari has called the "organizational crucible" of the intifada, sustaining high levels of political mobilization and confrontation against the Israeli occupation from December 1987 onward.[53]

For the PLO, the various component organizations of the PLO, and the Islamist movement, support for NGOs was thus an increasingly important part of the broader struggle against occupation. Yasir Arafat's dominant Fateh mainstream had little difficulty providing aid directly (at least until the Gulf War) by virtue of its access to the PLO's substantial financial resources. Smaller leftist PLO groups had less access to PLO resources but were able to generate resources either locally or by securing (usually unwitting) Western donor support for affiliated NGOs in the territories.[54] Here, the Left's much weaker popular support was offset by its substantial strength among the ranks of intellectuals, professionals, and NGO activists. Islamist NGOs appear to have raised the bulk of their resources locally, although some aid did come from outside, from sympathetic states,[55] individuals, and even Western donors.[56] Not surprisingly, Israel responded to the growing importance of grassroots nationalist and Islamist organizations in the intifada with its own countermeasures: popular committees were outlawed, activists were arrested and deported, and restrictions were placed on financial transactions in an attempt to staunch the flow of money.

Not all NGO-linked political mobilization was directed against Israel: factional competition was also an important political imperative shaping the growth of Palestinian civil organizations. Immediately prior to the Oslo Agreement, the Palestinian political spectrum was characterized by three major forces.

- *Fateh.* Since the late 1960s, Fateh (headed by Yasir Arafat) has been by far the largest Palestinian nationalist organization and historically has dominated the institutional machinery of the PLO. Fateh espouses a rather uncluttered Palestinian nationalism and contains supporters with a broad range of views. The bulk of the Fateh leadership had supported Palestinian participation in the Madrid peace process, and a majority endorsed (sometimes reluctantly) the Oslo Agreement.

- *The Left.* The Palestinian Left—represented by the Popular Front for the Liberation of Palestine (PFLP), the Democratic Front for the Liberation of Palestine (DFLP), the Palestinian Democratic Union (FIDA), and the Palestinian People's Party (PPP, formerly the Palestinian Communist Party) —had played a historically influential role in the evolution of Palestinian politics and the PLO and had a strong presence among intellectuals and NGO organizers. However, by the fall of 1993 their support and influence had waned. FIDA and the PPP had generally supported the peace process (while critical of aspects of Arafat's handling of this), while the DFLP and especially the PFLP had opposed the Palestinian presence at Madrid and were critical of the Oslo Agreement.

- *The Islamists.* In the place of the secular Left, the Islamist movement— Hamas and the much smaller Islamic Jihad, both of which lay outside the framework of the PLO—had emerged in the late 1980s as the primary opposition to Fateh and the nationalist mainstream. Hamas in particular was also linked, directly or indirectly, to a growing number of clinics, educational institutions, and other social welfare NGOs in the territories. Popular support for the Islamist groups was difficult to gauge but had grown substantially during the intifada, especially whenever confrontation grew or prospects for political settlement seemed faint. Hamas and Islamic Jihad opposed the peace process (and indeed any "two-state" solution to the conflict) altogether, although many individual Islamists expressed a broader range of views and interests.[57]

A number of smaller groups also existed, most of them rejectionist splinters of larger organizations or fronts established by Arab states. None enjoyed any significant support in the territories. Shortly after the Oslo Agreement, surveys suggested that around 45 percent of Palestinians supported Fateh, around 10 percent supported the various leftist groups (notably the PFLP), and some 20 percent or more looked to Hamas.[58] However, in the darker days of 1990–91 Islamist groups had taken almost half the vote in professional association elections in Gaza, underscoring their substantial potential threat to Fateh should the peace process falter.

Political factionalism shaped many aspects of associational life in the territories. When the Palestinian Left first promoted the vehicle of popular organizations and NGOs in the 1970s, the Fateh-PLO mainstream reacted with suspicion and discouragement. When discouragement failed, Fateh threw its own much larger financial resources into the fray, encouraging the creation of a broad range of pro-Fateh organizations. With the partial destruction of the PLO's base of operations in Lebanon in 1982, and even more so with the eruption of the intifada in 1987, the territories increasingly became the center of gravity of the Palestinian nationalist movement, creating greater incentive for factions to improve their relative influence there through the funding of politically compliant *dakakin* (shops). As a result, the West Bank and Gaza featured four major women's federations in the 1980s, each affiliated with a different Palestinian party.[59] Much the same occurred in the labor movement, in which factional competition encouraged the formation of rival trade unions. By the early 1990s there were three major labor federations and some thirty-eight registered trade unions in Palestine. When union splits are taken into account, the number of labor organizations reached 138 in 1993, serving only 6,000 active members.[60] Within professional associations, chambers of commerce, and Palestinian universities, internal elections became a key barometer of the balance of power among political groups, keenly watched by Palestinians and external observers alike.

The flow of financial resources to allied NGOs also served the purposes of consolidating party apparatuses and ensuring political control. Until the early 1990s, this allowed the PLO and its constituent groups to offer financial compensation to victims of the struggle and support for the families of prisoners. The PLO also supported student scholarships, as well as projects in areas such as housing, agriculture, and education. In addition, there was "a sizable amount of handouts in the form of patronage money to nationalist institutions and personalities."[61] This chain of patronage reached even into small rural villages. In the process, corruption was not infrequent.[62]

The use of such neopatrimonial mechanisms of political management had, in fact, a long history in Palestine. Variously the Ottomans, British, Jordanians, and Israelis had used patronage to consolidate their political position.[63] Within the PLO—long beset by the centrifugal political forces of factional competition, a dispersed population, and the tug-of-war of Arab politics—patronage had been used to cement both the organization as a whole and Fateh's leading position within it. The availability (until the early 1990s) of substantial petrodollar resources, the otherwise nebulous character of Fateh ideology, and Arafat's general historic reluctance to suppress political rivals increased the incentive to do so.[64] As a result, fealty was often prized over competence, and corruption by subordinates was often overlooked in the interests of power.[65] To the extent that this process was noted by observers, it tended to be attributed to political culture and traditional politics, or to Arafat's particular political style. In fact, it is much better understood as arising from a particular constellation of leadership, resource distribution, political economy, and organizational imperatives—a dynamic that would have important consequences for the post-Oslo construction of the Palestinian Authority.

THE PEACE PROCESS

The challenges of peacebuilding in Palestine have been fundamentally shaped not only by socioeconomic conditions, the legacies of Israeli occupation, and the dynamics of Palestinian nationalist organization, but also by the procedural and substantial content of the Palestinian-Israeli peace process and the various agreements it produced. These agreements determined, from the point of view of donors, the major raison d'être for the expansion of aid programs in the 1990s, as well as some of the framework of assistance and many of the opportunities for specific projects. From the perspective of the Palestinian Authority, the peace process and interim agreements determined the extent of its authority and defined the levers of policy that it had at its disposal. Moreover, the continuing process of negotiation loomed large in Palestinian development policy too, with the Palestinian Authority seeking to use aid and economic policy to consolidate its political situation and enhance its position in future interactions with Israel.

The Madrid Framework

The peace process began with the convening of the Madrid conference in October 1991, cochaired by the United States and Russia and based on the principles of UN Security Council Resolutions 242 and 338. Direct bilateral discussions subsequently followed in Washington, D.C., between Israel and the Palestinians, Jordan, Syria, and Lebanon.

Multilateral working groups were also initiated in Moscow in January 1992 on key issues of regional concern: regional economic development, refugees, water, the environment, and arms control and regional security. The Regional Economic Development Working Group (REDWG), "gaveled" by the European Union, organized a series of international activities and established a monitoring committee as well as a permanent secretariat in Amman. Perhaps the most visible manifestations of increased economic contact across the region among governments and private sectors alike were the Middle East and North Africa economic summits, held in Casablanca (October–November 1994), Amman (October 1995), Cairo (November 1996), and Doha (November 1997), and the establishment of the Middle East Development Bank. The Refugee Working Group (RWG), gaveled by Canada, addressed the difficult issue of Palestinian refugees, with work on databases, child welfare, public health, human resource development, economic infrastructure, and family reunification. The groups on water and on the environment, gaveled by the United States and Japan, respectively, sponsored a variety of activities focused on these critical areas.[66]

Given the very substantial issues between the parties and the constraining glare of publicity, the ten rounds of Palestinian-Israeli bilateral negotiations that took place through 1991–93 proved slow and difficult. Progress in the multilaterals was equally incremental and very much tied to the pace of the primary bilateral negotiations.

The Declaration of Principles

It was in this context that Israel and the Palestine Liberation Organization embarked, with Norwegian facilitation, on parallel but secret discussions. These ultimately bore fruit in the form of the Israeli-Palestinian Declaration of Principles (DoP, or "Oslo Agreement"), which was formally signed by Israeli prime minister Yitzhak Rabin and PLO chairman Yasir Arafat in Washington, D.C., on September 13, 1993.[67]

Central to the Oslo Agreement was mutual recognition between Israel and the PLO. The two parties pledged to begin "permanent status" negotiations in 1996, which would include the most difficult and important issues between them: borders, Israeli settlements, security arrangements, refugees, and Jerusalem. In the meantime, they agreed to immediately negotiate transitional arrangements for Palestinian elections and interim self-government. These would begin with the withdrawal of Israeli forces from the Gaza Strip and the West Bank town of Jericho and the establishment in these areas of the Palestinian Authority. Additional Israeli redeployments would occur at a later date, before Palestinian elections. Negotiations would also begin on "the modalities of admission of persons displaced from the West Bank and Gaza Strip in 1967" within the framework of a Palestinian-Israeli-Jordanian-Egyptian committee, and Israel agreed to establish a "safe passage" for Palestinian movement between the autonomous areas in the West Bank and Gaza. Finally, the two sides committed themselves to a range of initiatives to foster development and regional economic cooperation.

By securing mutual political recognition between Israel and the PLO, the agreement represented a breakthrough, setting the stage for more direct and intensive negotiations. Moreover, the Declaration of Principles was a careful experiment in forward-looking constructive ambiguity, which sought to create a productive political process (focused on immediately achievable objectives) without prejudicing the political ambitions of either party or predetermining the ultimate outcome of negotiations. Through such interim confidence-building measures and a growing volume of cooperative interaction, it was hoped, new future possibilities would emerge for a comprehensive and mutually acceptable resolution of the Palestinian-Israeli conflict. In practice, however, the extended nature of the "interim" period also provided opportunities for violence and unforeseen political developments to disrupt the process.

Implementing the Declaration of Principles

The Gaza-Jericho Agreement

The first of the transitional arrangements negotiated under the auspices of the Declaration of Principles was the Cairo Agreement (also known as the Gaza-Jericho Agreement) of May 4, 1994.[68] This established the framework both for Israel's withdrawal from Gaza and Jericho and for the establishment of the Palestinian Authority (PA). Under the terms of the agreement, the PA was assigned legislative authority in these areas in thirty-eight specified fields. However, Israel retained the ability to block unwanted Palestinian legislation through a joint "legislation subcommittee" of the Palestinian-Israeli Civil Affairs Coordination and Cooperation Committee. Moreover, Israel retained full control over the areas surrounding Jewish settlements in Gaza (map 2.1) and security control over some additional territories ("yellow areas"), as well as control of all West Bank areas outside Jericho.

On May 10 the first contingent of Palestinian police entered Gaza, and a little over a week later the last Israeli troops left the self-rule areas. On July 1, 1994, Yasir Arafat arrived in Palestine to assume the leadership of the Palestinian Authority, his first return to Palestine since 1967.

The Paris Protocol

Economic relations between Israel and the PA during the interim period were set forth in Protocol IV of the Cairo Agreement, previously signed in Paris on April 29, 1994.[69]

Under the terms of the Paris Protocol, a de facto customs union was established between Israel and the territories. Palestinian negotiators had not favored this model, which reinforced the continued integration (and dependence) of the Palestinian economy. Instead, they had pushed for an agreement that would give the PA greater control over its economic borders and maximize the range and independence of economic instruments at its disposal. However, Israel was reluctant to surrender too many symbols of sovereignty, and it was impossible to demarcate economic boundaries when the political borders remained undetermined pending final-status negotiations. Under the protocol, common tariffs were to be established for many products, with the PA permitted to set rates independently on some goods below certain quantities and import other goods duty-free. Israel, with control over all international crossing points, would collect customs and excise receipts on Palestinian goods and remit these to the PA. Palestinian exports were formally left largely unrestricted, although in response to the protectionist concerns of some Israeli producers, quotas were placed on the trade of six specified agricultural goods to Israel until 1998.

The PA was not authorized to establish its own currency, although a Palestinian Monetary Authority was mandated to oversee the local banking system and manage official foreign currency reserves. In the field of taxation, the PA was given independent control of direct taxation, but much less control over indirect taxation. Value-added tax (VAT) rates were pegged at 15–16 percent, so as to be in line with the 17 percent rate of Israeli VAT. Gasoline prices could be set somewhat below Israeli prices, but gasoline itself had to be distinctively colored to obviate sales into the Israeli market. Procedures were outlined for the clearance of customs, excise, and VAT revenues between the two parties. Finally, the parties committed themselves to attempt to maintain normal labor movement between them (in practice, almost entirely Palestinian workers traveling to Israel), "subject to each side's right to determine from time to time the extent and conditions of labor movement into its area."

Early Empowerment

Following Israel's withdrawal from Gaza and Jericho, new negotiations followed on both the immediate transfer of additional areas of responsibility to the PA ("early empowerment") and the eventual redeployment of additional Israeli forces from areas in the West Bank. In August 1994 the parties signed the Agreement on Preparatory Transfer of Powers and Responsibilities, whereby Israel undertook to transfer authority over education and culture, health, social welfare, tourism, and direct taxation and VAT on local production. In August 1995 a subsequent Protocol on Further Transfer of Powers and Responsibilities brought about the transfer of authority in eight more areas (agriculture, census and statistics, energy, insurance, labor, local government, postal services, and trade and industry).[70] In assuming control over these areas, the PA utilized both Palestinian employees of the previous Israeli civil administration and its own growing bureaucratic apparatus. It also established a series of different internal security agencies. The Cairo Agreement permitted the PA to employ up to 9,000 police, although the actual number would eventually grow much higher than this.[71]

The Palestinian-Israeli Interim Agreement: "Oslo II"

All of this set the stage for another political landmark: the Israeli-Palestinian Interim Agreement on the West Bank and Gaza Strip (better known as the Taba or Oslo II agreement), signed by the parties in Washington on September 28, 1995.[72] This lengthy and detailed agreement confirmed the process of expanding both territorial and functional control of the Palestinian Authority. The agreement contained a number of core elements.

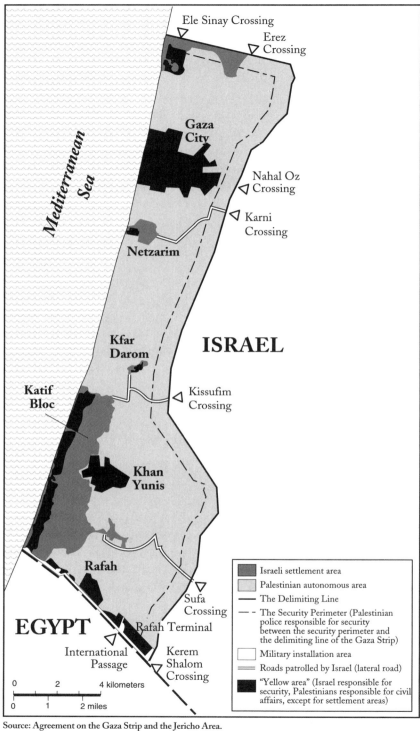

Ele Sinay Crossing

Erez Crossing

Gaza City

Nahal Oz Crossing

Karni Crossing

Netzarim

Mediterranean Sea

ISRAEL

Kfar Darom

Kissufim Crossing

Katif Bloc

Khan Yunis

Rafah

Sufa Crossing

EGYPT

Rafah Terminal

International Passage

Kerem Shalom Crossing

	Israeli settlement area
	Palestinian autonomous area
———	The Delimiting Line
– – –	The Security Perimeter (Palestinian police responsible for security between the security perimeter and the delimiting line of the Gaza Strip)
	Military installation area
═══	Roads patrolled by Israel (lateral road)
■	"Yellow area" (Israel responsible for security, Palestinians responsible for civil affairs, except for settlement areas)

0   2   4 kilometers

0   1   2 miles

Source: Agreement on the Gaza Strip and the Jericho Area.

Map 2.1. The Gaza Strip (1994). *By permission of the Foundation for Middle East Peace.*

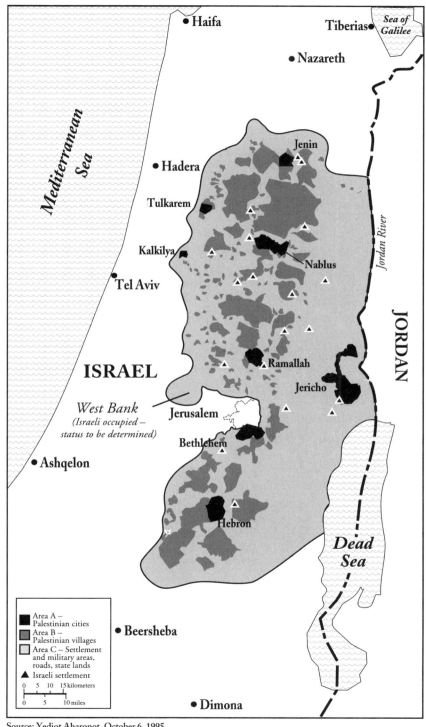

Source: Yediot Aharonot, October 6, 1995.

Map 2.2. The West Bank (1996). *By permission of the Foundation for Middle East Peace.*

Redeployment and security arrangements. Israel agreed to withdraw its military forces from the six Palestinian cities (area A) of Tulkarem, Qalqilya, Jenin, Nablus, Ramallah, and Bethlehem. In addition, special arrangements would be negotiated for the city of Hebron, to be followed by Israeli redeployment from that city too. In total, this made up some 2.7 percent of the West Bank and around 36 percent of its population (excluding Jerusalem). Israel also agreed to redeploy from other populated areas of the West Bank (area B), including some 450 Palestinian towns and villages, representing 25 percent of the West Bank and around 60 percent of its Palestinian population. The remaining areas (including sparsely populated areas, Israeli settlements, and military areas) were assigned to area C (map 2.2).[73]

Under the agreement, further Israeli redeployments would occur over an eighteen-month time frame, resulting in the enlargement of areas A and B to include all territories not subject to final-status negotiations. It was further agreed that "in order to maintain the territorial integrity of the West Bank and the Gaza Strip as a single territorial unit, and to promote their economic growth and the demographic and geographical links between them," the parties would protect the "normal and smooth movement of people, vehicles, and goods within the West Bank, and between the West Bank and the Gaza Strip." Territorial control of Jerusalem was not addressed in the agreement, as the issue was reserved for final-status negotiations.

The Palestinian Authority assumed responsibility for internal security and public order (civil policing) in area A. In area B the Palestinian police were to be responsible for public order, but with Israel retaining "overriding responsibility for security." Under the agreement Israel retained full security control of area C, subject to additional military redeployments over eighteen months and the possible transfer of additional powers and responsibilities to the Palestinian police. It was agreed that the maximum number of Palestinian police would be 18,000 in Gaza and 12,000 in the West Bank.

Expansion of Palestinian responsibilities. As the initial redeployment of Israeli troops occurred, all civil powers and responsibilities in areas A and B (some forty spheres, including those covered by the previous early empowerment agreements) were transferred to the Palestinian Authority. In area C, the PA was granted functional civil jurisdiction in areas not relating to territory. Moreover, powers and responsibilities relating to territory would gradually be transferred to Palestinian jurisdiction, excepting those areas (such as settlements) reserved for final-status negotiation. The agreement explicitly recognized Palestinian water rights in the West Bank—albeit subject to definition in final-status negotiations—and included water issues related solely to Palestinians among those areas of civil jurisdiction transferred to the Palestinian Authority. It was also agreed that the Palestinians would be permitted to develop some additional water resources in agreed areas to meet the shortfall in Palestinian water requirements, although the establishment of a Joint Water Committee gave Israel significant voice in water management issues.

The economic annex to the agreement (Annex V) comprised the earlier 1994 agreement between Israel and the Palestinians, with the addition of more detailed clauses regarding the clearance of import tax revenues from Israel to the PA and the implementation of direct and indirect taxation.

Palestinian elections. The agreement detailed the composition of an elected Palestinian legislative council and its executive authority (including a directly and popularly elected president). After the initial redeployment of Israeli forces, Palestinian elections would be held under international supervision throughout the West Bank and Gaza. Special arrangements were agreed to allow Palestinian residents in the city of Jerusalem to vote in the elections. The president and legislative council were to hold office for an interim period of up to five years.

Coordination and cooperation. Finally, the agreement provided for a host of coordinating mechanisms. The chief among these was the Joint Liaison Committee (JLC), previously established under Article X of the DoP. The Joint Security Coordination and Cooperation Committee was established in the security field, with the Joint Regional Security Committee and Joint District Coordination Offices. The agreement also broadly committed the PA to cooperate with Israel in combating terrorism and other security challenges. The Legal Committee addressed legal and judicial cooperation and provided a vehicle for Israel to raise concerns arising from Palestinian legislation. Unlike a similar committee established under the Gaza-Jericho Agreement, however, this committee had no power to delay or veto contentious Palestinian legislation. The Joint Civil Affairs Coordination and Cooperation Committee, together with a Joint Regional Civil Affairs Subcommittee for both the West Bank and Gaza and District Civil Liaison Offices in the West Bank, was to facilitate cooperation in civil areas. The agreement continued the Joint Economic Committee originally established by the 1994 Paris Protocol. Finally, the agreement contained a number of specific confidence-building measures, as well as an annex devoted to cooperation programs.

Following Israeli redeployment, Palestinian elections were held throughout the West Bank and Gaza on January 20, 1996, for both the presidency of the Palestinian Authority and the eighty-eight-person Palestinian Legislative Council (PLC). Despite some procedural weaknesses, international observers judged the elections to have been "an accurate expression of the will of the voters."[74] The overwhelming majority of those candidates elected supported the peace process, signaling Palestinian hopes for an end to decades of conflict. In April the Palestine National Council met in Gaza to formally amend the PLO Charter, eliminating those clauses contrary to the spirit of Oslo. In May final-status talks were formally opened, although the onset of substantive negotiations was delayed by forthcoming Israeli general elections. Before the elections, the Labor Party revised its electoral platform so as to eliminate its previous opposition to Palestinian statehood.

Despite the successful implementation of the initial stages of Oslo II, serious challenges continued to confront the peace process. In November 1995 Prime Minister Yitzhak Rabin was assassinated by an Israeli extremist opposed to the agreement. In February and March 1996, during the run-up to Israel's general elections, the Palestinian Islamist group Hamas launched four terrorist bombings in Jerusalem and Tel Aviv. Israel responded by imposing its most severe restrictions ever on the West Bank and Gaza. This resulted in very substantial Palestinian economic losses through forgone wages and exports and created price increases, shortages, and a steep rise in local unemployment. International development projects were severely disrupted. For its part the Palestinian Authority responded to terrorism by stepping up security measures against militant groups.

Hebron Protocol

Under Oslo II, Israeli redeployment from much of the city had been slated to occur in March 1996. Implementation was delayed, however, by the bombings of February and March and by Israeli elections. The elections themselves brought to power a new right-wing Likud-led coalition government, headed by Prime Minister Benjamin Netanyahu. This new government insisted on renegotiation of the Hebron agreement with the PA. This delayed the process still further, until a new accord was reached in January 1997.[75]

Under the agreement, Hebron was divided into areas H1 and H2, similar to areas A and B under the Interim Agreement. Israel retained control of the Israeli settlers in the heart of the city. Appended to the new Protocol Concerning the Redeployment in Hebron were a number of agreed minutes and notes. These included several mutual undertakings by the parties, including commitments by Israel to negotiate the possible establishment of a Gaza port and airport, as well as "safe passage" between the West Bank and Gaza. The final-status negotiations were to (re)start in March 1997. Furthermore, the Oslo II timetable for additional Israeli redeployments was relaxed considerably. A letter from U.S. secretary of state Warren Christopher to Prime Minister Netanyahu suggested that "the first phase of further redeployments should take place as soon as possible, and that all three phases of the further redeployments should be completed within twelve months from the implementation of the first phase of the further redeployments but not later than mid-1998"—a delay of approximately one year. Israel argued that the scope of such redeployments should be at its discretion, a view endorsed by the United States.

ECONOMIC CHALLENGES

In June 1994, as the PA assumed control over Gaza and Jericho, a substantial majority of Palestinians felt that the peace process would improve their economic situation. Less than a year later, 53 percent stated that their standard of living had actually declined, while only 8 percent saw any improvement.[76] By 1997 almost three-quarters of Palestinians believed that the peace process had "negative" (42.7 percent) or "very negative" (27.4 percent) effects on the economy, despite a general improvement in services and infrastructure since the PA had assumed control.[77]

Indeed, despite international assistance, economic conditions in the territories appeared to deteriorate in the aftermath of the Oslo Agreement. According to the United Nations, between 1992 and 1998 real per capita GNP fell by 21 percent.[78] Only in 1998 did this pattern of decline show signs of possible reversal, with the IMF estimating a modest increase of about 1 to 1.5 percent.

The decline was particularly notable in Palestinian labor remittances from work in Israel, as well as from the agricultural sector. Significant growth was evident only in the construction and public-service sector, both being areas affected by the inflow of donor assistance and by the establishment and expansion of the Palestinian Authority. Of equal concern was the erosion of the long-term productive foundations of the territories: Palestinian exports fell some 23 percent between 1992 and 1996, while private investment fell by 75 percent during the same period.[79] The social implications of this were evident in a variety of ways. Unemployment grew to an average of 23.9 percent in 1996 and 20.9 percent in 1997, before declining to around 15.6 percent in 1998. When discouraged, severely underemployed, and seasonal workers were counted, the proportion roughly doubled.[80] One study found more than one-third of Gazans and one-tenth of West Bankers living below the poverty line.[81]

A variety of factors accounted for this weakness in the Palestinian economy: the continued weakness of Arab oil economies, the weakness of Palestinian infrastructure, the reluctance of investors to risk capital in an uncertain political environment. However, not one of these factors alone was sufficient to explain the lack of growth. Indeed, in 1997 the IMF predicted that—barring external shocks— Palestinian real GDP could be expected to grow at a rate of 5.5 percent, and real GNP at around 8 percent.[82] UN analysts estimated that Palestinian GNP in

1998 stood at about one-third less than might be expected from growth rates in the early 1990s.[83]

The Impact of Closure

In December 1998, the owner of the small Pizza-Pizza restaurant in Gaza summarized the difficulties of business since Oslo: not only had the difficulties moving between Gaza and the West Bank made it impossible for him to open a second restaurant in Ramallah as he wished, but furthermore when Israel closed the border "sometimes I can't bring in cardboard containers for take-away pizzas . . . when the closure goes on for a long time I run out of cheese."[84]

Analysts too agreed that the single largest reason for poor Palestinian economic performance was Israel's policy of periodic closure of the territories. Restrictions on Palestinian mobility were nothing new: curfews and roadblocks had been used extensively since 1967 and had been used still more frequently with the eruption of the intifada. Despite these restrictions, until the early 1990s Palestinians generally enjoyed relatively easy access to Jerusalem, as well as mobility between and within the West Bank and Gaza. In the early 1990s, however, the situation began to change. During the Gulf War in 1991, an extended curfew was imposed throughout the territories. In March 1993 permits were required for Palestinians to enter Jerusalem or Israel, and permanent checkpoints were established to enforce the requirement. This had the effects of limiting mobility between Gaza and the West Bank (since travel through Israel was required); severely limiting Palestinian access to their main commercial and cultural center, East Jerusalem; and disrupting transport and communications between the northern and southern West Bank. Moreover, the borders were periodically closed altogether, usually in response to acts of violence or intelligence warning of impending terrorist attacks.

With the advent of Palestinian self-government (and its associated territorial autonomy in much of Gaza and major population centers in the West Bank), restrictions became more severe, particularly given the failure to establish a "safe passage" between the West Bank and Gaza as called for under the Oslo Agreement. In the words of one Israeli human rights organization, "movement between the Gaza Strip and the West Bank is currently almost impossible." Trade between the two areas declined sharply: whereas half the goods produced in Gaza were destined for the West Bank before 1993, by 1997 this had fallen to around 2 percent.[85]

Moreover, two additional measures were periodically adopted by Israel: *general,* or *comprehensive, closure,* which restricted all movement into and out of PA-controlled areas, and *internal closure,* which prevented movement between population centers within the West Bank.[86] Data compiled by the United Nations show the use of closure increasing, from seventeen working days ("effective closure days") in 1993 to sixty-one days in 1994, to seventy-three days in 1995, to eighty-two days in 1996, declining to fifty-seven days in 1997 and fourteen and a half days in 1998. In 1995–97, the West Bank and Gaza were closed for roughly one-quarter of all regular commercial days.[87]

The costs of this were devastating. First and foremost, Palestinian laborers were cut off from work in Israel, an important part of both their incomes and the overall Palestinian economy. In September 1997 the wages lost during closure were estimated at $1.4 million per day, while local unemployment increased by approximately one-half.[88] Of even greater effect was a longer-term decline in Palestinian employment in Israel, owing to a reduction in labor permits issued and the increasing replacement by Israeli employers of Palestinian labor with foreign labor—the latter often less productive but more reliably able to attend work. From around 100,000 workers in the early 1990s, the average number of Palestinians working in Israel fell to around 32,000 in 1995 and around 22,000–23,000 in 1996, rising again to 38,000 in 1997 and 44,000 in 1998. Sharp dips marked each sustained period of closure (figure 2.2).[89] Because of competition from imported labor, and because of a requirement that workers reapply for authorization anew after each round of closure, Palestinians were often unable to take up around one-third of the work permits authorized by Israel at any one time.

Employment losses from work in Israel were not the only consequence of closure. Businesses reported a 30–40 percent decline in sales during periods of closure. In Gaza, fishermen were frequently barred from putting to sea. The import of raw materials and consumer goods (including, at times, foodstuffs) was halted or restricted during periods of closure, resulting in sharp price increases in local markets. The export sector was unable to reach external markets. This had a particularly severe effect in Gaza, where cucumbers, tomatoes, citrus, strawberries, peppers, and cut flowers were among the major export crops. None of these products could easily withstand export delays or stand for days in the hot sun of border crossings awaiting security inspections.[90] UN and World Bank estimates suggested trade losses of $1.3 million per day during closure; overall, Palestinian exports fell by a quarter.[91] Furthermore, closure damaged the reputation of Palestinian exporters as reliable suppliers and deterred private investment in the territories, making it difficult for Palestinians to recoup trade losses or establish new export sectors.[92] With this, there was evidence of a reorientation of Palestinian trade, with West Bank–Gaza commerce declining and dependence on imports via Israel increasing correspondingly.

Closure also had serious effects on the public sector. On the one hand, trade interruptions and declining domestic sales affected the fiscal revenues of the Palestinian Authority. On the other hand, the social needs generated by closure increased demands on social services and state employment—thus compounding the budgetary problems of the PA.

Figure 2.2. Palestinian Labor in Israel (1990–98)

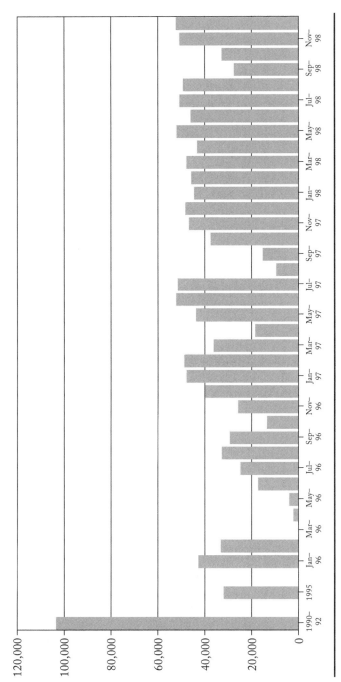

Source: UNSCO, *Quarterly Report and Report on Economic and Social Conditions in the West Bank and Gaza* (various).

Note: Figures are for permit-holders only, and include Palestinians working in Israeli settlements. Figures do not include Palestinian workers entering Israel illegally.

When all of these costs are combined, the result is substantial. One source estimates that between 1994 and 1996 Palestinian employment losses from closure totaled $685 million, with a further $1,809 million in trade-related costs.[93] Another estimate by UNSCO puts the costs of closure at some $4–6 million per day during severe closure, or between $864 million and $1.3 billion during 1994–96.[94] By either calculation, the costs of closure represent between 7 and 15 percent of Palestinian GNP, significantly exceeding the value of aid disbursed by the international donor community over the same period.

Closure was intended in part to prevent further terrorist infiltrations and also to force the PA to take firmer action against militant Palestinian rejectionists. These Israeli concerns were real enough; as one (Likud) government press statement noted, "More Israelis have been killed by Palestinian terrorists in the 5 years since the first Oslo Agreement was signed in September 1993 than in the 15 preceding years." Specifically, 279 Israelis died in Palestinian attacks between September 1993 and September 1998.[95] Thus, noted the government, "In view of the prevailing security situation, it is not always easy to implement the necessary steps in the economic sphere. Nevertheless, despite the calculated risks involved, Israel is doing its utmost to reduce to a minimum the impact of essential security measures on the Palestinian economy, and to enable it to grow and develop."[96]

Palestinian human rights organizations cast doubt on the effectiveness of closure as a security measure:

> Even during periods of severe closure thousands of Palestinian laborers were able to circumvent the checkpoints and cross the border. Furthermore, the total closure which began on February 25, 1996, in the aftermath of suicide bombings, did not prevent the subsequent suicide bombings of 3rd and 4th March. In 1995, according to the Israeli Police Ministry, over 40,000 arrests of Palestinian workers who were in Israel without permits were made. No suicide bomber has ever had a permit to legally enter Israel. The fact that it is possible to enter Israel even when an absolute closure has been imposed, particularly from the West Bank, is well-known, since there are a variety of roads which cross the Green Line and do not contain a checkpoint. Even in Gaza where there is a fence around the entire territory and only three checkpoints, car thieves have crossed into Gaza and Palestinians have dismantled areas of fence and sold pieces for scrap metal, despite the fact that the fence is supposedly electrified and secured.[97]

In fact, many Israelis—including many in the security establishment—agreed. Gideon Ezra (a Likud member of the Knesset and former official in Israel's Shin Beth internal security service) noted that "the value of the closure is psychological. It makes Israelis think they are safe. But in fact it has the opposite effect: it doesn't stop bombers. But it makes people angry, and that anger isn't good for anyone."[98] Closure also had adverse economic consequences for Israel. Although many Palestinians were replaced by foreign guest workers, the Israeli housing sector was particularly badly hit by interruptions to its supply of semiskilled workers.

But closure was driven as much by Israeli domestic political concerns as by counterterrorism or economic policy. Polls showed that up to 85 percent of the Israeli public wanted closure imposed in response to Palestinian terrorism.[99] Few politicians could be expected to ignore this sentiment, especially given the political catastrophe that would result were a bombing to take place because closure had *not* been imposed.

THE END OF OSLO . . . AND BEYOND?

While Palestinian-Israeli negotiations continued under Israel's Labor government and the onset of meaningful final-status negotiations approached, both the PA and the Palestinian public seemed willing to shoulder short-term pain (including closure) in the hope of long-term political settlement. With the election in May 1996 of Israeli prime minister Benjamin Netanyahu and a new hard-line Likud-led coalition government, however, the future looked rather bleak. During the election campaign Netanyahu had been critical of many aspects of the Declaration of Principles and subsequent interim arrangements, voiced opposition to any future establishment of Palestinian sovereignty, and expressed support for additional Israeli settlement activity in the West Bank. Following the elections, these attitudes were reflected in government policy.

In September 1996 Palestinians and Israeli troops had clashed in serious fighting following the Israeli government's decision to open a contentious tunnel in East Jerusalem. The new Israeli government also stepped up settlement activity in the West Bank, despite near-universal international condemnation that such activity constituted a violation of the Fourth Geneva Convention. The January 1997 Hebron Protocol, far from representing newfound Likud support for Oslo, was in essence an unavoidable obligation, given the PA's agreement with the previous Israeli government and substantial international pressure. Indeed, in many ways it seemed to represent a last gasp of the Oslo process. In March and again in November 1997 Israel outlined proposals for the first of what were supposed to be three "further redeployments" of Israeli forces in the West Bank. This was accompanied by "the necessary steps to continue the existence and strengthening of [Jewish] settlements in Judea and Samaria."[100] Since the Israeli offers involved returning only a small percentage of the occupied territories, the Palestinians quickly rejected them as inadequate.

As the peace process faded, terrorist attacks by radical Palestinian Islamist groups continued, notably a suicide bombing in Tel Aviv in March 1997 and more suicide attacks in Jerusalem in July and September. Further imposition of comprehensive closures of the West Bank and Gaza followed, and revenue transfers to the PA were temporarily suspended in the fall.[101] Netanyahu further declared that Israel would not stop settlement activity in the territories and would not be bound by its obligation under the Oslo Agreement to withdraw from additional territories unless the PA met Israeli security demands. In October, a failed Israeli assassination attempt against a Hamas official in Jordan further poisoned the regional atmosphere, including Netanyahu's already sharply deteriorating relationship with King Hussein.

Under Labor, general optimism about the peace process had led many Palestinians to oppose attacks against Israelis. The PA had also been in a strong enough position to take vigorous (even excessive, by human rights standards) measures against militant groups following the bombings of February and March 1996. With the new government's strong support for settlement activity and opposition to both the Oslo process and eventual Palestinian sovereignty, Palestinian frustrations grew—aggravated by deteriorating economic circumstances. Support for violence increased and the domestic position of the PA weakened, thus constraining its ability to suppress the radical wing of the Islamist movement.[102] While supporters of the Oslo process continued to outnumber opponents by a roughly 2:1 margin, public support for attacks against Israelis rose from 21 percent in March 1996 to 40 percent in April 1997, to 51 percent by October 1998.[103]

In this deteriorating context, diplomacy consisted of little more than crisis management. Negotiations on a host of issues—including the establishment of a "safe passage" between the West Bank and Gaza, the opening of Gaza's port and airport, and further Israeli redeployment—variously broke down, restarted, and appeared fruitless. Security cooperation and many other liaison mechanisms were also periodically suspended, restarted, and suspended again.

The United States, in an attempt to get the peace process back on track, invited both sides to intensive face-to-face discussions in October 1998. The resulting Wye River Memorandum saw Israel accept U.S. proposals (previously accepted by the PA) on further redeployment. These called for the phased transfer of 12 percent of area C to area B, 1 percent of area C to area A, and 14.2 percent of area B to area A—thus increasing the total size of areas B and A to 25 percent and 18 percent of the West Bank, respectively. For their part, the Palestinians agreed to intensify security measures and cooperation. Both sides agreed to open final-status talks, which had been stalled since May 1996.[104]

With regard to economic issues, the Wye River Memorandum contained an announcement that Israel and the Palestinians had "agreed on arrangements which will permit the timely opening of the Gaza Industrial Estate" and a "Protocol Regarding the Establishment and Operation of the International Airport in the Gaza Strip during the Interim Period." The memorandum also called for the parties to "continue or to reactivate all standing committees," to renew negotiations on establishing safe passage between the West Bank and Gaza and on the construction of a Gaza port, and to "launch a strategic economic dialogue to enhance their economic relationship." It noted:

> The two sides agree on the importance of continued international donor assistance to facilitate implementation by both sides of agreements reached. They also recognize the need for enhanced donor support for economic development in the West Bank and Gaza. They agree to jointly approach the donor community to organize a Ministerial Conference before the end of 1998 to seek pledges for enhanced levels of assistance.

Within days, however, full implementation of the agreement was put in doubt by terrorist attacks, criticism from the Israeli right wing, and disputes over interpretation. Israel soon found itself facing early elections in May 1999, as Netanyahu's parliamentary coalition imploded. On May 4 the Oslo Agreement itself expired. And the PLO, while postponing any unilateral declaration of independence, reserved its right to do so in the near future.

Shortly thereafter, on May 17, 1999, Ehud Barak led the Israeli Labor Party to victory at the polls. With this, the diplomatic process entered a new stage. The new government signaled its intent to move forward in peace negotiations with the Palestinians. Reflecting this, on September 4 the two sides signed the Sharm el-Sheikh Memorandum, calling for the implementation of the outstanding aspects of the earlier Wye River agreement. This included further Israeli redeployment in the West Bank, the opening of a safe passage between the West Bank and Gaza, and the resumption of final-status negotiations.[105] Israel also agreed that the PA could begin construction of a Gaza port, although the security arrangements under which it might operate were not yet agreed upon. While the challenges confronting the peace process were still formidable, the process itself was under way once more.

As the preceding survey has shown, many of the most severe challenges—and opportunities—confronting the aid effort in Palestine have arisen from the legacies of occupation and the contours of the peace process. With regard to the former, more than a quarter century of Israeli military rule after 1967 saw rapid economic growth, but with relatively little concomitant development of the productive base in the territories. Although Palestinians clearly benefited from relatively good social indicators, developed human resources, the small nucleus of a public administration, and a vibrant NGO sector, they also suffered from a weak industrial sector, poor infrastructure, and little in the way of legal institutions. Israeli settlements proliferated. The Palestinian economy was also highly dependent on trade and labor flows to Israel, a fact that would have important consequences in the post-Oslo period.

Occupation also shaped the political dynamics of the West Bank and Gaza in fundamental ways. The most prominent features of this terrain included a politically dominant Fateh challenged by a growing Islamist movement; high degrees of political mobilization and factionalization; and an established pattern of using external resources to strengthen political constituencies.

Finally, the enormous complexity of the peace process, with its various agreements and complex rules, provided the immediate context into which the aid effort proceeded. These agreements generated fragmented territorial and economic authority, complicating the task of development. The cycle of terrorism and closure had devastating economic effects. The entire process, moreover, was also adversely affected by the loss of political commitment during the Netanyahu administration in Israel between May 1996 and May 1999.

In this context, sustainable development became an elusive, and perhaps meaningless, concept. Yet at the same time, in moments of crisis and stalemate external aid also became more important—in the absence of political movement, perhaps the only "life support" available to an otherwise moribund peace process and the only mechanism available to avert an explosion of local political frustrations.

3

Mobilizing Assistance

The Politics of Pledging

E VEN AS PREPARATIONS WERE UNDER WAY for the signing of the Israeli-Palestinian Declaration of Principles, U.S. secretary of state Warren Christopher announced the intention of the United States to convene an international donors conference for the West Bank and Gaza. According to Christopher:

> The purpose of this conference will be to mobilize resources needed to make the agreement work. The international community must move immediately to see that the agreement produces tangible results in the security and daily lives of the Palestinians and the Israelis. If peace is to be achieved, this must be translated directly and visibly—vividly into real progress on the ground. . . .
>
> All agree we must take immediate steps to address the high unemployment rates that rob families of hope and fuels extremism in the West Bank. Housing, roads, and other permanent improvements must be quickly developed. We must also act to provide assistance in public administration, tax collection, and social services. . . .
>
> Ladies and gentlemen, the real barrier to peace between Israelis and Palestinians, the psychological barrier, has already been breached. Compared to that obstacle, the resource challenge we face can surely be met. I'm convinced that, working with our international partners, we can and will succeed.[1]

The meeting, cochaired by the United States and Russia (in their capacity as cosponsors of the Madrid peace process), was subsequently held in Washington on October 1. At it, participants pledged over $600 million for the first year of the interim period, with indications of planned support of around $2 billion. On this basis, the cosponsors announced that they were "confident that the

$2.4 billion of five-year external assistance needs identified by the World Bank will be met."[2] In fact, this target was exceeded considerably. At subsequent donor meetings, the total would rise to over $4 billion by late 1998 (table 3.1).

Why this growth in assistance? Several reasons can be identified. Some donors (such as Saudi Arabia) periodically announced new assistance packages, rather than committing themselves in advance for the full five-year period. As a result, their total pledge amount increased from year to year. Pledges also tended to rise as economic conditions in the territories deteriorated, as key political developments took place (such as the Israeli redeployment and Palestinian elections), or as deterioration in the political process underscored the need for a renewed sign of international support. The continued media attention to, and the strategic salience of, the peace process also had a positive effect.

Frequent pledging conferences and other donor meetings (see chronology) likely played an important role in mobilizing assistance, in several respects. They provided a useful venue for fund-raising by both PA and UN agencies. They created pressure (both domestic and international) on donor countries to bring something to the table and thereby demonstrate tangible support for the peace process. Such meetings facilitated efforts by donor and foreign ministries to concentrate the attention of their senior management and political leadership on the economic dimensions of the Palestinian issue. Visits by donor ministers or heads of government to the region, or trips by senior Palestinian leaders to donor capitals, also had a similar effect, often resulting in new projects or initiatives ("announce-ables"). Although these did not always involve new money, many did—and this, along with the factors noted earlier, contributed to the growing level of aid pledges over the years. Pledging conferences and other aid coordination structures (discussed in chapter 4) also created somewhat greater scope for donor transparency.[3]

Nevertheless, in evaluating donor pledges—or, for that matter, the announcements emanating from other international pledging conferences in support of war-to-peace transitions—several caveats are in order. First and most important, these donor pledges represent *pledges* of assistance rather than *commitments* against specific projects or *disbursements* to projects "on the ground."[4] The lag in translating such general undertakings into specific project support will be discussed in greater detail in chapter 5. Approximately one-quarter of the pledges for the West Bank and Gaza were in the form of hard or soft loans rather than outright grants.[5] In the short term, the immediate monetary value of loans and grants is similar; in the longer term, however, the former involves the additional burden of eventual repayment (albeit often at concessional rates).[6] A portion of aid to Palestine has been tied, thus requiring that it be spent on goods and services originating

Table 3.1. Pledges of Donor Assistance to the West Bank and Gaza (1993–98)

Donor	Pledge ($ thousands)	Donor	Pledge ($ thousands)
Algeria	10,000	Italy	156,837
Arab Fund	150,000	Japan	312,023
Argentina	1,368	Jordan	20,211
Australia	13,010	Kuwait	25,000
Austria	25,350	Luxembourg	11,500
Belgium	39,080	The Netherlands	154,166
Brunei	6,000	Norway	244,021
Canada	43,568	Portugal	825
China	15,935	Qatar	3,000
Czech Republic	2,718	Republic of Korea	15,000
Denmark	50,1311	Romania	2,880
Egypt	17,210	Russia	4,778
European Investment Bank	300,000	Saudi Arabia	208,000
European Union	421,580	Spain	147,152
Finland	13,904	Sweden	95,774
France	80,549	Switzerland	90,316
Germany	355,422	Turkey	54,971
Greece	28,231	UNDP	12,000
Iceland	1,300	United Arab Emirates	25,000
India	2,000	United Kingdom	128,656
Indonesia	2,000	United States	500,000
International Finance Corporation	70,000	World Bank	228,700
		World Food Program	9,334
Ireland	7,074		
Israel	75,000	Total	4,181,574

Source: MOPIC, December 1998.

within the donor country.[7] In other cases, assistance has taken the form of commodity rather than cash donations. Although tying and commodity assistance were undoubtedly less common in assistance to Palestine than in "ordinary" cases of development assistance, they nonetheless have imposed some restrictions on the utility of assistance to the Palestinian Authority.

Finally, donors often announced the same project in several different fora, making it difficult to distinguish "new" money from "old." Indicative of the problem of "pledge inflation" was the special ministerial-level Conference on Economic Assistance to the Palestinian People, held in Paris in January 1996. This meeting issued statements announcing pledges of some $1,365 million—consisting of $865 million toward the Palestinian Public Investment Program (PPIP) and $500 million in unspent commitments yet to be disbursed in the next fifteen months. In practice, these two sums overlapped considerably, with some of the "undisbursed funds" already committed to the PPIP. However, both donors and Arafat had wanted the total to exceed $1 billion so as to bolster the PA on the eve of the elections for the Palestinian Legislative Council and hence double-counted these amounts. One participant reported that "most pledging statements . . . mixed past pledges, disbursements and future projects such that it was impossible to determine totals," which in any case seemed to differ also from the summary that the World Bank produced immediately after the conference.[8] After the conference, the $1.3 billion figure was often repeated, even in a January 19 follow-up letter from Norwegian foreign minister Bjørn Tore Godal to foreign ministers of donor countries. Yet at the end of the year, actual donor disbursements for 1996 would total only $528 million.[9]

In order to establish who had really promised—and delivered—what, the World Bank and later the PA's Ministry of Planning and International Cooperation (MOPIC) issued regular reports on donor pledges and commitments. Although the accuracy of these reports was hampered by differing donor accounting systems as well as by the slowness with which some aid agencies initially responded to requests for information, these—together with the five-year pledging period—proved very useful in tracking donor assistance. The five-year pledging period adopted for 1994–98 also proved useful by making it difficult to reannounce unspent funds as a "new" pledge for the forthcoming year.[10] Indeed, the system of aid monitoring adopted for Palestine seemed to compare favorably with many other cases of transitional assistance. By contrast, one comparative research project on pledges of international aid notes that, in Cambodia, "lack of transparency has been a major problem in tracking aid flows into the country." Moreover, pledge disbursement gaps were apparently so great that some donors pressed the government not to publicly release data on aid flows. Similarly, in Bosnia "there are major difficulties determining donor commitments and disbursements. . . . The data themselves are a political function, a fact underlined by the presence of rival, inconsistent databases. The discrepancies between them are occasionally enormous. The overall muddiness of the tracking is complicated by double accounting—the tendency to count the same funds twice."[11]

In November 1998 a second major donor conference was again held in Washington, D.C., to pledge assistance for the *next* five years of assistance. A total of $3.4 billion was apparently pledged, significantly more than was originally promised at the first conference in 1993. Despite concerns about potential donor fatigue, most countries appeared to maintain their previous levels of support. Two of the largest donors—the United States and the European Union—substantially increased their pledges, to $900 million and around $480 million, respectively. Clearly, donors thought their support to be of continued political importance.

ENOUGH SUPPORT?

Was this level of donor support adequate to the challenges facing the West Bank and Gaza? Not surprisingly, different views emerged. In announcing the initial 1993 Washington pledging conference, Secretary of State Warren Christopher had suggested that some $3 billion over ten years needed to be raised by donors. This figure was based on a then recently completed six-volume World Bank study of the West Bank and Gaza, *Developing the Occupied Territories: An Investment in Peace,* which had been initiated by REDWG and was fortuitously published by the World Bank in September 1993. Specifically, the bank estimated medium-term (1994–98) financing requirements of around $2.5 billion. A portion of this, however, would be met by private capital inflows, leaving donors with the primary task of mobilizing $1.35 billion for medium-term public-sector investments and $85 million for technical assistance. A further $1.6 billion in public investment would be required in the longer term (1999–2003). Subsequently, World Bank estimates for external donor assistance for the five-year transitional period were increased to $2.4 billion to include the costs of institution building and current expenses.[12] Given these sorts of estimated requirements, donor mobilization appeared fully adequate. Indeed, larger sums might only risk wastage: in the words of one bank spokesperson, "it is a standard rule of thumb that to use money effectively, and without waste, an economy cannot absorb investments exceeding 10–12 percent of GNP annually . . . which means that the absorptive capacity of the public sector is about $300–360 million a year."[13]

Before Oslo, the PLO had drawn up its own assessment of economic needs, the *Programme for Development of the Palestinian National Economy for the Years 1994–2000.* Produced under the direction of Palestinian economist Yusif Sayigh, this study called for some $14.4 billion in investments over seven years.[14]

Although the gap between this and *Developing the Occupied Territories* was not quite as large as might first appear—the PLO plan covered a somewhat longer period and called for 60 percent of investments to be provided by the private sector—nevertheless, it proposed around twice the level of donor assistance called for by the World Bank. Moreover, for the Palestinians there was another relevant point of comparison: Israel. By the early 1990s Israel was receiving some $3.7 billion per year in U.S. economic and military assistance, and some $50 billion since 1979.[15] Not surprisingly, Arafat—after thanking donors—complained that amounts raised in the October 1993 meeting were not enough and that around $2 billion per year would be required.[16]

International Comparisons

It is also instructive to compare the level of aid mobilized for the Palestinians with assistance generated by the international community for other war-to-peace transitions. In Bosnia, the international community agreed in 1995–96 on a medium-term Priority Reconstruction Program of some $5.1 billion, with $1.9 billion committed (and about half of this disbursed) for 1996 alone. Annual aid disbursements to the West Bank and Gaza also lagged behind those to Mozambique and Rwanda in 1996. Faced with such comparisons, some Palestinian officials argued that donors demonstrated an ethnocentric Western bias in favor of the "European" conflict in the Balkans. Others visibly bristled at any suggestion that the (self-evidently important) Arab-Israeli conflict should have to compete with needy and postconflict countries in Africa, Asia, and the Americas for aid.[17]

In fact, when Palestine's relatively small size and lesser need are taken into consideration, aid for the West Bank and Gaza appears to have been extremely generous. This can be seen in a comparison of data on aid receipts per capita by various countries involved in war-to-peace transitions (table 3.2).[18] By this measure, the priority assigned by the international community to Bosnia and Palestine stands out clearly: annual Palestinian per capita aid receipts were the highest in the world in 1996, representing more than twice per capita official development assistance to postgenocide Rwanda and around ten times average per capita ODA for the least-developed countries.

The reasons for this seem clear enough. Bosnia and Palestine—and, more recently, Kosovo—are conflicts in parts of the world that are geostrategically and economically important to the Western donor community. They also garner—for both these reasons, and for reasons of history and cultural affinity—much greater attention in the Western media. This has consequences not only for the level of resources mobilized but also for the type of assistance generated and the degree of political priority, diplomatic encouragement, and institutional support devoted by donors to implementing assistance programs.

Table 3.2. Per Capita Aid Receipts for Countries in War-to-Peace Transitions (1996)

Country	Annual Aid Receipts ($ millions)	Per Capita Aid ($)
Palestine	596 (DAC data) 572 (MOPIC data)	275.93 (DAC data) 225.21 (PCBS data)
Nicaragua	954	212.00
Bosnia	838	190.02
Rwanda	674	100.15
Liberia	207	73.67
El Salvador	317	54.56
Mozambique	923	51.19
Haiti	375	51.09
Cambodia	453	44.07
Least-Developed Countries		23.88
All Developing Countries		12.72

Sources: DAC, *ODA Receipts and Selected Indicators for Developing Countries and Territories* (8 February 1999); MOPIC, *1998 Third Quarterly Monitoring Report of Donor Assistance* (15 November 1998).

This disparity has sometimes created resentment among aid officials, some of whom have felt that the West Bank and Gaza receive a disproportionate share of declining ODA resources, despite social conditions and income levels that place the territories in the top one-third of developing countries. Indeed, in some donor agencies (such as those of Denmark and Norway) special authority had to be sought to provide "transitional" development assistance to Palestine, which might not otherwise have qualified on the basis of need.[19] John Stackhouse, a well-regarded development journalist, noted:

> [Comparatively] high incomes weren't the only shock I suffered coming from South Asia to visit the West Bank and Gaza Strip. Smooth roads, brightly lit schools, contained sewers, wide-open spaces and some of the cleanest, neatest refugee camps I'd seen made my head turn again and again. . . .
> The moral tragedy is that every dollar of aid spent in the Palestinian areas comes directly from aid budgets meant for the world's poor—the

one billion people who go to bed dizzy with hunger dripping in malarial sweat, walk barefoot on gravel, deliver babies in screaming pain, and cower in fear of every public official who passes by.[20]

Paucity amid Plenty: The Paradox of UNRWA

Another perspective on the tension between the political priority of mobilizing support for the Palestinian-Israeli peace process and humanitarian or developmental needs elsewhere around the world was provided by the experience of the United Nations Relief and Works Agency. Despite growth of over 3.5 percent per year in the Palestinian refugee population and increases in the local cost of living in many of its areas of operation, donor support for UNRWA's general budget remained essentially flat in the 1990s. In real terms, per refugee, it dropped by about one-third between 1992 and 1997.[21] As a result, the agency was forced to cut services, plead with donors, periodically delay payments to contractors, plead still more, and even borrow against its own project funds. It was also forced to adopt a variety of cost-containment and -reduction measures. These included reduced or suspended teacher recruitment, the cancellation of hospitalization programs, and a 15 percent reduction in international staff.[22] As the UNRWA commissioner-general noted to the UN General Assembly:

> UNRWA was fortunate in enjoying strong support from donors, host authorities, regional bodies and the international community at large. It was unfortunate that support was not always translated into the tangible assistance required for the Agency to effectively carry out its mission and provide the basic services on which so many refugees depended. The Agency was well aware that many donors were faced with reductions in aid budgets, other global demands, new emergencies and increasing domestic needs, and wished to see an expansion of UNRWA's traditional donor base. At the same time, strong support was frequently expressed by donors for the continuation of UNRWA services, for an enhanced role by the Agency in the interim period of the peace process and for special activities such as the European Gaza Hospital project and the move of Agency head-quarters to the Gaza Strip. In many cases, funds were not available for the Agency to carry out activities that had been specifically called for, or for overall priorities.[23]

This shortfall occurred despite the substantial increase in international assistance to the Palestinians during the same period. How can this be explained when UNRWA was generally recognized as providing effective health, education, and social services to refugees—indeed, perhaps the best basic education system and most cost-effective health care in the Arab world—and when the entire budget shortfall represented only 5–10 percent of annual aid disbursements in the West Bank and Gaza?

Part of the reason for this arose from donor unwillingness to assume the burden for an ever-expanding pool of UNRWA-registered refugees, as well as concerns over UNRWA's financial administration. Some donors also preferred the political benefits of providing project assistance directly to the territories, rather than through budget support for a UN agency. For similar reasons, donors may have also diverted some assistance otherwise intended for UNRWA's core programs to the agency's project-oriented "Peace Implementation Program."

However, much of the funding crisis was also rooted in the trade-offs between support for UNRWA and other priorities. In many donor agencies, support for UNRWA was lodged within that part of their aid bureaucracy responsible for all UN, multilateral, or humanitarian agencies, where institutional expertise in dealing with such agencies was also located. Canada, for example, supported UNRWA out of the same CIDA budgetary envelope as the UNHCR and the Red Cross, lodged in its International Humanitarian Assistance division. This historical allocation of responsibilities, once set, was difficult to change: bureaucratic procedures prevented responsibility for UNRWA being easily shifted within any agency, and particular divisions were reluctant either to surrender budget lines or to acquire new funding responsibilities. However, at a time when aid budgets were declining, such donor officials could only preserve (or increase) support for UNRWA by making even larger cuts to critical UNHCR or International Committee of the Red Cross (ICRC) programs in such places as Central Africa, where humanitarian needs were intense and life expectancies half of those in Gaza refugee camps. At a time when UNRWA was receiving some $78 per registered refugee (compared with only $55 per UNHCR "person of concern"), it was only natural that some Western humanitarian relief officials viewed UNRWA with an increasingly jaundiced eye.[24] In the blunt words of one official, the cost of maintaining support for UNRWA was more dead children in the Congo.[25] The result was a CIDA decision to reduce UNRWA funding by $1 million.

Anecdotal evidence suggests that in those agencies where UNRWA financing was lodged in either foreign ministries or Middle East aid divisions, and where the budgetary trade-offs were consequently very different, support for UNRWA was more robust. Thus, while the relatively large amount provided by donors for Palestinian refugees reflected the overall strategic priority of the Palestinian issue, the responsiveness of individual donors to political versus humanitarian imperatives was also shaped by institutional factors and the nature of budgetary envelopes. It could also be shaped by more idiosyncratic and serendipitous factors: in Canada, the case for supporting the UNRWA core budget was given a strong boost during and after visits by the ministers of foreign affairs and international cooperation to the region. The latter in particular was swayed by some of the arguments in support of UNRWA made to her during her trip (notably by

Canadian diplomats), which ran counter to the policy advice of CIDA's International Humanitarian Affairs division back at headquarters. She then directed that the cut to CIDA funding for UNRWA be replaced with a significant increase.

These dynamics were poorly understood outside donor circles. Many refugees, NGOs, and local officials—faced with the paradox of a growing UNRWA budget deficit and cuts in UNRWA services amid the apparent plenty of donor aid programs—tended to settle on another, more simple explanation: the international community was deliberately starving the UN agency of funds so as to "liquidate" the Palestinian refugee issue.[26] Even some senior UNRWA program directors were convinced that budgetary problems reflected "political agendas aimed at closing the page on the refugee problem by writing off the Agency."[27] In September 1997 such dissatisfaction was registered in the form of widespread protests by refugees and a strike by UNRWA employees. Protesters complained:

> The steps taken by the so-called Refugees' Relief Agency coincide with and are in harmony with the [Israeli] closure policy, from which the occupied territories and the PNA areas have [long] suffered. . . . This confirms that UNRWA is part and parcel of the political scheme, and that—especially since the Madrid conference—the Agency has played that suspicious role of which we have warned several times; a role which is in complete harmony with the plans to end the Palestinian refugee question by disregarding all internationally legitimized resolutions, the foremost among them Resolution 194 on the refugees' right of return.[28]

The following year UNRWA was again hit by strikes and protests. In Gaza workers complained that the agency and donors were "working systematically to destroy the international institution, hoping to liquidate its services to Palestinian refugees."[29] The peculiar dynamics of donor mobilization thus not only affected the level of resources available for specific purposes, but also had unintended, adverse political consequences.[30]

BURDEN SHARING

In any multilateral pledging process, questions arise regarding the fair allocation of cost within the international community. In the Palestinian case as well, debates over "burden sharing" have arisen, with some donors complaining that they shoulder an unfair portion of the financial load.

The European Union has been the largest donor to the territories, with over $400 million pledged for the period 1994–98, plus up to $300 million in loans offered through the European Investment Bank, plus another $1.3 billion or so pledged bilaterally by individual EU members.[31] The United States was the second-largest donor in 1993–98, at $500 million, followed by Germany, Japan, Norway, Saudi Arabia, Italy, and the Netherlands. The World Bank has pledged some $228 million in loans (for full data on donor pledges, see table 3.1).[32]

These differences generated some tensions within the donor community. The Europeans saw themselves as shouldering a disproportionate share of the aid burden, while the United States dominated the political process. The United States, by contrast, considered its aid levels appropriate. It also tended to view its aid to Israel, Egypt, and Jordan as part of its general contribution. (Privately, some other donors questioned this, quietly wondering whether unqualified U.S. aid might actually reduce Israel's willingness to reach a political accommodation with its neighbors.)

Within Western countries, complaints were sometimes voiced by donor officials and legislators that Arab states failed to shoulder an appropriate share of the burden of aid to the West Bank and Gaza.[33] There was also debate over the level of the Israeli contribution: the Palestinians and the Arab states suggested that the modest level of Israeli assistance hardly made up for the harm inflicted on the territories by past and present Israeli policies, while Israel argued that it faced significant costs of its own in withdrawing from Palestinian territory. Indeed, in the summer of 1998 the Netanyahu government suggested that the further redeployment of Israeli forces from an additional 13 percent of the West Bank might have a price tag of $1.2 billion in additional U.S. assistance.[34]

Here again, aggregate totals are misleading, since they fail to reflect the differing sizes of donor economies and hence their differing ability to generate financial resources. A far better indicator of donor burden (or generosity) is the measurement of annual pledges as a percentage of donor GNP (figure 3.1).

By this measure, Norway stands out as the most generous among Western donors, devoting around 0.0359 percent of GNP annually to the Palestinian territories. The United States, by contrast, fares poorly by this indicator (0.0014 percent), despite its preeminent position in the peace process. In general, more distant states (Australia, Canada, Japan, and the United States) have shown much less commitment than do European countries, especially when EU contributions are taken into account. Among European states, the so-called like-minded donor countries (Norway, Denmark, the Netherlands, and Sweden) have made a particularly strong contribution.[35]

Measured relative to the size of their economies, Arab donor states generally rank well ahead of their Western counterparts, even more so when the pledges of the Arab League's Arab Fund for Economic and Social Development are included. Indeed, on this basis even low-income Egypt and low-middle-income Jordan seem to have attained greater relative aid mobilization than most developed economies. As for Israel, its relative rate of aid mobilization has been

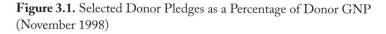

Figure 3.1. Selected Donor Pledges as a Percentage of Donor GNP (November 1998)

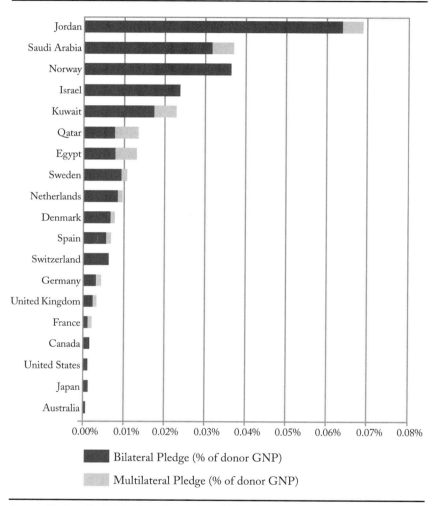

Sources: Pledges for 1994–98 are drawn from MOPIC, *1998 Third Quarterly Monitoring Report of Donor Assistance* (15 November 1998) and divided by five to represent annual averages. Data for total GNP are drawn from UNDP, *World Development Report 1998* (New York: Oxford University Press, 1998).

Note: Multilateral pledges include those from the European Union or Arab Fund for Economic and Social Development, calculated as a percentage of total EU or Arab League GNP.

at around the level of Arab donors and ahead of the Europeans', but behind that of Jordan, Saudi Arabia, and Norway. None of this, of course, says anything about the actual amounts disbursed (later highlighted in table 5.5). If this were the basis of calculations, Norway (with a high rate of aid implementation) would appear even stronger, while Israel (with one of the worst rates) would fall behind most European donors.

The substantial variation in rates of donor generosity underscores the need to examine a range of factors affecting aid mobilization. Certainly, realpolitik or commercial interest provides part of the explanation. EU assistance, for example, can be seen as part of its broader Euro-Mediterranean policy, which has clearly been driven by political and economic concerns.

However, realpolitik does not provide a full explanation, as evidenced by high levels of Nordic mobilization and low levels of U.S. mobilization. In the former case, broad political and societal support for foreign assistance has played a significant role, although Norwegian aid is also motivated by that country's central role in the negotiation of the Oslo Agreement. In the United States, by contrast, domestic political resistance to foreign aid partly accounts for relatively low levels of aid mobilization for the West Bank and Gaza. Another factor in the U.S. case is the unusual degree of U.S. ODA concentration on a limited number of states, notably Israel and Egypt. However, it is also true that U.S. officials do not perceive any substantial imbalance in American assistance. Indeed, many were surprised to learn how low the American contribution is relative to U.S. GNP or population.[36]

Such variations in rates of aid mobilization can have important negative political implications, not only for resource availability, but also for relations among donors. Where significant imbalances exist, disputes over aid leadership and unfair allocation of the financial burden can inhibit the development of effective mechanisms of donor coordination and hence further complicate the already formidable challenges of peacebuilding.

Interestingly, in the Palestinian case disagreements over appropriate burden sharing did not seem to significantly increase the propensity of parties to "free ride"—that is, lead donors to restrict their contribution in the expectation that others would assume the financial costs of the peace process. On the contrary, the initial pledging period had actually seen substantial pledge *escalation* between the United States and European Union as each sought to enhance its political position in the peace process, and others sought to offer (relatively) comparable amounts.

✦   ✦   ✦

Overall, the record of aid mobilization in Palestine is an impressive one, with well over $8 billion pledged for the decade following 1993. This clearly reflected the strategic importance of the conflict and the historic opportunity presented by the peace process. Whether such assistance was delivered in a timely fashion and whether it was allocated to the appropriate purposes, however, are altogether different issues, to be explored later. Moreover, the burden of economic assistance to the West Bank and Gaza has been unevenly distributed among members of the international community. This fact has had—as detailed in the next chapter —significant implications for both the coordination of donors and the political rivalries among them.

4
Coordinating Assistance
Donors, Agencies, and Institutions

THE ASSISTANCE PROGRAM for the West Bank and Gaza has been a complex one, involving more than forty countries, over two dozen UN and other multilateral agencies, a score of Palestinian ministries, and hundreds of Palestinian and international NGOs. The array of coordinating mechanisms that have emerged after 1993 has been equally complex (figure 4.1).

THE ARCHITECTURE OF DONOR COORDINATION

At the outset, two major structures were established to provide some overall external direction to the aid effort: the Ad-Hoc Liaison Committee (AHLC) and the Consultative Group (CG). The AHLC, a high-level political group of key donors, was charged with political oversight of the international aid effort. The Consultative Group, a typical World Bank mechanism, was used to coordinate donor programs and win support (and funding) for assistance programs. In addition, the special ministerial-level Conference on Economic Assistance to the Palestinian People was held in January 1996 to give added impetus to the recently signed Palestinian-Israeli Interim Agreement. On average, Consultative Group meetings were held once per year from 1994 through 1999 and formal or informal AHLC meetings every few months (see chronology).

Subsequently, a number of other sectoral or local coordination mechanisms were established. The first of these—the aptly named COPP (Coordinating Committee for International Assistance to the Palestinian Police Force)—was composed of Egypt, the European Union, Israel, Japan, Norway (as chair), the PLO, Russia, and the United States. It sought to secure and coordinate donor pledges of police funds and equipment, as well as to promote transparency by all parties and to

Figure 4.1. Structure of Donor Coordination in the West Bank and Gaza (1998)

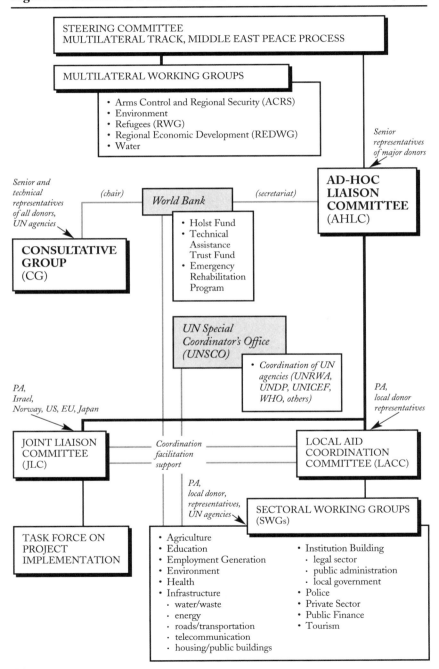

STEERING COMMITTEE
MULTILATERAL TRACK, MIDDLE EAST PEACE PROCESS

MULTILATERAL WORKING GROUPS

- Arms Control and Regional Security (ACRS)
- Environment
- Refugees (RWG)
- Regional Economic Development (REDWG)
- Water

Senior representatives of major donors

Senior and technical representatives of all donors, UN agencies

(chair)   *World Bank*   *(secretariat)*

AD-HOC LIAISON COMMITTEE (AHLC)

- Holst Fund
- Technical Assistance Trust Fund
- Emergency Rehabilitation Program

CONSULTATIVE GROUP (CG)

UN Special Coordinator's Office (UNSCO)

- *Coordination of UN agencies (UNRWA, UNDP, UNICEF, WHO, others)*

PA, Israel, Norway, US, EU, Japan

PA, local donor representatives

JOINT LIAISON COMMITTEE (JLC)

Coordination facilitation support

LOCAL AID COORDINATION COMMITTEE (LACC)

PA, local donor, representatives, UN agencies

SECTORAL WORKING GROUPS (SWGs)

TASK FORCE ON PROJECT IMPLEMENTATION

- Agriculture
- Education
- Employment Generation
- Environment
- Health
- Infrastructure
  - water/waste
  - energy
  - roads/transportation
  - telecommunication
  - housing/public buildings

- Institution Building
  - legal sector
  - public administration
  - local government
- Police
- Private Sector
- Public Finance
- Tourism

monitor developments within the Palestinian police force(s).[1] The importance of establishing an effective Palestinian police force was recognized early, and Norway held an initial meeting of police donors in Oslo in December 1993. As the implementation of self-rule in Gaza and Jericho approached, the question became more urgent, and Norway subsequently convened the first COPP meeting in Cairo in March 1994. In addition, the appointment of two senior Norwegian police officers as advisers to COPP (one of whom, Major General Arnstein Överkils, was also appointed as police adviser to Arafat) also facilitated coordination.[2] Yet despite vigorous Norwegian efforts, the actual delivery of appropriate security assistance lagged dangerously in 1994–95, as will be discussed in chapters 5 and 6.

At its June 1994 meeting, the AHLC recognized—in part owing to the COPP experience of in-region coordination among interested donors—that some form of local aid coordination structure would have to be established in the territories. In November 1994 it thus decided to establish the Local Aid Coordination Committee (LACC) in the West Bank and Gaza. This would facilitate coordination on the ground among the major aid agencies and with the PA.[3] The LACC, cochaired by Norway (as AHLC chair), the World Bank, and UNSCO, met approximately monthly, with around thirty local donor representatives attending each meeting. In turn, the LACC established twelve thematic Sectoral Working Groups (SWGs), each with one or more PA ministries as "gavel holder," a donor as "shepherd," and a UN agency as "secretariat." In the police working group, for example, Norway acted as shepherd and UNSCO as secretariat; the other SWGs addressed agriculture (Spain and UNDP); transport and communications (France and UNDP); education (France and UNICEF); public works/employment (Sweden and UNDP and the International Labor Organization [ILO]); environment (the Netherlands and UNRWA, later UNSCO); health (Italy and the World Health Organization [WHO]); institution and capacity building (European Union–World Bank and UNSCO); infrastructure and housing (Germany–World Bank and UNSCO); private sector and trade (United States–World Bank and UNDP); public finance (United States–World Bank and the IMF); and tourism (Spain and UNDP). A number of SWG subsector groups were also subsequently established, while the PA established internal "core groups" parallel to the SWGs to improve its own interagency cooperation. In April 1997 a joint review of the LACC structures resulted in minor changes in the organization of groups and subgroups,[4] a shift in the leading role in the groups from (donor) shepherds to (PA) gavel holders, and an expanded role for the Palestinian Ministry of Planning and International Cooperation. More far-reaching reforms were introduced in 1999. These reduced the number of major SWGs to four: productive sector, infrastructure, social sector, and institution building. Within each of these sectors a variable number of thematic subgroups were established. At the same time, MOPIC established a special coordination unit as a first step toward assuming the secretariat function for all of the SWGs.

In November 1994 the AHLC also decided to establish a Joint Liaison Committee (JLC), consisting of the LACC cochairs and the PA (chair), to deal with significant obstacles in the way of the prompt and effective delivery of assistance, as well as to review Palestinian budgetary performance, revenue generation, and priorities for technical assistance. The European Union, Israel, Japan, and the United States subsequently joined the JLC, which initially met quarterly or more frequently. However, its meetings became less frequent and its effectiveness was undermined owing to the breakdown in Israeli-Palestinian relations after the May 1996 Israeli elections.

As is clear from this discussion, a number of multilateral agencies and international financial institutions have performed important roles in the assistance process. Most prominent among these has been the World Bank, which has acted as secretariat of the Ad-Hoc Liaison Committee and chair of the Consultative Group, in addition to its role in developing and packaging projects and programs for donor support. The IMF has assisted in monitoring and strengthening PA fiscal management.

Among UN agencies, the most important has been the United Nations Relief and Works Agency. UNRWA has by far the most developed infrastructure and capacity of any aid-relief agency in Palestine, employing more than 8,300 local staff and 65 internationals in the West Bank and Gaza at the time of the Gaza-Jericho agreement.[5] In addition, UNRWA headquarters was transferred from Vienna to Gaza as a sign of UN commitment to the Palestinians and the peace process. The United Nations Development Program (UNDP) also assumed a significant role, not only by providing technical and project development assistance to the Palestinian Authority, but also by acting as a conduit and implementing agency for aid projects in the territories. UNDP's substantial role as an implementing agency is not typical for the organization. UNDP officials defended this on grounds of their expertise and efficiency. Moreover, the earnings from such activities help to finance other aspects of UNDP programs in Palestine.[6] The Office of the United Nations Special Coordinator (UNSCO) was established in June 1994 to coordinate various UN activities and to facilitate cooperation among the United Nations, the Palestinian Authority, Israel, and donors.[7]

The initial Palestinian counterpart to the World Bank was the Palestinian Economic Council for Development and Reconstruction (PECDAR), established in 1994 to track donor assistance, channel it into specific projects, and generally act as the Palestinian Authority's interface with the donor community. The subsequently established PA economic ministries—notably the Ministry of Planning and International Cooperation (MOPIC) and the Ministry of Finance—as

well as line-sectoral ministries, the office of the president, and municipal governments, have all played increasingly important roles in the aid process. In particular, MOPIC has assumed the function of primary Palestinian interlocutor with
the donor community, while PECDAR has increasingly specialized in the role of
implementing agency.

Leading the Effort

In the immediate aftermath of Oslo, significant competition emerged between
the United States and the European Union on who would assume the leading role
in the donor effort. For the United States, Washington's leadership was essential:
no other actor had comparable leverage over the parties. Moreover, the Europeans
were viewed by some in the State Department as inclined to appeal to the Arab
world by adopting rhetorical positions that only antagonized the Israeli government and polarized the situation.[8] The United States also found the complex
decision-making process within the European Union and European Commission
cumbersome and difficult to deal with and sometimes avoided consultation with
the European Union for that reason.[9]

     For their part, most of the Europeans felt that it was unfair that the United
States intended to maintain a dominant political role while Europe shouldered
the primary financial burden for the peace process. Initially, they also wished to
see the coordination of international assistance occur within the framework of
the multilateral Regional Economic Development Working Group, of which the
European Union was gavel holder. The European Union was more likely to favor
a substantial Palestinian role in the aid process. European countries viewed their
relations with the Middle East as more even-handed than those of the United
States, which was seen to have a chronic pro-Israeli tilt. Finally, the Middle East
peace process was seen as an early test case for the European Union's new Common
Foreign and Security Policy (CFSP). Indeed, EU governments explicitly made
the Middle East—and "accompanying the peace process with the mobilization
of all political, economic, and financial resources of the Union"—a priority of the
CFSP.[10] Within the European Union, the need to chart a distinctive European
(or non-American) path in the Middle East was perceived differently by member states, with the French often particularly critical of Washington and the
United Kingdom generally much more willing to support U.S. initiatives. For
their part, the Palestinians generally preferred to maximize the role of both the
European Union and supportive regional states, although with the frank recognition that U.S. diplomatic clout was preeminent and irreplaceable.

     These tensions manifested themselves in a variety of ways. As noted earlier,
one positive effect was some escalation in aid pledges as the October 1993 aid
conference approached, with the U.S. pledge growing from $250 to $500 million

between late September and early October and the EU commitment rising to 500 million Ecu (or about $600 million).

Less positively, there were disputes over the structure of the aid process. Shortly before the Washington pledging conference, the European Commission had noted, "It is the Commission's view that the Community, as the main financial contributor, should seek to play a central role in [donor] coordination." To do so, it proposed that a Palestinian Economic Development Working Group should be established as a subgroup of REDWG, with all donors represented and meetings held every three months.[11] Not surprisingly, Washington preferred a structure (like that of the overall Madrid process) in which the American role was preeminent. The United States also favored a leading role for the World Bank in donor coordination and mobilization. The European Union, by contrast, tended to see the World Bank—headquartered in Washington—as a U.S. proxy, and one that would further undercut the role of REDWG. Immediately before and after the October 1993 pledging conference, tensions on these and related issues were high. There were additional disputes over the presence of the United Nations in the AHLC, with Israel and the United States reluctant to grant the United Nations full membership, and the United Nations pressing for an expanded role.

In the end the structure that emerged was the Ad-Hoc Liaison Committee, formally established in November 1993 to provide overall political guidance for the aid process. Reflecting European concerns, the AHLC was formally linked to the Steering Committee of the multilaterals, with its membership consisting of Canada, the European Union, Japan, Norway, Russia, Saudi Arabia, and the United States. Egypt, Israel, Jordan, the PA, and Tunisia became associate members. All decisions within the AHLC were to be taken by consensus. The World Bank was assigned responsibility for acting as secretariat to the group, and the United Nations was admitted only as an associate member and only after lengthy debate and a Norwegian-brokered compromise.[12] In an effort to deal with competing U.S. and EU ambitions, Norway was eventually assigned the role of AHLC chair.[13] From Washington's perspective, the Norwegian chair had relatively little influence over donors—"the Saudis aren't going to provide aid because of a letter from the Norwegian foreign minister"[14]—but could serve to bridge differences between participants. Later, complaints were sometimes heard from others that the Norwegians seemed excessively willing to accept a U.S. lead.

By the time of the November 1994 meeting of the AHLC, major U.S.-EU conflict over leadership of the aid effort had faded somewhat. Even the venue of the AHLC—formal meetings held in Brussels or Paris and "informal" meetings held in Washington—reflected a symbolic effort to assuage European concerns. In practice, the United States assumed the leading role in the AHLC, preparing the diplomatic groundwork for each meeting in consultation with other leading members.

However, irritants continued to arise from time to time. In the field, UNSCO officials directly attributed the structure of the LACC (cochaired by Norway, UNSCO, and the World Bank) to the desire of both U.S. and EU officials to prevent each other from assuming a leading role in local aid coordination. With all EU assistance (including bilateral programs) representing almost half of donor support—compared with the U.S. contribution of around 12 percent— Europe generally felt that it should acquire a larger political role in the peace process. The perception that Washington's unilateralism and pro-Israeli stance sometimes endangered either the aid effort or the broader peace process reinforced this position. Even senior World Bank officials—who had initially been perceived by the European Union as too close to Washington—sometimes complained that high-level aid coordination risked losing credibility because of periodic American high-handedness.[15]

In 1998—as donors approached the end of the initial five-year pledging period and attention was devoted to the need for future assistance—such tensions resurfaced once more. One indicator of them came in a formal policy analysis prepared by the European Commission for the European Parliament. The analysis noted that "the EU has accepted a role which is diplomatically and politically complementary to that of the United States. This is an arrangement which has worked imperfectly so far and which can be improved to boost the effect of international community efforts to put the peace process back on track." Specifically, the European Commission suggested that "while the European Union should continue to support the crucial political role of the United States," this role "would be much improved if the parties and the United States acknowledged the need for the European Union, both at Ministerial level and through its Special Envoy, to participate alongside the United States in all fora set up to assist bilateral negotiations between the parties." Furthermore, "if the international assistance effort is to be renewed, it must be redefined. It is clear that the basic shareholder should be the key coordinator. Therefore, the international economic effort should be coordinated by the European Union on the basis of the Ad-Hoc Liaison Committee model: Palestinians, Israelis, the Bretton Woods institutions, the United Nations and the active participation of key donors." Thus, "Being by far the first donor, the European Union (Presidency and Commission) should play a substantially enhanced role in the co-ordination of international assistance, according to a formula to be negotiated with other donors."[16] The Japanese too expressed quiet dissatisfaction with the mismatch between their economic contribution and coordinating role.

Discussions followed among major donors on possible modification of the AHLC structure, including the role of AHLC chair. Some senior EU diplomats expressed vocal discontent with Norway's status as "permanent chair" of the

AHLC. Other EU member states, however, felt that Norway—which had put much effort into the peace process—should not be sacrificed on the altar of European-American rivalries. In an effort to protect its position, the Norwegian foreign ministry circulated a "non-paper" proposing that it retain its position, but that AHLC meetings held in Europe be cochaired by the European Union. It also proposed that the JLC (which includes the European Union) assume a greater role in preparing for AHLC meetings.[17] Reflecting the counterbalancing of these various views and ambitions, the February 1999 meeting of the AHLC subsequently "reaffirmed the Committee's existing structure, including Norway's role as permanent chair," but agreed that "formal meetings of the AHLC will be cochaired by the AHLC member hosting the meeting." It also agreed that the next meeting should be held in Japan and that "future AHLC meetings will be regularly held in the European Union."[18]

International Financial Institutions

Case studies of other war-to-peace transitions have often been highly critical of the international financial institutions (notably, the World Bank and the International Monetary Fund) created by the Bretton Woods Conference of 1944, accusing them of undercutting peacebuilding through a rigid application of stern (and politically destabilizing) economic medicine[19] or failing to use "peace conditionality" to encourage politically constructive behavior on the part of local parties.[20] Concern has also been expressed about the lack of cooperation and communication between Bretton Woods and UN institutions.[21] In the West Bank and Gaza, however, the World Bank and the International Monetary Fund have both played generally very constructive roles, in coordination with the UN system and the international community. Still, there have been some shortcomings.

As noted, the World Bank assumed a particularly important role in the coordinating and facilitation of donor assistance to the West Bank and Gaza, serving as AHLC secretariat, chair of the Consultative Group, cosecretariat of the LACC, the JLC, and four of the Sectoral Working Groups. The World Bank has assumed a major role in assessing economic conditions and in developing (in association with the Palestinian Authority) broad development priorities. The first such schema for donor priorities—the Emergency Assistance Program (EAP) for the Occupied Territories—was presented by the bank to the first Consultative Group meeting in December 1993. Drawing from the larger six-volume study earlier prepared by the bank, the EAP identified sectoral needs and priorities totaling $1.2 billion through 1994–96. Later, the bank played an important role in the design of the Palestinian Public Investment Program (1996–98) and the first Palestinian Development Program (1998–2000).

Another aspect of the World Bank's role in donor coordination has been the design and administration of multilateral donor programs aimed at key Palestinian needs. All told, around one-sixth of all donor assistance to Palestine was disbursed through World Bank channels during 1994–98.

Two World Bank–administered, quick-disbursing channels were established early in the donor process: the Technical Assistance Trust Fund (TATF) and the Johan Jürgen Holst Peace Fund (or Holst Fund). The TATF received some $19 million from twelve donors through 1994 to assist in the development of nascent Palestinian technical and administrative infrastructures. However, three years later it had disbursed only a little more than half of this sum.[22] The Holst Fund supported the start-up and recurrent costs of the Palestinian Authority, providing some $212.8 million for budget support and $39 million for emergency employment over the period 1994–98. In 1999, the bank determined that the Holst Fund was no longer needed and recommended it be terminated.[23]

In addition to these, the World Bank group put in place more than a dozen other programs. These have included the Emergency Rehabilitation Project (ERP) I and II (education, water, road, sewage, and labor-intensive microprojects), the Education and Health Rehabilitation Project (EHRP), the Municipal Infrastructure Development Project (MIDP), the Gaza Water and Sanitation Services Project, the Microenterprise Project (with the International Finance Corporation), the Community Development Project, the Housing Project, the Legal Development Project, the Palestinian Expatriate Professional Program, the Palestinian NGO Project, and the Investment Guarantee Fund (with the Multilateral Investment Guarantee Agency).[24] Together, these projects have involved commitments of $186 million in World Bank loans and $96 million in donor cofinancing (as of March 1998), with Saudi Arabia ($52 million) emerging as the leading cofinancer of bank activities.

Early on, the World Bank came under heavy criticism for moving too slowly. While the Holst Fund moved funds quickly, the TATF was initially held up by extended wrangling between the bank and PECDAR. The other programs were even slower, with only $2 million in bank funds and none of the $31 million received from donors for its Emergency Rehabilitation Program being disbursed in 1994. As one bank official admitted in late 1994:

> The program, from any objective evaluation, is a failure . . . little has happened on the ground . . . the money that has been disbursed has not shown much to the people. . . . Like it or not, [we are] viewed as the leaders of this program. If we sit and do not react we will ultimately be blamed. More than this, the peace process will fail.[25]

The World Bank had expected that donors would seek to speed assistance by delivering it under a World Bank umbrella, with pooled resources, cofinancing arrangements, and simplified procedures:

> From the outset, the Bank strongly advocated to donors that they consider financing and coordinating their investment projects under the umbrella of a single program . . . and, to simplify procedures, that they pool their resources into more substantial operations, including joint financing with the Bank. Donors were generally supportive . . . but, to our knowledge, no donors chose the option of simplified procedures and only two donors chose the joint cofinancing option during the critical first two years. The result was that the ill-equipped, novice and fragmented Palestinian institutions and decision-makers were overwhelmed by donor missions, paperwork and procedures. This set of factors alone accounts for much of the delay in getting projects implemented.[26]

Indeed, overall the degree of donor support for World Bank projects (other than the Holst Fund and the TATF) was disappointing. As of March 1998, less than $100 million in donor cofinancing had been received, two-thirds of this for the initial ERP I (table 4.1).[27]

Another internal assessment identified a series of World Bank and donor assumptions that had proved unrealistic: that progress in political negotiations would be steady; that a well-functioning PA administration would be rapidly established; that there would be a vital development impetus imparted from the private sector; that the PA would become financially viable by the end of 1994 and hence not need continuing budget support; and that donor commitments would be more timely. These expectations had not been met, however: negotiations generally took longer than first anticipated; the bank found itself entangled in Palestinian turf battles, particularly between PECDAR and MOPIC; the private sector lagged; Palestinian budgetary needs remained high; and donor coordination and implementation lagged, with few donors opting for the umbrella of a single program and joint cofinancing with the bank. For their part, Palestinian officials not only complained about the pace of bank and donor programs but also criticized what they saw as the bank's "inflexibility" and its failure to empower Palestinian institutions: it "did not help build Palestinian capacity, but replaced it."[28]

In order to speed responsiveness, a series of internal institutional reforms were made. In Washington, the office dealing with the territories was effectively upgraded from its initial status as part of a larger country division, thereby effectively reducing the number of management layers it had to report to. More important, authority over the program was moved out of headquarters and to the bank's dynamic resident representative in the field, Odin Knudsen (and his successor, Joseph Saba).

Table 4.1. World Bank Activities in the West Bank and Gaza
(as of March 1998)

	Bank Commitment ($ millions)	Donor Cofinancing ($ millions)	Disbursement of World Bank Funds ($ millions)	Disbursement of Donor Funds ($ millions)
ERP I	30.00	66.00	28.97	57.68
ERP II	20.00	3.50	18.45	2.23
EHRP	20.00	22.26	17.10	2.84
MIDP	40.00	0	21.95	0
Water and Sanitation	25.00	0	8.98	0
Other Projects	51.00	4.55	16.02	0.43
Technical Assistance Trust Fund	—	19.00	—	12.37
Holst Fund	—	255.00	—	246.90
Total	186.00	370.31	111.47	322.45

Source: World Bank, *West Bank/Gaza Update* (March 1998), archived at www.palecon.org.7.

This move faced significant initial resistance within the World Bank, representing as it did a major departure from past practice. One bank insider characterized the political infighting around the issue as "vicious":

> It is impossible to properly service clients from 4,000 to 5,000 miles away. The hard part, however, is divesting authority—the center of gravity always tends to pull things back towards Washington. Administrators who have spent their careers in the bank can't always appreciate the desirability of divesting authority to the field. It also requires a different kind of person in the field, not a "post office box" as Resident Representatives have been in the past. You have to find a "doer." Bureaucracies like the World Bank always try to diffuse accountability and responsibility in a way that no company or business would or could.

The bank's role in supporting war-to-peace transition, moreover, required flexibility, innovation, political savvy, and risk taking—all of this in a bank that tended to be a "technocratic" and "zero-error organization," and wherein "the political consciousness of staff is limited." Decisions tended to be made slowly and often by committee. It was, noted one official, rather like being in "a Grand Prix race with a slow moving Fiat, with many bodies hanging off it, including across the windscreen."

U.S. officials say that they "weighed in heavily" with the World Bank in support of greater flexibility and field autonomy. In fact, such donor pressures proved critical when efforts were made by some bank officials to pull authority for the West Bank–Gaza program back to Washington in late 1994: praise for Knudsen's role voiced during an AHLC meeting convinced senior bank management to retain the field-driven model. Later, these reforms came to be seen as a significant success, to be copied in Bosnia and held out as a potential model for other cases of postconflict reconstruction assistance.[29]

In addition to the organizational politics of the issue, there were practical problems adjusting field operations, both physically and conceptually. Although establishment of the World Bank's field office in the West Bank was begun as soon as it was announced in August 1994, it took almost a year to finalize an agreement on the office's operations with the PA and the PLO.[30] Knudsen initially favored a decentralized model, with his officials working out in the field, but later had to establish a more centralized operation to improve communication—which facilitated better teamwork but sometimes led to complaints that he was being too "Napoleonic." Initial shortages of field staff were met through the use of extended missions by externally based task managers, which increased flexibility but also put greater stress on some of the personnel involved.

Complaints, meanwhile, continued to be heard from the PA that the World Bank was still not accepting enough Palestinian input. Ironically, when the bank did demonstrate greater responsiveness, this created other difficulties. The most notable example of this occurred in the spring and summer of 1996, when the bank utilized the Holst Fund to support an emergency job creation program implemented through PECDAR, following urgent appeals by Arafat himself. This initiative brought complaints (notably from Norway, the United States, and UNSCO) that the bank was financing unsustainable make-work projects, that it was diverting precious and difficult-to-raise Holst funds, and that it had inadequately consulted with donors. Bank officials refuted all of these, noting that the bank was authorized to make use of Holst in this way, that it had informed donors, and that the Palestinian Authority itself had pressed for such measures in response to the economic havoc wrought by Israeli closure of the territories. Indeed, it seemed that American officials were most perturbed by a multilateral agency showing independent initiative ("activism" and "politicization," as one U.S. State Department official put it), and not necessarily by the job creation itself.

Devolution of authority into the field turned out to be key to the effective operation of the World Bank, both with regard to its own programs and its broader role in the donor effort.[31] Over time, the importance of some bank functions declined: the Palestinian Ministry of Planning and International Cooperation took over preparation of the periodic donor matrices, while budgetary support through Holst became generally less important by 1997–98. However, other aspects of the bank's activities—its various multidonor projects, its support for PA policy planning, and its work in facilitating both high-level (AHLC, CG) and local coordination activities—remained important. In one 1997 survey of donor officials by the Center for Palestine Research and Studies (CPRS), 38 percent rated the World Bank's performance as "positive" and only 9 percent rated it as negative. However, both Palestinian NGOs and PA officials were more mixed in their assessments, with 31 percent of the latter rating the bank's performance as "positive" and 30 percent rating it as "negative."[32]

The International Monetary Fund played a valuable role in providing oversight and advice to the Palestinian Authority on its fiscal affairs from late 1994 onward. This included an "exceptionally large" program of technical assistance intended to help the PA establish a modern revenue and public expenditure management system; improve audit capability; establish a Palestinian Monetary Authority; and enhance the ability to generate statistical data.[33] At the request of donors, the IMF also assisted the Ministry of Finance in reporting revenue and expenditure developments to the AHLC and CG, through a quarterly *Report on Fiscal Developments*.

Although the recurrent costs of the PA proved larger than donors had first anticipated and concerns about PA expenditure remained, in general the IMF did help to establish an effective revenue-collection system, as well as a reasonable system of cost control. Indeed, some PA officials—chafing under expenditure restrictions—complained of excessively close relations between the Ministry of Finance and the IMF.[34] The periodic monitoring reports and other analyses became a useful tool for donors, not only in reporting on Palestinian budgetary measures but more broadly in providing information on the current situation and facilitating future donor planning.

UN Coordination

Within the UN system, the secretary-general first responded to the challenge of the Oslo Agreement by appointing the High-Level Task Force on the Socio-Economic Development of the Gaza Strip and Jericho, which issued a report on current and potential UN efforts on September 23, 1993.[35] This report suggested that UN agencies could mount an additional $138 million in program activities in the West Bank and Gaza during the first year of the interim period, in addition to existing activities by UNRWA and others. It also urged the appointment of a UN coordinator in the territories.

Subsequently, in June 1994 Norwegian scholar-turned-diplomat Terje Rød Larsen was appointed the first UN special coordinator in the occupied territories.[36] UNSCO was given a fivefold mandate:

- Provide overall guidance to and facilitate coordination among United Nations programs in the West Bank and Gaza Strip.
- Represent the United Nations at donor coordination meetings and assist the Palestinian Authority and donors in coordinating international donor assistance.
- Maintain contact with the many NGOs operational in the West Bank and Gaza Strip.
- Support the implementation of the Declaration of Principles at the request of the parties.
- Represent the Secretary-General at multilateral working groups set up under the Palestinian-Israeli Peace Accords.[37]

Coordinating the UN system, however, was more easily said than done.[38] Between 1993 and 1997 the number of UN agencies with a presence in the territories increased from three (UNRWA, UNDP, and UNICEF) to twenty-five, fifteen of these maintaining field offices.[39] Although this occurred for many good reasons (the services and expertise that UN agencies could deliver), there was also a more negative side (a desire to share the limelight of a prestigious peace process). There were initial delays getting adequate funding and staff in place, and recurrent battles between UNSCO and some UN officials back in New York; in the view of many UNSCO officials, the office fell "very uncomfortably within the UN bureaucracy" (being originally lodged within the Department of Peace-Keeping Operations) and was "ill-managed from HQ." Larsen's lack of previous UN experience didn't help matters, especially when he did not have a New York–based desk officer, responsible to the field operation, to sort out headquarters problems.

Moreover, there were substantial turf wars, exacerbated by the fact that, as one staffer put it, "there are probably more senior UN officials per square kilometer in Gaza than anywhere outside New York." UNRWA—by far the largest UN actor in the field—felt that it should be the senior partner in any UN development effort. Indeed, when UNSCO was first established, UNRWA commissioner-general Ilter Türkman ordered that his office give prior approval to all communication with the special coordinator's office. (UNRWA staff, out of practical necessity, largely ignored the instruction; cooperation subsequently improved when Peter Hansen became UNRWA commissioner-general.) Similarly, the United Nations Development Program—which has often assumed the coordinating role in other countries—felt that it should be assigned this role. The perception of Larsen as an outsider compounded matters. At both UNRWA and UNDP, many were critical of what they claimed was UNSCO's ineffectiveness.

Given a lack of both line authority and budgetary control, UNSCO had little formal power within the UN system beyond its ability to urge UN agencies to cooperate more effectively. However, other mechanisms were utilized to counterbalance this. Larsen was able to use generally good relations with senior UN officials (including UN secretary-general Boutros Boutros-Ghali and the UNDP administrator) to occasionally go over the heads of local actors. Indeed, UNSCO officials actively lobbied UN headquarters to replace one UNDP special representative who was seen as particularly uncooperative. In addition, UNSCO assumed the role of the exclusive UN spokesperson in the Consultative Group. Because of this, UN agencies had to maintain good relations with UNSCO if they wished to ensure that their programs received best exposure at donor meetings. Larsen's broader effectiveness as a fund-raiser for UN programs also gave him somewhat greater powers of suasion within the UN system.

One manifestation of UNSCO efforts was a series of documents that combined project listings, proposals, priorities, and sectoral analyses, starting with *Putting Peace to Work* (1995–96) and thereafter the United Nations' *Programme of Cooperation for the West Bank and Gaza Strip* (1997–).[40] Although one UNDP staffer decried *Putting Peace to Work* as "essentially a series of organizational shopping lists festooned with children's drawings"—and it was certainly true that UNSCO was in little position to impose priorities—it did at least give somewhat greater cohesion to the UN effort. This was also served by the establishment of a UN compound headed by UNSCO. This provided physical space and support in Gaza for many of the smaller UN programs. Some felt that it was excessively ornate, inviting unflattering comparisons between the condition of UN offices and the rest of the Gaza Strip.[41] It was intentionally impressive, however—intended to send a sign of international commitment to the Palestinians. It was also built with one of the few large meeting rooms in Gaza, thus ensuring that UN, LACC, and other similar coordination meetings would take place on UNSCO's turf.

As noted, UNSCO was also tasked with assisting in the broader role of donor coordination. In this capacity it acted as cochair of the LACC (along with Norway and the World Bank), cosecretariat of the LACC and the JLC, and secretariat of some of the Sectoral Working Groups.[42] Its effectiveness here was constrained by limited staff resources and technical capacity. Moreover, the initially extremely good working relationship between UNSCO and the World Bank in 1994–95 began to deteriorate in 1996. UNSCO officials privately accused the bank of being slow and of sometimes showing poor political judgment; bank officials accused Larsen of grandstanding and being excessively concerned about his future political career in Norway. This friction reached a peak during the summer of 1996, when the World Bank–PECDAR and UNSCO-UNRWA-UNDP seemed for a period to become virtual competitors in the business of emergency job creation.[43]

Finally, it is important to note that although UNSCO's formal mandate emphasized coordination, Larsen was also appointed for his political skills. He had played the central role in the original secret Oslo peace negotiations and continued to play a periodic role in facilitating subsequent negotiations. He also combined personal dynamism, media savvy, personal ties to the senior Israeli (Labor) and Palestinian leadership, and a close working relationship with the United States and Norway. In both public and private Larsen encouraged and cajoled donors, Israel, and the PA alike to respond to the urgent situation on the ground. Although critics (many within the UN system) accused him of being pushy, arrogant, excessively close to the Americans, publicity seeking, and/or politically ambitious, he was generally very highly regarded by donors. According to one U.S. official, Larsen was "tremendously dynamic," and without him, "the UN agencies would be doing much less, and even doing some political damage."[44] Certainly, Larsen was careful to coordinate closely with both the United States and the European Union. For example, a September 1995 UNSCO–World Bank paper entitled *Strategies and Priorities for the Second Phase of the Development Effort in the West Bank and Gaza Strip* was partly written in the home of the U.S. consul in East Jerusalem, with a senior EU aid official in attendance.[45]

Larsen resigned his position in October 1996 to briefly serve as a Norwegian cabinet minister and later as Norwegian special ambassador. He was succeeded temporarily by Peter Hansen, UNRWA commissioner-general. Quite apart from the sheer workload involved in overseeing both UNRWA and UNSCO, the two functions were rather different and did not easily rest in the same hands. In turn, Hansen's temporary responsibilities passed on to an Indian diplomat, Chinmaya Gharekhan, who was appointed special coordinator in February 1997. Following a rather lackluster performance by Gharekhan, Larsen returned to the helm of UNSCO in October 1999, this time with an expanded mandate as UN representative to the overall peace process.[46]

With these changes, UNSCO's role in donor mobilization and coordination weakened somewhat. Differing approaches and leadership accounted for only part of this, however. By late 1996 donor programs in the West Bank and Gaza were quite mature and there was little possibility of mobilizing substantial new funds. The consolidation of MOPIC also had an effect. Most important of all, the May 1996 change of government in Israel also limited the influence of Larsen and his successors, as did the consequent rise in Palestinian-Israeli tensions.

Less visibly, however, UNSCO continued to undertake quieter but nonetheless important work. Supporting the LACC and SWGs was one part of this.

In addition, the fall of 1996 saw UNSCO's economic monitoring unit issue the first of what would be a series of useful reports on economic trends in the territories. These provided clear and readable warnings of economic deterioration, produced in a style that caught the attention of policymakers and others. UNSCO also co-wrote, in conjunction with the World Bank, a series of briefing papers on the impact of Israeli closure of the territories, which were widely distributed among donors and journalists alike. Finally, it produced some special reports on thematic topics, such as the state of the Palestinian private sector.[47]

THE EFFECTIVENESS OF COORDINATION

Some have criticized the aid coordination structure that developed to support donor assistance in the West Bank and Gaza as a "multilateral morass."[48] The welter of committees and acronyms could certainly be confusing, especially given the rotation of aid and foreign ministry staff and the consequent imperfections of institutional memory. When Norway proposed changes to the Joint Liaison Committee in the fall of 1998, for example, an official of one foreign ministry complained, "No one here is sure what the JLC does or if it really even exists. At our most recent interdepartmental coordination meeting, our [aid agency] colleagues were unsure of the nature and purpose of the JLC, too, and we didn't even know what the acronym stands for."[49]

In practice, however, it is difficult to see what other architecture might be more effective. On the one hand, donor coordination required meetings of senior policymakers and technical experts from the donor community (hence the Consultative Group); at the same time, the CG was clearly too large a group to effectively discuss overall donor policy, which was much better pursued in a smaller setting involving the principal donors and regional actors (the AHLC). Although the United States might have preferred a less multilateral framework, it could not—given that it contributed only a fraction of total donor pledges—have insisted on anything else. Moreover, the inclusive character of the Consultative Group in particular undoubtedly facilitated the mobilization of additional pledges after the initial donor meeting in October 1993.

At the same time, it soon became clear that the AHLC and the CG were not enough, since neither could provide the frequency of meetings or detailed follow-up that would be necessary at the project level. Hence the need for local structures of donor coordination. Here, too, some key policy issues and aid impediments were better discussed in a smaller setting involving only the key actors (hence the JLC), while other issues were best dealt with in a more inclusive setting (the LACC) or at a technical or sectoral level (the SWGs).

Table 4.2. Perceptions of Aid Coordination in the West Bank and Gaza

	Positive	Fair	Negative
Evaluation of Donor Coordination with Other Donors			
By Donor Officials	24%	36%	33%
By Local NGOs	24%	22%	31%
By PA Officials	34%	19%	34%
Evaluation of Donor Coordination with PA			
By Donor Officials	46%	39%	9%
By Local NGOs	36%	29%	23%
By PA Officials	35%	37%	24%
Evaluation of PA Coordination with Donors			
By Donor Officials	21%	55%	15%
By Local NGOs	28%	21%	46%
By PA Officials	32%	34%	34%

Source: CPRS, *Prevailing Perceptions on Aid Management,* Research Reports Series no. 9 (Nablus: CPRS, December 1997), 11–12. Table excludes "Don't know" responses.

Given initial Palestinian technical and institutional weaknesses, it was only natural that the World Bank, UNSCO, and the IMF would assume key roles in facilitating all this. Similarly, the need to organize myriad UN agencies on the ground made UNSCO important, quite apart from its value as a general support to the LACC and SWGs and its role (particularly under Larsen) as a political "helpful fixer."

That the complex architecture that emerged after 1993 was *necessary*, however, does not automatically mean that it was as *effective* as its architects had hoped. One survey of donor officials, local NGOs, and PA officials found that opinions on the quality of coordination among donors were divided (table 4.2).[50] Evaluations of PA coordination with donors were also split. Interestingly, donors appeared to consider that they had better coordinated with the PA than with one another. PA officials agreed, although they did not rate donor-PA coordination as highly.

With regard to high-level coordination, a number of complaints could be heard. Some aid officials expressed dismay that AHLC meetings focused on political issues (such as the donors' political jostling or Palestinian-Israeli maneu-vering) rather than aid design and coordination,[51] or that the (theoretically more technical) Consultative Group meetings were similarly dominated by foreign ministries and political symbolism.[52] Some felt that AHLC and CG meetings were too infrequent: five to six major meetings were held each year in 1994–96, but only three (two AHLCs and a CG) in 1997, and two (AHLC and ministerial pledging conference) in 1998, reflecting both the routinization of the aid effort and the stagnation of the peace process (see chronology). For their part, Palestin-ian officials often expressed considerable frustration at the difficulty they encoun-tered converting general pledges of support for Palestinian public investment programs made at Consultative Group meetings into concrete commitments to specific projects.

Locally, participants found that raising issues in the JLC was not necessarily the same as resolving them: appropriate political will or follow-up by Israeli, Pales-tinian, and donor bureaucracies was often a different question. The Local Aid Coordination Committee proved to be a useful forum for raising broad issues of concern, and at times donor criticism of the Israelis and Palestinians could be quite pointed. However, some officials bemoaned the lack of opportunity for real sustained dialogue on development issues. Instead, they complained, they simply heard lengthy speeches by UNSCO, the World Bank, and Norway.[53]

The performance of the various SWGs and SWG subgroups was uneven, depending to a large extent on the degree of energy and initiative shown both by the (donor) shepherd and the (PA) gavel holder. As a result, whereas some groups met frequently, others hardly met at all. In some cases, the absence of a critical individual could delay meetings or de-energize those that were held. Moreover, most donors in most sectors continued to pursue their programs bilaterally, using the SWGs as an opportunity to share information on their activities rather than coordinate future plans (although this in itself could be very useful). Moreover, the SWG structure was increasingly deemed by the PA and donors as being "too complicated and labor-intensive."[54] The technical weakness of the SWG secre-tariats was another hindrance. In the words of one World Bank official, the SWGs "could have offered the potential for substantive forums and for strategizing, for moving ahead with implementation. They have largely failed [to do this]."[55]

As will be discussed later, the institutional weaknesses of the PA further com-pounded such problems of donor coordination. Here, donors faced a dilemma: when the coordination architecture was being established and the PA was still weak, it seemed more expeditious to assign the leading role to donors and inter-national agencies. Later, however, this lack of Palestinian "ownership" over the coordination of its own aid proved a point of friction and even inefficiency. Some donor officials argued that that had been a mistake; others argued that the problem was unavoidable. In any event, they belatedly agreed upon the goal of "gradually transferring total ownership to the Palestinian Authority."[56]

The performance of the SWGs also depended on the sector that each working group addressed. For example, the education SWG was reported to be relatively useful and effective, in part because of the unified nature of the area and the relatively small number of entities involved in coordination. By contrast, the infrastructure SWG involved a broad and potentially unwieldy array of actors. On top of this, the structure of the SWGs was increasingly out of synch with the planning mechanisms that gradually developed *within* the PA (notably the Palestinian Development Plan, discussed in chapter 6), thus further complicating the task of coordination.

Finally, it would appear that PA and donor appreciation of the SWGs has varied over time: what at first appeared to be a vital effort at coordination amid the chaos of the initial period of the aid program later came to be seen as a much more limited exercise in information sharing, as other relationships and structures were consolidated. It was in an attempt to address the weaknesses identified earlier that reforms to the SWGs were adopted in 1997 and even more sweeping ones proposed in 1999.

In broader perspective—and despite such criticisms—the situation in Palestine may still be very much better than is the pattern in many other cases of transitional assistance. Thus, one World Bank official noted: "Donor coordination is very elaborate. As a result, the exchange of information is one of the best. Other countries have no experience like this. Here, donors talk often. It's a lot better." (All this, it should be added, was facilitated by the small size of the West Bank and Gaza and the ubiquity of the cellular phone—advantages not always found in cases of peacebuilding.) Put differently, if donor coordination has been less than some had hoped for, it has still been better than many had feared.

CONDITIONALITY

In many cases of international peacebuilding, a degree of formal or informal conditionality has been imposed on assistance in order to encourage parties to abide by agreements and undertake the measures necessary for reconstruction.[57] Perhaps the obvious case of this has been in Bosnia, where the withholding of assistance was used as a tool to force greater Serbian compliance with the Dayton Agreement.

In the Palestinian case, there has been little effort to formally tie donor assistance to the fulfillment of specific clauses in the various Palestinian-Israeli agreements. However, donor concern over Palestinian transparency, accountability, and institution building did lead to the formal Understanding on Revenues, Expenditures and Donor Funding for the Palestinian Authority, signed by donors and the PA at the November 1994 meeting of the AHLC. This agreement, focusing on the requirements for continued donor budgetary support to the PA, was largely the result of a U.S. lead.

The November 1994 understanding flagged a number of issues—for example, budgetary clarity—that would be repeatedly raised by donors.[58] It also established procedures (such as the monitoring role of the IMF) that would be retained in future arrangements. It did not, however, establish any explicit conditionality, either by linking Holst Fund disbursements to the achievement of the objectives listed in the agreement or by establishing any other mechanism. Such a linkage had been considered[59] but rejected as unworkable or politically implausible.[60] The agreement also did not require any specific Israeli actions. Indeed, Israel was not a signatory of the understanding, although in a carefully negotiated side letter it promised its support for donor and PA efforts.[61]

The Europeans, who were likely to assume the largest share of external support for Palestinian recurrent costs, were anxious that future agreements also clarify Israeli responsibilities. This position was strengthened by the lag between the early empowerment agreements (August 1994, August 1995) and the yet unconcluded Interim Agreement (September 1995), which meant that the PA was assuming new policy and financial responsibilities while Israel continued to accrue most Palestinian tax payments.

The result was the Tripartite Action Plan (TAP) on Revenues, Expenditures and Donor Funding for the Palestinian Authority of April 1995. The TAP, signed by Israel, Norway (in its capacity as chair of the AHLC), and the PA, contained a number of specific commitments. Among these were:

- by the PA, to: improve its domestic revenue-collection systems; restrain civil service hiring; clarify the division of responsibilities among the main PA economic institutions; clarify regulatory frameworks and commercial codes; and make efforts to eliminate donor support for start-up costs by the end of 1996.
- by Israel, to: cooperate with the PA in establishing a functioning tax system; facilitate the transfer of goods between the West Bank and Gaza, and between the territories and neighboring countries; and finalize negotiations on industrial zones and on construction of a port for Gaza.
- by donors, to: extend budgetary support and police funding through 1995; support quick-disbursement job-creation programs; provide preferential trade access to Palestinian goods.

Finally, donors warned that "their own continuing efforts would be contingent upon performance by Palestinians and Israelis in implementing the steps described in this action plan." The AHLC and the IMF were to monitor implementation of the agreement, in conjunction with the JLC and the LACC.[62] The TAP was subsequently revised in January 1996 and then extended through 1997–99. Later versions included new Palestinian commitments to abide by budgetary targets, strengthen fiscal expenditure management and budgetary controls, consolidate revenue accounts, establish a commission on public administration, and clearly identify development priorities. Israel undertook to "remove measures which have proven impediments to the achievement of sustained economic growth in the West Bank and Gaza Strip" (while recognizing Israel's obligation to provide for the "security of its citizens"), and particularly to facilitate movement to and from Gaza (including the establishment of safe passage between the West Bank and Gaza, as called for in the original Oslo Agreement). Finally, donors agreed to promptly pay outstanding pledges, support the PA's medium-term economic strategy, and provide budgetary support through 1996 "on the clear understanding that donor support for recurrent cost will not continue beyond 1996."[63]

The TAP provided a useful mechanism for signaling donor concerns, focusing the attention of the PA (and Israel) on specific issues, and monitoring (through the AHLC, IMF, JLC, and LACC) specific actions taken or not taken. At the same time, however, many of its provisions went unfulfilled. According to periodic TAP status reports to the AHLC, the PA continued to delay civil service reform and the consolidation of accounts, while "much work still needs to be done to strengthen the budgeting, financial control and internal audit systems within major spending ministries." Israel continued to impose periodic closure on the territories in the name of "security." Furthermore, until late 1999 "no progress" had been reported "on the safe passage between the West Bank and Gaza Strip," while negotiations on Gaza Port could not "be deemed expeditious." Implementation of industrial estates was also delayed by Israeli security concerns, as well as by the ups and downs in the broader political negotiations.[64]

The Norwegian chair of the AHLC, commenting on this situation in May 1998, noted that "frustration was expressed [by the AHLC] at the lack of mechanisms to implement TAP provisions."[65] The more fundamental problem was a lack of leverage—or, perhaps, a lack of willingness to exercise leverage—on the part of donors. In general, however, donors were unwilling to halt assistance to the territories at a time when the Palestinian economy was in sharp decline for fear of further damaging the peace process. As a consequence, support for Palestinian recurrent budget expenditures continued longer than many donors would have wished.

At times, very specific incentives were offered by particular donors in connection with very specific objectives. The United States, for example, pledged USAID support for a series of specific urban renewal programs in Hebron as part of the negotiations culminating in the Hebron redeployment. Similarly, an offer of substantial increase in U.S. assistance (to $300 million per year in 1999 and 2000) was used to cement the October 1998 Wye River Memorandum and may have been intended to deter any unilateral Palestinian action upon the expiry of the Oslo process in May 1999. However, the United States was alone in its ability to marry political and economic incentives and disincentives—and even here, the result was not always the desired one. Attempts by USAID to encourage moderation by the Palestinian Broadcasting Corporation (PBC) by providing equipment, training, and access to Voice of America programming were ultimately deemed unsuccessful. Charging that the PBC was "unhelpful to the peace process, at times inciteful, and at times anti-semitic," the United States eventually withdrew its support of the PBC in 1998. Palestinian officials rejected this as a form of Israeli pressure, and the PBC continued much as before.[66]

More frequent than such direct conditionality was a more diffuse linkage: the inefficiency of a particular ministry might deter donor support for its projects, while general concern at reports of corruption and administrative inefficiency tended to sap already reluctant donor support for recurrent costs. Such indirect and uncoordinated linkages, however, were generally ineffective at eliciting the desired changes on the part of the PA. This was particularly true when the Palestinian behavior that donors were trying to modify was itself driven by strong local political imperatives. The confusing lines of authority in the PA, for example, were part of a broader strategy by Arafat to fragment potential rival power centers; both the existence of revenue accounts outside the control of the Ministry of Finance and the growth of quasi-official monopolies reflected Arafat's desire to retain flexible control of financial resources for patronage and other political purposes. In 1997 the European Union tried a different approach to this problem, based on incentives for compliance rather than punishments for noncompliance. Specifically, it offered to establish a facility that the PA could draw upon in the event of future closures of the territories or Israeli refusal to provide tax clearances—but only if the PA got its financial house in order. Nothing really came of the proposals, however.

With regard to Israeli policy (arguably the single largest reason for Palestinian economic decline), donors have had even less leverage and have been unwilling to use what leverage they have.[67] It should be noted, moreover, that many of the actions that angered donors were—rightly or wrongly—regarded by Israeli governments as vital to national security. Even had pressure been exerted, it is doubtful how much effect such pressure would have had.

In one rare exercise of economic pressure, the European Commission did insist in May 1998 that Israel stop labeling as "made in Israel" any goods originating from Israeli settlements in the occupied territories.[68] The Palestinians, though strongly supporting the spirit of the EU move, expressed concern that the dispute might adversely affect Palestinian exports to Europe via Israel—thereby underscoring the dependence, and continued vulnerability, of the Palestinian economy. In the meantime, the French and British parliaments delayed ratification of a European Union–Israel economic association agreement, citing the absence of progress in the peace process. Subsequent negotiations between the European Union and Israel suggested that Europe might overlook the origins of Israeli products in exchange for partial exemption from the Paris Protocol and the ability to form closer trade links with the PA, and the issue fizzled out shortly thereafter.[69] Similar examples of linkage could be found in Britain's refusal to sign a bilateral defense research memorandum of understanding with Israel until after the latter had approved the Wye River Memorandum, or the European Union's threat to exclude Israel from European research and development funding because of its suspension of that same agreement.[70] Once more highlighting the weakness of donor conditionality, the latter threat soon evaporated. The United States, by contrast, did withhold additional aid offered to Israel when it failed to redeploy its forces as promised in the Wye River Memorandum.

Within the context of the aid coordination process there was even less scope for (or effort at) joint donor action vis-à-vis Israel. The European Union at one point suggested that the TAP include a compensation clause whereby Israel would assume the costs of closure, but this proposal went nowhere in the face of Israeli opposition and a lack of U.S. (and full intra-European) support. In the words of Swedish foreign minister Lena Hjelm-Wallen: "It is true that the European Union is one of the most important economic partners of Israel; however, it is the United States that is the largest aid donor to Israel. Moreover, any economic pressure on Israel will be rejected by the Americans, and this [veto] makes the exercise of economic pressure somewhat difficult."[71]

Given both the difficulties of EU decision making and the rather weak record on independent European economic pressure, however, it is unclear whether the United States can really be held responsible for this. Just as the United States tended to marginalize Europe's political role in the peace process while depending on European financial generosity, the European Union often tended to blame Washington (or Israel, or the Palestinians) for problems that also had roots in Europe itself.

The international aid effort in the West Bank and Gaza involved an extensive role for international financial agencies and UN agencies and a highly complex system of donor coordination. The system was clearly imperfect and at times unwieldy. Yet it also reflected not only the complicated economic and political environment of Palestine but also several other imperatives: the need to accommodate donor rivalries; the need to strike a balance between inclusive participation on the one hand and purposive direction (and hence a narrow membership) on the other; the need to move forward in a timely fashion while Palestinian institutional capacities were still weak. In this context, moreover, the capabilities of key individuals could often be at least as important as the coordination structures that were erected. Perhaps the most serious weakness of the architecture was its failure to systematically build Palestinian capacities, something that was evident in the early, dominant role of the World Bank, UNSCO, and key donors in priority setting and in the later, growing mismatch between the structure of the SWGs and the internal structure of development planning that was emerging within the PA.

The use of conditionality in peacebuilding in Palestine was much less successful than efforts at donor coordination. Lack of leverage and lack of political will largely accounted for this: donors either lacked effective policy instruments or were unwilling (or unable) to use what instruments they did have. As well, many of the key issues raised by the donor community were intrinsically difficult to resolve, even had real pressure been applied. For Israel, concerns over national security shaped many of its policies toward the aid effort. For the Palestinians, aid was closely linked to the dynamics of regime consolidation. And for both parties, aid was intimately bound up with the broader process of diplomatic negotiations. As will be discussed later, these considerations—among others—would have profound effects on the prompt and effective delivery of assistance.

5

Delivering Assistance

From Pledges to Practice

DONORS: SLOW TO DELIVER?

AS THE PALESTINIAN AUTHORITY assumed control of Gaza and Jericho in the summer of 1994, it soon became apparent that—despite the large and very public pledges of aid made in Washington in October 1993—donor funds would be slow in arriving. Indeed, when Palestinian security forces first deployed to Gaza in May 1994, PLO negotiator Nabil Sha'th was forced to obtain emergency monies from other sources to meet the forces' immediate needs. Angered by this lack of resources, Arafat delayed his return to Palestine in apparent protest of the lack of support forthcoming. However, after U.S. secretary of state Warren Christopher stressed the linkage between the consolidation of the PA and the delivery of American assistance, Arafat arrived in Gaza on July 1.[1]

Thereafter, the PA continued to complain that "the international community is moving very, very slowly"[2] and that delays were "an attempt to politically pressure us, to make us accept conditions."[3] Arafat told one interviewer, "No doubt, the delay in extending aid has an impact on the process of building, on building establishments and on setting up economic, social, and other structures. . . . the aid is still promised and we have received only meager amounts. I say frankly that a failure to honor these promises will endanger the entire peace process."[4]

Donors too recognized the need to accelerate disbursements. The first and immediate priority had been to secure support for start-up and recurrent costs, as well as funding and equipment for the police. This gap was closed, largely through the Holst Fund, by the time the AHLC met in Brussels in November 1994. At that same meeting, however, the AHLC chair warned that the reconstruction program too was proceeding slowly, with disbursements predicted to fall 40 percent below the targets set by the World Bank.[5]

113

Table 5.1. Aid Commitments and Disbursements to the West Bank and Gaza

	Committed ($ millions)	Disbursed ($ millions)	Disbursed (% Commitments)
1994	789	524	66
1995	605	416	69
1996	886	537	61
1997	620	486	78
1998	655	330	50

Sources: MOPIC, *1997 Fourth Quarterly Monitoring Report of Donor Assistance* (31 December 1997), for 1994–95; MOPIC, *1999 First and Second Quarterly Monitoring Report of Donor Assistance* (30 June 1999), for 1996–98.

In the end, donors committed some $789 million for specific projects in 1994 and actually disbursed $524 million, or 66 percent of commitments (see table 5.1 and box 5.1).[6] Although much better than first anticipated, much of this occurred in the final quarter of the year, amid mounting criticism of the slow pace of aid delivery.

Such criticism of the pace of assistance was, in part, politically motivated. By criticizing donors, the PA diverted attention from its own shortcomings and exerted pressures for accelerated disbursements. Donors argued that support for Palestinian recurrent costs, transmitted through the Holst Fund, was delivered in a timely fashion and indeed represented a large share of 1994–95 disbursements. In the case of investment and rehabilitation projects, however, planning and engineering cycles could only be compressed to a limited extent. Still, it was clear that the aid was much slower arriving than anyone would have wished.

By the end of 1995, donors argued that they had turned the corner. In October of that year, Terje Larsen noted that "[in 1994] I called the donor effort a failure . . . but now donors are moving speedily."[7] In fact, in 1995, 1996, and 1997 the level of disbursements fluctuated and the rate of aid implementation remained more or less steady. More important than the annual disbursement figures, however, was the fact that an aid "pipeline" had now been established, consisting of an array of projects in the preparatory, planning, implementation, and wind-down phases. Unlike in the initial cash-starved period in 1994, this ensured a relatively smooth and constant flow of donor resources. Moreover, improvements in Palestinian revenue generation meant that the PA was increasingly less dependent on donors for immediate budgetary support, although it did continue to rely on external sources for virtually all public investments. In 1998, however,

Box 5.1. A Methodological Note on Aid Disbursement

International assistance to the West Bank and Gaza has benefited from what, in comparison to many other cases of peacebuilding, has been a relatively sophisticated system of tracking donor pledges (offers of assistance), commitments (the commitment of specific funds against specific projects), and disbursements (the transfer of funds to implementing agencies). This was initially undertaken by the World Bank and later transferred to MOPIC; in the case of the LACC and the SWGs, periodic sector summaries have been provided by UNSCO.

However, it is important to note that this system is dependent on donor reporting, which was less than fully reliable in the early years of the donor effort. Moreover, the category of "disbursements" only tracks whether funds have been transferred to an implementing agency, not whether that agency has begun to expend the funds "on the ground." In 1994, for example, bilateral donors disbursed $39.7 million to UNDP, but only $12.4 million (31 percent) of this was in turn disbursed by UNDP to actual projects during that same year. With the carryover of funds to following years, cumulative disbursements rose to 48 percent in 1995, and 68 percent in 1996. A roughly similar pattern would be evident for other multilateral agencies, while donor support for NGOs would also face smaller but still significant lags between donor disbursement and actual NGO spending.

Moreover, donor policy on "pledges" varies substantially. Some donors do not announce multiyear pledges but rather make annual announcements. Others may subsequently revise earlier pledges. Exchange rate variations may also play a role where pledges are made in U.S. dollars but budgeted by donors in national currencies.

Finally, rates of donor disbursement must be viewed in reference to the *type* of assistance delivered. Russia, for example, shows a very impressive 95 percent rate of pledges disbursed (table 5.5), but almost all of this is accounted for by equipment donations to the Palestinian police soon after the establishment of the PA. For other donors, a large portion of their initial assistance took the form of check-writing to the Holst Fund. While this was a fast, efficient, and useful mechanism, equally useful bilateral aid programs could lag significantly.

donor disbursements suddenly dropped sharply, as did the rate of aid implementation—generating new concerns about the flow of aid.

Although the PA might have preferred higher rates of delivery, by international standards such results seemed comparable to, or better than, those for other peacebuilding programs. By the end of the initial 1994–98 pledging period,

Table 5.2. Overall Disbursement Rates in the West Bank and Gaza (1994–98)

	Amount ($ millions)
Total Pledged	4,181.6
Total Committed	3,802.2
Total Disbursed	2,566.2
	Percentage
Proportion of Pledges Committed	90.9
Proportion of Pledges Disbursed	61.4
Proportion of Commitments Disbursed	67.5

Source: Personal communication, MOPIC official, 1998.

over 90 percent of pledges had been committed by donors for specific projects, and over 60 percent had already been disbursed (table 5.2).[8] In Cambodia 59 percent of funds pledged for 1992–95 were disbursed within that period. In Bosnia the annual ratio of disbursements to commitments has stood at around 50 percent, significantly behind the ratio (67.5 percent) in the West Bank and Gaza.[9]

There were several reasons for the slow start of the aid program, as well as for subsequent delays. Some of these constraints were structural in character, associated with the immediate political and economic context within which development and donor assistance programs have operated. Others arose from the actions and characteristics of the Palestinian Authority or from Israeli policies. Finally, still others have been related to strategies, structures, and procedures of the donors themselves.

STRUCTURAL CONSTRAINTS

Many of the structural constraints that have confronted the aid effort have been attributable to local economic conditions, which have set the context for all development programs in the area. As noted earlier, the Palestinian economy under occupation had been characterized by an underdeveloped infrastructure, heavy economic dependence on Israel, and a weak and fragmented public sector. In addition, donor programs faced particular constraints associated with both the absorptive capacity of the territories and the responsiveness of the private sector.

Finally, many constraints and needs were associated with the various political agreements that have characterized the interim period of the peace process.

The commitment of assistance was often timed to support certain political developments. Also, the complex territorial and functional division of jurisdiction that emerged from these agreements, as well as the model of economic policy laid down in the Paris Protocol, had important effects on what the PA and donors alike could, and could not, do in the territories.

Absorptive Capacity

Clearly, donor assistance to the West Bank and Gaza—representing around 12 percent of Palestinian GNP—has pushed the upper margins of what is generally considered the "absorptive capacity" of aid-recipient economies. The promise of both development assistance and private-sector investment caused land prices to skyrocket in some areas (notably in Gaza and Ramallah) and caused price increases in some construction materials. More serious still—at least in the initial years of the aid program—were bottlenecks arising from the limited technical and physical capacities of the local construction sector, the underdevelopment of the financial services sector, weaknesses in local infrastructure, and other constraints.

A number of efforts were made to deal with this. The World Bank, for example, designed the first Emergency Rehabilitation Project (ERP I) around smaller projects. Although the projects were best suited for the capacities of the construction sector, they also proved too small and geographically scattered to attract the interest of the larger regional and international contractors, who might otherwise have become engaged. The second Emergency Rehabilitation Project (ERP II) addressed this in part by emphasizing labor-intensive activities that had less requirement for physical plant and that had the additional benefit of addressing the growing need for local employment generation. A parallel approach— evident in the World Bank's Municipal Infrastructure Development Project—was to leave open the possibility of combining odd subprojects with larger packages so as to attract international consultants and contractors "if serious local capacity constraints materialized."[10]

Of course, project design could also build in the necessary lead time to bring contractors and others up to the required level of capacity and technical expertise. Yet, here and elsewhere in the assistance effort, donors faced a trade-off: should they design programs so as to maximize long-term capacity building, even if these delayed implementation, or should they stress timely implementation, even if it meant short-circuiting such capacity building?

The Palestinian Private Sector

From the outset, donor assistance programs assumed that substantial private-sector investment (spurred by the peace process and by an inflow of expatriate investment capital) would play a major role in sustaining economic growth in the territories. In practice, investment flows were disappointing. Although a few substantial Palestinian holding companies (notably PADICO, with $200 million in capital and up to $1 billion in planned investments by the end of the 1990s) have been active, and despite extensive real estate speculation in Gaza, Ramallah, and elsewhere, Palestinian expatriate investment has still not reached hoped-for levels. On the contrary, investment in the Palestinian economy fell from around 19 percent of GDP in 1993 to 10–11 percent by 1997, with the vast bulk (85 percent) in the form of investment in residential housing and very little (less than 5 percent) in capital equipment and machinery.[11]

Several factors have accounted for this decrease. Perhaps foremost has been political and economic uncertainty and hence the high degree of risk associated with investments in the West Bank and Gaza. Even expatriate investors, who might be ideologically attracted to the notion of supporting Palestinian development, often proved wary of risking capital in this environment. Broader private-sector growth has also been hampered by the weaknesses of local infrastructure in such areas as transportation, communication, and energy. It is not clear that the West Bank and Gaza offer obvious comparative economic advantages for foreign investment, especially given competition from Israel and Jordan. Moreover, the legal and regulatory context—based on a complicated amalgam of Turkish, British, Jordanian, Egyptian, Israeli, and PA regulations—"is far from ideal, characterized by numerous regulatory hurdles and a lack of legal transparency which increases the burden, risk, and confusion involved in doing business."[12] Potential investors also cite concerns regarding corruption, the free movement of goods and people, and the transferability of capital. Another significant bottleneck confronting development in the territories concerned the underdeveloped financial services sector. The number of banking institutions has grown (from twenty-six branches in 1992 to eighty-six in 1996), and deposits have roughly tripled.[13] However, bank behavior was slower to change: lending remained constrained (with a credit-to-loan ratio of 29 percent, only a slight improvement on the pre-1993 period and less than half the rate in Jordan or Israel), venture capital was difficult to raise (despite a nascent stock market), and mortgage lending remained extremely rare. One 1997 survey of Palestinian NGOs providing business consultancy "ranked the closure policy and the unclear operating environment as the main obstacles facing their clients with almost equal frequency. Managerial deficiencies were ranked nearly as high, followed by problems of market access and marketing, technical deficiencies, credit constraints and finding qualified workers." An earlier 1995 market analysis of potential Palestinian, Israeli, and external investors found free movement, corruption, security, rule of law, capital transferability, electrical supply, risk insurance, telecommunications, and risk insurance as major areas of concern.[14]

Not all of these constraints, of course, were purely structural; they were also bound up with politics and policy decisions. Businesspersons, for example, often complained about high rates of taxation on the private sector, arguing that these and other PA actions sapped private-sector competitiveness and deterred entrepreneurship. The excessively interventionist policies of the PA; the proliferation of semipublic, semiprivate monopolies (discussed later); a sometimes coercive partnership with the private sector (or at least with some unscrupulous businesspeople); and corruption also undermined the investment climate.

In order to redress the lack of private-sector investment, the PA has held high-profile meetings with Palestinian entrepreneurs. The Palestinian Investment Law announced by the PA in April 1995 sought to attract external investors by offering tax exemptions of up to five years, but it did little to resolve the more fundamental obstacles to private-sector development. Moreover, many external experts criticized it as unclear, inadequate, and outmoded.[15]

Over time, the donor community increasingly pressed the PA to address weaknesses in the private-sector environment. This pressure reflected growing recognition of both the weakness of private-sector activity and its central role in any future Palestinian economic growth. It also reflected a refocusing of donor attention on structural and policy issues that had received inadequate initial attention. Under the terms of the Tripartite Action Plan, the PA agreed to regularize and update its commercial codes. Later, in January 1998, Arafat and World Bank president James Wolfensohn agreed to an action agenda addressing six key areas of reform: the legal environment, privatization, institutional development, Palestinian-Israeli economic relations, infrastructure and environment, and open markets. The PA announced its intention to introduce or revise laws on taxation, competition, companies and agencies, investment, industrial zones, securities, insurance, arbitration, rental, banking, intellectual property, and other issues. A joint committee of the PA, the World Bank, and the International Finance Corporation (IFC) was also established to monitor progress in these areas.[16] In February 1998 both UNSCO and the IMF prepared special reports on the Palestinian private sector; these were followed in May 1998 by a discussion paper requested by the Norwegian chair of the AHLC. The latter identified more than two dozen priority areas for action. Tellingly, half of these were dependent on Israeli action, notably with regard to freer movement of goods and persons.[17]

Although the donor community paid growing attention to the needs and weaknesses of the Palestinian private sector, donor programs themselves were slow to develop in this sector. The most serious problem involved donor export, credit, and investment guarantee agencies, such as the American Overseas Private Investment Corporation (OPIC). These agencies often cited the risky local environment as a justification for not supporting projects in the area, thus essentially negating any meaningful contribution to peacebuilding. Belatedly, the IFC began lending operations in the territories in March 1997. By April 1999 it had provided some $130 million in project financing for thirteen planned investments worth $459 million.[18] Also, the Multilateral Investment Guarantee Agency (MIGA) established an Investment Guarantee Fund. Questions were raised, however, about how effective this latter program was likely to be, given local conditions: although the fund did cover losses from border closures under its war and civil disturbance coverage, this only addressed losses due to business interruptions lasting for 180 consecutive days. Even when MIGA made special allowances for the West Bank and Gaza—by reducing the waiting period to 90 days on a case-by-case basis—this seemed unlikely to address the problems generated by the typically short-term but recurrent interruptions to trade experienced by Palestinians. Indeed, at the time the fund was introduced no Israeli closure had lasted as long as 90 consecutive days.

A $100 million Peace Technology Fund was also established, cofinanced by the IFC, to facilitate joint ventures in the territories. Other donor programs have also sought to inject greater flexibility into the local financial services sector, whether through microenterprise schemes (notably those operated by UNRWA and by several NGOs), capacity building in the banking sector, or attempts to encourage the emergence of local mortgage lending.[19] With regard to the critical area of legal reform, initial progress was slowed by "a lack of adequate financial resources," although the situation was largely remedied by 1997 as more and more donors became active in this area.[20] Finally, one of the most evident projects in support of private-sector development was the export-oriented Gaza Industrial Estate project, located at Karni on the northeastern border with Israel and supported by private investors (the Palestinian Industrial Estate Development and Management Company, a subsidiary of PADICO), bilateral donors (notably USAID), and the World Bank. This project, it was hoped, would provide some 20,000 jobs on-site, and 30,000 more indirectly.[21] Here again, however, implementation was often mired in negotiations with Israel over security and transportation issues.

Donors also sought to promote trade and investment in the territories by negotiating trade agreements with the PA. The United States guaranteed duty-free access to the U.S. market for Palestinian goods, while the European Union negotiated an Interim Association Agreement on trade and economic cooperation with the PA. Canada, Denmark, Egypt, several Gulf states, Jordan, Norway, and Sweden also signed trade agreements with the PA.

One interesting U.S. initiative was Builders for Peace, an NGO formed in November 1993 by American Arabs and Jews, at White House urging and with USAID support. The group had the aim of encouraging and facilitating U.S. investment in the West Bank and Gaza.

Despite hard work, Builders for Peace was dissolved in August 1997 with few concrete achievements to show for its hard work. The cofounders disagreed slightly on what was the primary reason for this: Mel Levine, a former member of the House of Representatives, identified a lack of Palestinian accountability, transparency, and predictability as the major obstacle, while Arab-American activist James Zogby pointed to Israel's policy of closure and lack of direct Palestinian access to outside markets. Both agreed that setbacks in the peace process were another major source of problems, and both were also critical of the performance of OPIC in financing potential investments. In short, their experience proved representative of the broader challenges of promoting private-sector development in Palestine.[22]

Interim Agreements

All donor assistance has taken place against the backdrop of a series of interim Palestinian-Israeli agreements: the Declaration of Principles; the Gaza-Jericho Agreement and the Paris Protocol; the early empowerment agreements; Oslo II. The interim and incremental nature of these agreements has naturally inhibited long-term planning. Moreover, with each of these agreements have come specific needs and imperatives, such as the establishment of the administrative structures of the PA and its expansion into an increasing number of policy areas. The various agreements have also altered the physical area under PA control, modified the authority it exercises, and altered its revenue base. They have also determined the political space within which donor programs have had to operate. Donor mobilization and coordination efforts were thus closely tied to such agreements. The first Washington pledging conference closely followed the signing of the Declaration of Principles; AHLC meetings in 1994 were timed to discuss the needs of (and build on the momentum of) the Gaza-Jericho and early empowerment agreements; the October 1995 Consultative Group meeting largely addressed the requirements of Oslo II, while the January 1996 ministerial conference on assistance was deliberately convened shortly before the Palestinian elections.

Two aspects of the agreements deserve particular attention because of the extent to which they have structured the environment for donor programs and Palestinian development efforts. The first is the degree of *functional and geographic fragmentation* built into the agreements. The second is the *limited range of economic policy instruments* available to the Palestinian Authority.

With regard to the first aspect, the territorial arrangements established—with their patchwork quilt of areas A, B, and C (map 2.2) and the declining degree of Palestinian governmental authority as one moved from one area to the next—proved complex and unwieldy, creating a variety of problems. Lack of Palestinian control over land registration in area C and delays in establishing a registration system for area B, for example, introduced significant distortions in local property prices. Environmental and water policy was also hampered by the complex political geography of the West Bank, as well as the need to coordinate many policies with Israel (for example, within the framework of the Joint Water Committee, wherein Israel retains an effective veto). The disarticulation of the West Bank and Gaza has sometimes hampered the development of "national" policies by the PA. Administratively, geographically divided Palestinian ministries have also faced challenges in communicating effectively. Staff members have often been unable to meet one another, and physical separation has increased the danger of rival power centers emerging within supposedly unified government departments. Such fragmentation has accentuated complexity in an already very complex situation.

As for the second aspect, the specific provisions of the agreements allowed the PA to manage the main sectors of the economy (such as health, education, and the tax system), but with only partial control over instrumentalities and without the full ability to make important strategic choices (for example, with respect to the type of fiscal instruments or the choice of external economic relations).

Furthermore, the customs union model adopted under the Paris Protocol and the subsequent Interim Agreement has proven to have a number of weaknesses. Because taxes are levied on the basis of the initial destination of imported goods, for example, tax leakage (perhaps as high as 4–6 percent of GDP) occurred on goods purchased by Palestinians through Israeli intermediaries.[23] VAT clearance procedures (and other aspects of the agreements requiring cooperation) also proved highly cumbersome.

The Paris Protocol also resulted in considerable limits on PA policy independence on trade issues by closely linking these to Israeli trade policy. Thus, although the PA signed a number of bilateral trade agreements with the United States (November 1996), the European Union (February 1997), Jordan, Egypt, and a number of other countries, "these must be in compliance with the Israeli trade regime [and] the PA cannot offer import concessions, or export incentives, that differ from Israel's."[24] Both closure and other impediments limited Palestinian access to both Israeli markets and external markets, while preserving Israeli access to the Palestinian market. Jordanian officials, for example, frequently complained that differing trade agreements, "strict and bureaucratic Israeli policies," and various other obstacles hindered their trade with the PA.[25] These served to create an unstated pattern of trade discrimination in favor of Israeli concerns. The problem was compounded by the fact that the Palestinian side—lacking Israel's negotiating resources—agreed to some import quotas without accurate information on actual market needs. The estimated market for cement in the agreement, for example, was only one-tenth of actual need.

Finally, some argued that a significant gap had emerged between the spirit of the agreement and actual practice. As one analyst noted, "although the Paris Protocol was negotiated by economists, academics, and politicians, it is being implemented by [the] military."[26] As a result, a range of de facto trade barriers existed, many arising from security procedures of the Israeli Defense Forces (IDF). This process also facilitated the rise of commercial monopolies linked to Israeli firms and Palestinian security agencies.

As a result of such shortcomings, many Palestinian officials, outside experts, and even the World Bank called for the economic agreement to be renegotiated or for a new trade/fiscal model to be adopted.[27] However, it proved politically impossible to reopen the agreement once it was in place, and the Paris Protocol continued to provide the basic framework for Palestinian-Israeli economic relations throughout the interim period.

ISRAELI CONSTRAINTS

In addition to the constraints on rapid aid implementation presented by limited Palestinian institutionalization and absorptive capacity, assistance to the West Bank and Gaza has had to cope with a number of fundamental obstacles arising directly or indirectly from Israeli actions. Indeed, many donors—and even some Israeli diplomats[28]—would argue that these have been the single most important constraint on development.

Some of these constraints—the structural legacies of ongoing Israeli occupation, the structural constraints imposed by the various interim agreements—have already been discussed. Others arose from the need to protect Israel, and Israelis, from very real security threats, as well as intense public pressure on authorities to "do something" in response to acts of terrorism. The slow pace of the peace process itself was an important drag on development, exacerbating both political and economic uncertainty. As one AHLC discussion paper noted, "It would be unrealistic to expect any rapid take-off in private investment unless there is significant forward movement in the peace process."[29]

Two aspects of Israeli policy deserve particular attention. The most important of these has been closure, which has had devastating effects on the territories and, at times, has severely hampered development assistance. In addition, however, a number of other obstacles—either bureaucratic in nature or motivated by political or security concerns—have often inhibited development.

Closure

In the view of donors, "the unanticipated, dominant fact of Palestinian economic life since the signing of the Declaration of Principles has been the introduction of complex restrictions on the movement of Palestinian people and goods. For an economy so dependent on its neighbor, these restrictions have been crippling."[30]

The impact of closure on donor programs has been equally profound. The hardship imposed by closure created the need for emergency job-creation programs and the rapid injection of donor assistance into the territories. Projects were disrupted by interruptions in both the flow of building materials and the mobility of project personnel (especially locally engaged Palestinian staff). The costs of closure also placed increasing strain on the PA budget, depressing tax revenues and creating additional pressures on expenditures. In the longer term, closure made it difficult for both donors and the PA to envisage a strategy whereby sustainable development could best be promoted in an environment characterized by the periodic (and generally unpredictable) interruption of trade, uncertain Palestinian access to external markets, and severely corroded private-sector confidence.

Because of this, donors repeatedly called on Israel to refrain from the use of closure. In September 1997, for example, the Local Aid Coordination Committee issued a pointed statement that noted:

> Deep concern was expressed about the effects of continued closure on the Palestinian economy and society.
>
> The parties to the peace process realized at the outset that there remained the potential for violence at the hands of those opposed to the peace process. It would be unfortunate if that violence were allowed to achieve its objectives by constricting Palestinian development and reversing the peace process itself. Actions which would result in destruction of economic and social development or in donors reducing their commitment to development of the West Bank and Gaza would validate the actions of these extremist minorities. The political and economic tracks of the peace process are inextricably linked to each other.
>
> The basis of donor engagement in Palestinian development was the expected transformation which the peace process would bring to Palestinian lives through economic and social development. While security issues concern all, the impact of closure and withholding of revenue transfers are considered counterproductive to security concerns by undermining the key cornerstone on which the donor community participates in the peace process.
>
> Donors are committed to building capacity for Palestinian development and welfare, on the basis of viable Palestinian institutions. If those institutions cannot be built and become financially sustainable, donors cannot be expected to be responsible indefinitely for recurrent budget support or more generally the welfare of Palestinians. The responsibility for Palestinian welfare does not rest with donors alone.
>
> Donors are answerable to internal budgetary processes which will question the continuing commitment of resources to a development process damaged by closures.

By July 1997, considerable institutional and economic gains were realized and the donors were intending to build on these gains. The present closure and the withholding of Palestinian revenues will impact heavily on those gains.

The Palestinian Authority said losses were being sustained in the agriculture, industrial and tourism sectors, and medical services were threatened. Further, lack of movement on issues such as the port and airport prevents reasonable remedies to the situation.

The Palestinian Authority said that "security" meant not only personal security for Israelis, but also economic security for Palestinians. . . .

Project implementation is impeded through material shortages, increasing costs, and restrictions on personnel movement.

Some donors feel that—rather than achieving sustainable development—they are merely alleviating the detrimental effects of closure. There is no net gain from the presence of donors where the losses from closure exceed donor disbursements.

Essentially, donors were unsure of how to proceed in the circumstances.[31]

Successive UN special coordinators were particularly outspoken in this regard, and UNSCO issued detailed assessments of both the general impact of closure and specific incidents.[32]

The Tripartite Action Plan called on Israel to facilitate the movement of goods and persons to and from the West Bank and Gaza, although at the same time donors recognized Israel's obligation to protect its security.[33] At one point the European Union had pressed for more than this, but State Department officials rejected the notion of pressuring Israel on the issue of closure, much to the chagrin of other donors and many of their colleagues in USAID.[34] Instead, the United States preferred to politely suggest the "need to balance Israeli security concerns with making this a more business-friendly environment,"[35] while finding workarounds to the problem of closure. These included equipment and procedures to facilitate the inspection of trucks leaving Gaza, close diplomatic monitoring of closure, and support for border industrial zones that would enable Palestinians to work without entering Israel. It was also hoped that technological fixes—notably special scanning equipment for pallets and containers—would speed inspections.

At times, Israeli spokespersons sought to downplay the effects of closure and place the blame for poor economic performance elsewhere—suggesting, for example, that if the donors "would merely implement the commitments they took upon themselves, most of the economic difficulties would be alleviated."[36] Privately, however, senior officials did recognize the devastating effects of Israeli policies on the territories. They also recognized the paradox that closure policies, utilized both for security reasons and in response to pressure from the Israeli public, had the perverse effect of destabilizing the peace process and strengthening the position of Palestinian extremists.

Consequently, the Israeli government sought some mechanisms for lessening the economic impact of closure. This was true under both Labor and Likud: although Likud might be expected to be tougher on security issues, its long-term desire to retain substantial control over the Palestinian territories meant that it was also anxious to promote greater economic integration rather than reinforce the Green Line—the borders of the West Bank and Gaza—through the imposition of economic frontiers. Indeed, the use of closure dropped substantially after the change in Israeli government in May 1996, although this was also due to greater PA success in fighting terrorism.

Both Israeli governments also supported the idea of industrial estates, although in practice extended delays arose from negotiations over a Palestinian-Israeli framework agreement. In December 1997 Israel also announced that it would issue up to 30,000 "closure-proof" labor passes to Palestinians considered a low security risk and establish a program to allow Palestinian workers to remain overnight in Israel. Pointing to increases in the number of workers in Israel from 1996 to 1997, and from 1997 to 1998, it declared that such measures had resulted in "a significant improvement in employment, which has been recognized both by foreign representatives and by PA officials in recent [donor conferences]."[37] Economic data partially supported this contention, with unemployment declining in 1998 and the Palestinian economy showing modest per capita growth (or, at least, no further decline) for the first time since Oslo.

Other Impediments

In addition to the substantial effects of closure, other Israeli policies have also had negative effects on aid implementation in the territories. Not surprisingly, PA officials took a dim view: in the CPRS survey of PA, NGO, and donor officials, 29 percent described Israeli actions as "obstructive" and 69 percent as "very obstructive." Palestinian NGOs offered a similar assessment.[38] However, even donor officials had an overwhelmingly negative impression: none described Israel's role as positive, while 39 percent described its policies as "obstructive" and 27 percent as "very obstructive."

One problem was the initially slow pace of Israeli tax clearances to the Palestinian Authority under the terms of the Gaza-Jericho Agreement. The PA also complained about the rate at which Israel transferred tax records and other economic data, and the formats in which some data were received. For this reason, the Interim Agreement (Oslo II) included a rewrite of articles of the earlier Protocol on Economic Relations (Paris Protocol), detailing with greater specificity the process for VAT clearances between the two parties. Later, in August–

September 1997, Israel temporarily withheld customs and excise clearances as a way of exerting pressure on the PA. Given that these clearances account for over 60 percent of the PA budget, Israel's action posed a serious threat to political stability and was widely criticized by the donor community.

A second major problem concerned the ease—or more accurately, the difficulty —with which goods and persons flowed even when the borders were open. Palestinian imports and exports faced time-consuming and sometimes damaging searches. Because of these searches, Palestinian exporters were unable to use containerized or standardized pallets for exports, and goods such as textiles were often unpacked, unfolded, refolded, and repacked when searched. U.S. officials publicly expressed doubts as to why Palestinian exports needed to be inspected at all.[39] Such procedures, and other obstacles to mobility, effectively tripled the costs of transportation between the West Bank and Gaza, choking off intra-Palestinian trade. Palestinian businesspeople also had difficulty moving. Although a "safe passage" between the West Bank and Gaza was promised in the 1993 Oslo Agreement, it wasn't until October 1999 that such a route was finally established.

Both donors and the PA have complained about the sclerotic rate of some Israeli customs procedures, which could leave imported materials languishing on Israeli docksides for weeks or months. To these were added ever-present Israeli concerns about security, which tied up some goods for even longer because of their possible "dual use." Moving a U.S. donation of two hundred pickup trucks destined for Gaza through the Rafah crossing from Egypt took eight days and the full-time efforts of two U.S. officials. Among the delays was Israeli insistence that the trucks obtain separate insurance for the time they spent at the (Israeli-controlled) border crossing before entering Gaza and that all headlights be changed to conform to Israeli road standards.[40] A donation of $2.8 million in fire-fighting equipment from Japan was held back either because the Palestinian civil defense organization is technically a police agency or because the equipment might be destined for use at the disputed Gaza airport. During this period, PA officials blamed damage caused by a major fire in Gaza on the absence of the required equipment. A Canadian shipment of small inflatable boats (intended for search-and-rescue missions) was held back because their top speed was a few knots too high. A shipment of sewer-cleaning pumps was delayed until the Israeli Defense Forces ascertained whether the pumps could be turned against Israeli troops. Although the IDF eventually overcame its concern at this potential threat to Israeli national security, another was identified: the pump trucks lacked ABS brake systems. These then had to be retrofitted (at an additional cost of $40,000) for the thirty-five-kilometer trip to the Gaza Strip. European construction equipment intended for the Gaza port and airport has been deliberately delayed because of the political sensitivity of these disputed projects.

While goods lay delayed in port, storage costs mounted, payable by the donors or the PA, and sometimes exceeding the value of the shipment. Frustrated, the Netherlands at one point threatened to deduct the costs of port clearance from its bilateral cooperation programs with Israel.

Other problems include securing the necessary visas and other documents for foreign experts working on development projects, VAT clearances, disputes over product standards, and so on. Many of these problems arose simply from inefficiencies within the Israeli bureaucracy or poor interagency coordination. Obstacles were also sometimes created by right-wing customs and other officials hostile to the peace process. In one public manifestation of the tensions this could generate, in April 1999 the World Bank resident representative was forced to apologize to the Israeli government after a heated argument with an Israeli military officer over restrictions on the mobility of the bank's Palestinian personnel. To counter this hostility, some local donor representatives cultivated "friendly" (that is, Labor or Meretz) Israeli port and customs officials, who could then help to smooth over some of the bureaucratic obstacles.

Still other delays have clearly reflected official policy. One case in point was the slowness with which the Israeli telephone company Bezeq responded to PECDAR's initial requests for telephone lines when the latter agency was first being established. The lines were not installed until December 1994, forcing PECDAR staff to depend on a limited number of UNDP-financed cellular phones in the meantime. While some Israeli officials claimed that this was simply an example of Bezeq's legendary lethargy, others admitted that the delay signaled Israel's disapproval of PECDAR's location on the fringes of the Jerusalem municipal boundary.[41]

Another example has been the water sector, a contentious area that is reserved for final-status negotiations. Although under the Interim Agreement the PA was authorized to develop additional water resources, projects that potentially increased water production (rather than improved distribution) seemed to encounter frequent obstacles and delays.

Perhaps most visible, however, have been the political delays surrounding the establishment of industrial estates, Gaza airport, and a Gaza port. In all three cases, issues of security control were central, as was the desire to minimize any apparent signs of Palestinian sovereignty.

In the case of the industrial estates, Israel wanted strong inspection and security measures for any goods exported, as well as the ability to close the estate (located in PA territory) in the event of security concerns. Although the parties inched toward agreement and implementation of the Gaza Industrial Estate, others proposed for the West Bank bogged down, in part because they were to be located in areas B and C.

In the case of the Gaza airport, Israeli officials pressed for the right to control airport security, including the control of the tarmac and the power to inspect Arafat's own aircraft. They also argued that the airport, rather than having its own international airport code, should be considered an extension of Israel's Ben-Gurion Airport. One small section of the runway approaches jutted into an Israeli-controlled part of Gaza, further complicating the situation: the Israelis refused to clear this area of trees or otherwise allow the airport to operate, although the physical facilities were essentially completed by the end of 1996. Much of the technical equipment for the airport, provided by Germany and Spain, was impounded at the Israeli port of Ashdod. The PA was required to pay storage fees or face having its equipment auctioned off.[42] At least the airport was eventually opened: even less progress was made on authorization of a port for Gaza, thereby placing in limbo the almost $60 million committed to the project by the European Investment Bank, France, and the Netherlands.[43]

The establishment of the JLC—which allowed donors and the PA to raise such irritants directly with senior Israeli officials, and in so doing also flag them for the attention of the AHLC—eased some problems. The JLC subsequently established the Task Force on Project Implementation to follow up on reports of such obstacles. Furthermore, under the Tripartite Action Plan, Israel committed itself to facilitating the movement of aid officials, as well as to expediting the establishment of three industrial estates and the port negotiations. However, the effectiveness of this Israeli initiative was often stymied by another bureaucratic factor: while delays were usually associated with the actions (or lack thereof) of the IDF, MATAK (the Israeli civil administration for the territories), the Israeli Ministry of Finance, or Israeli port and customs officials, it was the Israeli Foreign Ministry that was represented in the JLC. Both aid officials and Israeli Foreign Ministry officials expressed periodic frustration at the bureaucratic disconnection.[44]

Whatever goodwill existed largely evaporated after Israel's May 1996 change of government. Cooperation and facilitation mechanisms also languished. Some of the coordination mechanisms established under the architecture of both the interim agreements and the AHLC-LACC stopped meeting altogether; others were attended by lower-level officials. Eventually, the JLC Task Force on Aid Implementation was reestablished, and the Palestinian-Israeli Joint Economic Committee resumed its meetings. However, all such coordination remained vulnerable to unexpected political shocks.

Faced with negative press and criticism from the international community, the Netanyahu government went on the diplomatic offensive, arguing that its economic policies toward the PA were positive rather than negative. In a May 1998 speech to the diplomatic corps, the Israeli prime minister asserted, "We believe that if the Palestinians have a good economy, have a good life, then the chances for peace are increased significantly." As proof of this, he pointed to recent growth in the number of Palestinian workers in Israel, reductions in the number of closure days, increases in the number of merchants crossing from Gaza, increases in tax clearances, and growth in the export of some Palestinian goods. "There has never been," he argued, "a more liberal, more conciliatory, more open, more generous treatment of the Palestinian economy than under this government. . . . There has been a material change for the good in the Palestinian economy as a result of Israel's policies." According to Netanyahu, donors who thought otherwise were being misled by the PA or simply lacked the correct facts.[45] Few donors were swayed by Netanyahu, and even many Israeli commentators appeared unconvinced.[46] Israel also argued that many of the delays were the responsibility of the PA, which refused to negotiate many issues in the absence of forward movement on the central issue of Israeli military redeployment. General Yaaqov Or, the Israeli coordinator for activities in the territories, complained that "it is easy to blame Israeli security" for obstacles, "but it isn't always only a matter of security." Specifically, he claimed that the Palestinians had failed to utilize the maximum number of work or truck permits available to them.[47] Regardless of this specific claim, it was certainly the case that the Palestinians did seek to use Israeli economic impediments—and perceptions of Israeli economic impediments—to maximum gain in the battle for public and donor opinion.

With the signing of the Wye River Memorandum in October 1998, hopes rose for significant progress in resolving these economic impediments. The memorandum included agreement on the opening of both the Gaza airport and the Gaza Industrial Estate, as well as on finalizing two safe passages between the West Bank and Gaza and accelerating talks on the Gaza port. However, although the airport and the industrial estate were promptly opened in December 1998, the remaining issues were put on hold when the Netanyahu administration suspended implementation of the agreement. Only after the election of a new Israeli government in May 1999 was further progress achieved.

PALESTINIAN CONSTRAINTS

Structural constraints on aid implementation, although substantial, explain only part of the difficulty in transforming aid pledges into concrete projects on the ground. Palestinian factors also slowed the delivery of assistance, with many donors (and Palestinian NGOs) critical of the PA's ability to identify projects, prepare proposals, coordinate, and manage projects in a financially transparent manner (table 5.3).[48] Palestinian NGOs were generally seen by donors as performing better in these areas, although both PA officials and local NGOs themselves were often somewhat more doubtful of this.[49]

Table 5.3. Perceptions of Palestinian Authority Aid Management

	Positive	Fair	Negative
Evaluation of PA Project Identification and Prioritization			
By Donor Officials	34%	38%	25%
By Local NGOs	31%	21%	43%
By PA Officials	31%	39%	29%
Evaluation of PA Preparation of Project Proposals			
By Donor Officials	6%	44%	38%
By Local NGOs	13%	21%	57%
By PA Officials	17%	18%	64%
Evaluation of PA Coordination with Other PA Institutions			
By Donor Officials	3%	36%	49%
By Local NGOs	11%	28%	56%
By PA Officials	20%	39%	42%
Evaluation of PA Coordination with Local NGOs			
By Donor Officials	3%	23%	65%
By Local NGOs	25%	34%	28%
By PA Officials	30%	45%	21%
Evaluation of PA Project Management			
By Donor Officials	16%	28%	31%
By Local NGOs	7%	13%	72%
By PA Officials	14%	20%	56%
Evaluation of PA Financial Transparency			
By Donor Officials	13%	28%	34%
By Local NGOs	6%	18%	63%
By PA Officials	21%	25%	42%

Source: CPRS, *Prevailing Perceptions on Aid Management,* Research Reports Series no. 9 (Nablus: CPRS, December 1997), 10–11.

Among the factors that most donors failed to anticipate were the lack of Palestinian preparedness and the associated institutional growing pains of the PA. Following the assumption of control in Gaza and Jericho, the PA had to staff ministries; acquire the necessary office space, equipment, and other supports; delineate bureaucratic responsibilities; establish coordination and communication mechanisms; reform legal and regulatory systems; and set national priorities—all essentially from scratch. In the meantime, the PA's ability to operate effectively was seriously constrained. One consultant's report, for example, noted that in June 1995—a year after the establishment of the PA—the headquarters of the Ministry of Labor in Jericho still had only two telephone lines, one for the minister and one shared by some 150 employees.[50] In some ways, building a (para-)state administration has presented a task more daunting than that confronting other war-torn societies, where the skeleton of a bureaucratic structure might already be in place—although the PA did have the advantage of a relatively highly educated population, access to considerable technical skills in the diaspora, and a reasonable tax base. Furthermore, as in other cases, external assistance was a significant local political resource, and the delivery of assistance had profound local political ramifications and dimensions. Aid, institution building, and the political consolidation of the PA proved to be inextricably bound, further complicating an already complex environment.

Technical Expertise

Part of the problems encountered by the Palestinian Authority in handling assistance stemmed from human resource shortages; although the PA did inherit some of the civil structure of the former Civil Administration (notably in the education sector), it lacked both trained senior management and technical experts required in many policy areas. Even when these skills existed elsewhere in the Palestinian diaspora, many Palestinian professionals were understandably reluctant (or simply could not afford) to uproot themselves in order to work under difficult conditions in the territories. Compounding this shortage of expertise, appointments to administrative and technical units were often driven by political favoritism and nepotism rather than qualifications.

To alleviate this weakness, donors established a World Bank–administered Technical Assistance Trust Fund, which disbursed some $23 million in support in 1994. To tap diaspora skills, the UNDP's TOKTEN program provided short-term support for Palestinian expatriates working with the PA, and later the World Bank established the Palestinian Expatriate Professional Fund. Such programs, however, have faced problems owing to pay and status differentials between local and expatriate Palestinians and have sometimes provided technical expertise of uneven quality. All told, donors committed roughly $479 million to technical assistance by the end of 1997, representing around 16 percent of all commitments.[51]

The passage of time, growing experience, and the provision of technical assistance all gradually helped to relieve shortages of expertise within the PA. However, this was only part of the problem. Another—and, indeed, much more serious —impediment has concerned the efficiency, transparency, and accountability of the administrative institutions of the Palestinian Authority.

Institutional Effectiveness

The institutional constraints experienced by the PA, like the human resource constraints, have stemmed in part from inexperience and the challenges of assembling the bureaucracy of a proto-state. Above and beyond this, however, the senior leadership (and Arafat in particular) seemed unwilling to create meaningful structures or clarify decision-making authority. This unwillingness inhibited the ability of the PA to formulate and implement economic policy—an ability already limited by lack of access (under the various agreements) to key policy tools. Moreover, the mechanisms of accountability and transparency required by donors were, initially at least, absent. Aid agencies were required to demonstrate —and hence required from the Palestinian Authority—a fairly demanding level of accountability and transparency in the disbursement of assistance, which slowed assistance significantly. Indeed, the PA found itself subject to audit, with a portion of its (Holst Fund) expenditures reviewed by the accounting firm of Touche-Ross Saba and its revenue collection process overseen by the IMF.[52] In the absence of solid project proposals and sufficient procedural guarantees, funds were simply not released: many harried aid officials were reluctant to undertake what they saw as Palestinian responsibilities.

Emerging bureaucratic structures also became personal and political power bases, enmeshed in competition with one another and with preexisting NGOs. One initial manifestation of this was an unclear demarcation of authority between the remnants of the PLO's Tunis-based bureaucracy and the emerging power centers in the territories. The PLO's Tunis-based foreign minister, Faruq Qaddumi, wrote key donors in October 1994 to stress that the PA was a local arm of the PLO and that the "Political Department of the PLO, which is in charge of foreign relations, will therefore continue to negotiate and conclude international economic agreements *for the benefit of the Palestinian Authority*."[53] In one memorable case, confused lines of authority led to the simultaneous announcement in Tunis and Gaza of a contract for long-distance telephone service—to two *different* companies. Soon, however, the PLO's Tunis-based bureaucracy slid into irrelevancy. While Qaddumi himself remained in exile, funding for external PLO institutions withered, offices were closed and telephones disconnected, and most cadres sought to return to Palestine and seek jobs with the PA.

A more important example of the intensely political dynamics of institution building was the Palestinian Economic Development and Reconstruction Authority (PEDRA). Later renamed the Palestinian Economic Council for Development and Reconstruction (PECDAR), it was intended to be the primary—but transitional—conduit for international assistance.[54]

PECDAR was formally established on October 31, 1993. Donors were uncomfortable with a variety of aspects of PECDAR, however, including the apparent predominance of political rather than technical personnel at the top of the organization, its lack of clear lines of authority and responsibility, and the absence of solid auditing mechanisms.[55] Some members of the PECDAR board expressed similar concerns over the preponderance of political appointees within the governing structures of the council. These issues were raised as early as the first AHLC meeting in November 1993 and repeated frequently by donors thereafter. As a consequence of these disputes, there were extended delays in initiating donor programs and concluding the necessary World Bank agreement with the PLO-PA. Finally—following more than six months of active follow-up by the Norwegian chair of the AHLC, bilateral diplomatic representations, a diplomatic démarche by donors, and final negotiations with the World Bank[56]—the revised bylaws of PECDAR were approved by Arafat, the PLO Executive Committee, and the PA in mid-May 1994.[57]

Subsequently, the establishment of separate PA economic and line ministries raised further questions about PECDAR's future role and the locus of economic authority. This was accentuated by institutional rivalries between MOPIC and PECDAR and personal political rivalries between Nabil Sha'th (of MOPIC) and Ahmad Qurai' ("Abu Alaa," who served for a period as minister of economy and director-general of PECDAR). Donor meetings were sometimes preceded by arguments over which minister would represent the PA, while the World Bank and other donors often encountered difficulties in getting both PECDAR and the Ministry of Planning to agree on a new common set of project proposals. A variety of committees and other mechanisms (including the JLC) were delayed by internal arguments among PA bodies over representation. Even seating arrangements at Local Aid Coordination Committee meetings could sometimes be the subject of dispute.[58] As one donor official noted:

> PECDAR [was] established to act as a transitional institution to fill a gap
> in implementation capacity. . . . Unfortunately, PECDAR did not mature
> or function as assumed. Rivalries traditional within the PLO continued
> and the impetus became more control than implementation . . . [and] did
> not overcome the culture of power developed over thirty years of struggle.

The monopoly power of PECDAR became an impediment to implementation.... On the other side, the ministries emerged extremely slowly, both because of a lack of staff and funding. Centralized decision making, compounded by the view of PECDAR that the ministries were potential rivals, impeded development.[59]

In the end, MOPIC emerged victorious and was designated as the official intermediary between donors and the PA, with the Ministry of Finance acting as the central agency for receiving donor funds. With this, tensions between MOPIC and PECDAR faded in their practical importance. PECDAR officials downplayed reports of turf battles with MOPIC as past history, "exaggerated" and "more imaginary than real."[60]

Perhaps so, perhaps not. Qurai' went on to serve as speaker of the Palestinian Legislative Council (PLC), and some suspected that he encouraged the rough treatment MOPIC sometimes encountered in the PLC. Meanwhile, as PECDAR's political fortunes declined (and some donors were heard to call for winding down the "transitional" organization), its new director-general, Muhammed al-Shatiyyah, ambitiously promoted the organization, with its glossy annual report noting that "PECDAR's role as the principal Palestinian Development Agency has become even more important than originally perceived."[61] Tellingly, MOPIC's quarterly monitoring reports on donor support contained only incomplete information on PECDAR operations. MOPIC officials complained that "it may be alive but since January 1, 1997, it has had no mandate. The Governors of PECDAR have not met [during 1997]. According to its internal law and regulation, PECDAR is illegal.... The World Bank is trying to keep this institution alive."[62] Bank officials responded that the "much-maligned" PECDAR had become a relatively effective mechanism for project design and management and implementation, capable of providing the necessary financial safeguards: "if there was sufficient capacity within the PA, [the World Bank] would push strongly for PECDAR to be dissolved. But the thing is, PECDAR works."[63] PECDAR officials also stressed—with some justification—that PECDAR was "one of the most transparent Palestinian institutions."[64] A number of donors evidently agreed, continuing to channel a portion of their assistance through the agency.[65]

Meanwhile, within MOPIC—once the wunderkind of the PA, with superior access to Arafat, donors, and resources—there were problems too. In 1997 the PLC called for Sha'th's resignation and a criminal investigation following findings of corruption inside his ministry.[66] Rivalries erupted between MOPIC's Gaza- and West Bank–based offices. Other battles over bureaucratic turf were also commonplace. Sha'th himself had initially been highly popular with donors for his urbane and cooperative manner, but this eroded over time. Moreover, he

Box 5.2. The Politics of Institution Building:
The Case of Environmental Policy

The development of Palestinian environmental policy—and the structures necessary to oversee it—represents another case study in the complexities and politics of Palestinian institution building.

Environmental protection was among those areas identified in the Oslo Agreement for Palestinian-Israeli "joint and/or coordinated measures" —with Palestinian concerns for autonomy reflected in the language adopted. Subsequently, the Gaza-Jericho Agreement also included a number of clauses regarding environmental protection, several of them reflecting Israeli concern for the protection of the Palestinian aquifers from which Israel drew water supplies.

Institutionally, the Oslo Agreement also called for the establishment of a Palestinian Environmental Authority, and following the establishment of the PA there was discussion of establishing a Palestinian Environmental Protection Agency. None of this came to pass, however. Instead, various ministries established their own environmental directorates.

The most developed of these, not surprisingly, was MOPIC's Environmental Planning Directorate (EPD). Through 1995–97, roughly $4 million in technical assistance and other support was provided to the EPD from Canada, Denmark, the Netherlands, and other donors.

In December 1996, however, a new agency, the Palestinian Environmental Authority (PENA), was established (by presidential decree) entirely separate from MOPIC and the EPD. Immediate confusion followed about the mandate of PENA and its relationship to the EPD. External support for the expansion of the new agency came from other donors, notably from UNDP, Japan, Switzerland, and Italy. Further assistance was provided to local and international NGOs for initiatives in the environmental sector.

Further complicating the picture, a new minister—but not ministry —of the environment was established in August 1998. Although the new

tended to be "very distant" from the operation of his ministry,[67] and often absent from it altogether because of his close involvement in the Palestinian-Israeli negotiating process. Because authority was seldom delegated—and because internal communication among senior MOPIC bureaucrats was imperfect—the result could be frustrating to donors.

Complicating the picture still further, in August 1998 Arafat announced that he would chair a new committee (including MOPIC, PECDAR, the Ministry of Finance, and later the Ministries of Local Government and of Industry

Box 5.2. *(cont.)*

minister, Yusif Abu Safieh, was well qualified—he had chaired the PLC Natural Resources Committee and held a Ph.D. in environmental science —his appointment seemed largely motivated by Arafat's desire to bring additional PLC members into the cabinet rather than by any institutional forethought. In any event, the Palestinian Environmental Authority, which had learned of the initiative in the newspaper, resisted the move. Abu Safieh, frustrated at being named minister of a nonexistent ministry, resigned. He "unresigned" the following day, after Arafat agreed that the phantom ministry would, in fact, be established. The EPD at MOPIC was effectively closed, and most of its staff moved to the ministry. As a result, as one donor official noted, "now both PENA and the Ministry deal with environmental affairs, and have different budgets and different staff." In the end, the ministry finally emerged as the responsible institution.

Although the environment was a key thematic priority of many donor programs in Palestine as elsewhere, on the ground general environmental issues were either ignored (as being of secondary importance to economic development and the national struggle) or heavily politicized. Despite the existence of a legislative committee on natural resources, the PLC had yet to pass an environmental law of any kind at the time the ministry was established. The PA regularly complained of environmental damage caused by settlers, emphasized Israeli exploitation of Palestinian water supplies, and bemoaned its lack of authority over the major portion of the West Bank (area C). Israeli critics of Oslo, by contrast, frequently recounted tales of Palestinian environmental mismanagement as evidence that Israel could ill afford a Palestinian state adjacent to its borders and astride major aquifers.

Sources: Palestine Economic Pulse 2, no. 2 (March–April 1997): 2-3; *Palestine Report,* 25 September 1998.

and Trade) to develop future PA economic strategy. PECDAR quickly emphasized that this (and, by implication, not MOPIC) would be the "new address [for] donor assistance."[68] Others were simply confused: noted one donor official, the new committee had "god-knows-what reasoning behind it, and nothing was ever formally conveyed to donors about it, or what it was supposed to do."[69]

Similar tales could be told of institutional development in other policy areas, for example the environmental sector (see box 5.2), or within the Ministry of Agriculture (box 5.3). Meanwhile, Palestinian line ministries, municipalities, and other agencies continued to make their own bilateral approaches to donor agencies, rather than operate through MOPIC or any other centralized mechanism. Some donors complained about this circumvention.[70] Most, however,

---

Box 5.3. A Minister's Travails

The PA's first minister of agriculture, 'Abd al-Jawad Saleh, was a longtime independent critic of Arafat and often denounced PA mismanagement and corruption. Indeed, his appointment to the cabinet in 1996 probably reflected Arafat's intention to give his administration greater political credibility and possibly quiet some of the criticism. None of this, however, enhanced Saleh's influence within the PA. Moreover, many of the ministry's senior staff were political appointees, with different loyalties. The problems this created were highlighted in an August 1997 press interview:

Q: What would you characterize as the major problems you found within the Agriculture Ministry when you took over as minister?
A: Well, I have seen three directors-general in one department. I have seen abuse of money; money which was donated for research was mismanaged by an assistant director-general and a director-general and they bought a car with it. One director-general also tried to transfer another director-general without any justification and without informing me.
Q: And are those people still in their jobs?
A: Yes, of course.

A few months later, Saleh complained to a session of the PLC that a number of senior officials in his ministry were involved in producing false licenses for Israeli citrus products so that they could be illegally marketed in Jordan. Saleh noted that he had twice reported the scam to the PA attorney-general, but no action was taken. During the same session, he also protested that his ministry's Planning Center in Nablus did little but "sabotage and cause disruption."

In the cabinet reshuffle of August 1998, Saleh was demoted to the position of minister without portfolio. He refused the position and resigned from the cabinet instead, complaining that the PA had become a "school for corruption" in which "effective ministers are kicked out and corrupt ones are retained."

Sources: Palestine Economic Pulse 2, no. 2 (March–April 1997), 2–3; Palestine Report, 25 September 1998.

pursued the path of least resistance, arranging whatever projects seemed easiest with whatever level or branch of Palestinian authority or society seemed most amenable—further complicating economic planning. One senior PECDAR official described this process as "signature-shopping."[71] In defense of this practice, some donor officials cited the need to disburse funds expeditiously: "[We] need to get development money in Palestine so we can't wait for capacity in the PA to be built. Absorption capacity has come a long way, but institutions are [still] shallow."[72] One effect was for donors to target their assistance in those sectors where Palestinian counterpart institutions were stronger (for example, education or health), rather than those where institutional capacity or competence seemed weaker (for example, agriculture or tourism). This, of course, served to further exacerbate differences in institutional capacity.

In addition to the economic policy and line ministries, the Office of the President retained a role in a great many projects and economic decisions. Surrounding the president were a bevy of assistants, advisers, and sometimes shady hangers-on, all of whom claimed some influence, authority, or *wasta* (intermediation), and who further clouded economic accountability. In the early days of the aid program, virtually all Western aid officials could recount a similar experience: the approach of a business agent, seeking donor cofinancing or other support, brandishing a letter of authorization from some PA official or another. Generally it was doubtful on what authority the letter had been issued and by what process it had been obtained—and there were almost always several other versions of the letter (issued by the same official or others) in circulation.

Although this problem diminished as PA ministries developed, donors also expressed concern about the existence of funds outside the control of the Ministry of Finance and under the apparent direct control of Arafat. Most notable among these was the over $100 million per year in petroleum excise taxes collected by Israel and paid to a separate numbered Bank Leumi account in Tel Aviv believed to be under Arafat's direct control. Although the PA repeatedly pledged to consolidate all accounts, in the Tripartite Action Plan and elsewhere, by the end of 1999 this consolidation had yet to occur. The result was a growing liquidity crisis, with the Ministry of Finance increasingly unable to meet its budgetary obligations because of unreliable access to the "missing" funds.

Finally, institutional development within the PA has been accompanied by another problem: the rapid (and, in the view of most donors, excessive) growth of the Palestinian bureaucracy. Between October 1994 and the end of 1997 public-sector employment more than doubled, from some 35,000 employees (including 12,000 members of the security services) to 86,800 (including around 38,400 members of the security services), representing some 16 percent of the labor force (figure 5.1). By September 1998 the total stood at 90,000. As a consequence, wage costs grew to consume some 55 percent of Palestinian recurrent budgetary expenditures and around 12 percent of GDP—a very high proportion by international standards, although not dissimilar to the pattern in neighboring Jordan. The introduction of a new civil service law, mandating pay increases for many public-sector employees, further aggravated the PA's liquidity crisis. It also provoked a wave of labor unrest in 1999 by those who felt disadvantaged under the new law. Faced with this, Arafat ordered that implementation of the law be suspended until new arrangements could be worked out.

The PA argued that the growth in the public sector was necessitated by rapid population growth and widespread unemployment. Donors, however, saw it as a continuing drain of scarce fiscal resources. Both were right. However, a complete understanding of the evolution of the Palestinian public sector also requires attention to the imperatives of regime consolidation, an issue discussed later in this chapter.

Corruption

Donor concerns about Palestinian transparency and accountability, which had proved to be a real drag on rapid implementation of aid programs in 1994–95, increasingly resurfaced in 1996–98 with reports of growing corruption. Some reports suggested that aid funds were being mishandled within ministries, that officials were enjoying excessive perks at public expense, that favoritism and kickbacks were involved in the granting of some contracts, and that excessively close connections existed between some officials (and ministries) and some private-sector companies.[73] The PA's failure to consolidate all financial accounts heightened donor concern. Perhaps the most obvious manifestation of corruption, however, was the rise of semiprivate, semipublic monopolies. These controlled the import trade in a number of sectors—fuel, cement, gravel, cigarettes, flour, steel, building materials—typically with an exclusive Israeli supplier[74] and one of the myriad PA security agencies. Some estimates suggested that twenty-seven or more such monopolies were operating in the territories by 1997.[75] These in turn spawned an expanding array of second-generation commercial activities, in the form of fully legal enterprises established with the probable proceeds from somewhat murkier business operations.

In May 1997, the PA's own Public Monitoring Department (PMD) issued a report detailing some $329 million in forgone revenues and irregular or excessive expenditures by PA ministries and official bodies.[76] In an explanation presented to an informal AHLC meeting in Washington, PA representatives argued that many of the items cited as forgone revenues were deliberate policy decisions rather than evidence of wrongdoing.[77] Arafat subsequently appointed a special commission to examine the question of corruption, while a special committee of

Figure 5.1. Growth in PA Public Sector

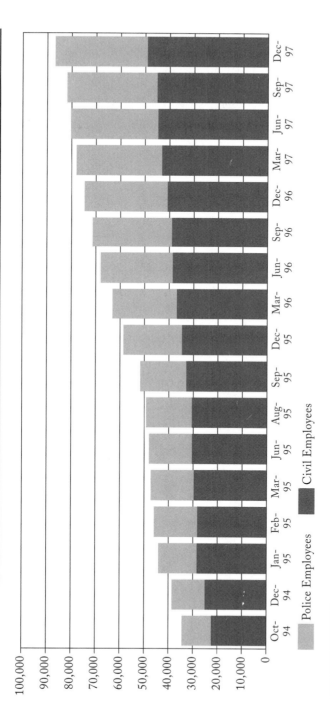

Sources: World Bank and the Palestine Economic Policy Research Institute, *Development under Adversity? The Palestinian Economy in Transition* (discussion draft, 30 October 1997), box 8.1 and table 12 in the appendix; Palestinian Authority, *Report on Fiscal Developments in April–September 1997 and Outlook for the Remainder of 1997* (31 October 1997), 5; UNSCO, *Economic Conditions in the West Bank and Gaza Strip: Summer 1997 Quarterly Report* (4 October 1997), 9; AHLC Secretariat, *Report on the Status of Tripartite Action Plan Provisions* (13 May 1998).

the Palestinian Legislative Council issued a follow-up on the PMD report detailing alleged abuses in a number of PA ministries.[78] Not dealt with in either report, however, were the problem of semiofficial monopolies, the operations of Arafat's office, or the role of the security services. In July 1997 the PLC adopted a resolution (by a vote of 57 to 1) calling for the entire PA cabinet to be replaced. In June the attorney-general was fired for pocketing bail money; in September some members of the security forces were arrested for their involvement in extortion and the smuggling of spoiled foodstuffs.[79] However, thereafter the corruption issue withered somewhat amid the continued uncertainty of the peace process. In late 1997 discussions between PLC members and Arafat resulted in agreement on eighteen recommendations concerning greater transparency, improved legislative-executive cooperation, reliance on the rule of law, and other issues. With this, the PLC explicitly agreed to effectively close its file on the 1996 PMD report.[80]

In August 1998 Arafat, responding to long-standing demands from the PLC, announced a cabinet reshuffle. However, none of the ministers named in the PMD and PLC reports was removed from his or her position; instead the cabinet was enlarged through ten new ministerial appointments—all largely drawn from the PLC, thereby assuring parliamentary endorsement. In effect, nothing changed, leading a few ministers to resign in protest.

It remains difficult to get a sense of the true scope, and effect, of corruption within the PA. In the words of one Gaza merchant and former Fateh cadre:

> We live in amazing, shameful times, but you should know that every revolution has its fighters, thinkers and profiteers. Our fighters have been killed, our thinkers assassinated, and all we have left are the profiteers. These don't think even primarily of the cause, they don't think of it at all. They know that they are just transients here, as they were in Tunis, and, as with any regime whose end is near, they think only of profiting from it while they can.[81]

With regard to both the motivations of many former PLO officials and the institutional accomplishments of the PA, clearly this judgment was excessively harsh. However, it did echo the perception of a growing number of Palestinians: according to surveys, the proportion identifying corruption as a problem rose from 49 percent in September 1996 to 56 percent by August 1998, with 30 percent stating that corruption would diminish and 51 percent believing that it would worsen.[82] Only 7 percent maintained that *wasta* (meaning, in this context, connections and nepotism) was unnecessary to secure employment. Most respondents believed that corruption was present in government ministries (78 percent) and the security forces (69 percent); somewhat fewer believed it existed in the PLC (45 percent) and the president's office (36 percent). Similarly, some 45 percent of donors (and 75 percent of local NGOs) expressed the view that there has been a "very strong" or "strong" misuse of funds by the PA.[83]

The Palestinian Legislative Council drew greater attention to the issue of corruption, although its investigation was weak in a number of respects.[84] A variety of political and media dynamics also amplified the issue, which has been seized on by local opponents of the PA, the international media, the Israeli government (under Netanyahu, but not Labor), and external critics of the aid program (notably in the United States). Local press reporting has been rather more muted, reflecting the constraints imposed by a degree of official intimidation.

From one perspective, it is possible to argue that corruption, though very serious, has been somewhat exaggerated. Some activities—notably the operation of the monopolies—combine elements of an extortion racket and an inefficient and extralegal system of taxation, with some of the funds going into private pockets but a substantial share likely being used to finance the off-the-books expenses of the Palestinian Authority. Indeed, two of the largest companies involved in such activities—Sharakat al-Bahr (co-owned by the director of Arafat's office) and the Palestinian Company for Commercial Services (headed by Arafat economic adviser Mohammad Rashid, also known as Khalid Salam)—have close links to Arafat's office. As the monopolies attracted greater public and donor attention, the PA moved to officialize some and privatize or even dismantle others. Significantly, Rashid himself was appointed as the senior PA representative to the joint Public Sector Development Progress Committee.

Broader corruption in official agencies is certainly present, but in the words of one IMF official, "The PA is not any worse than other countries in corruption and tax evasion," with the Ministry of Finance described as "very clean."[85] Official corruption in Palestine would appear to be less widespread than in neighboring Egypt, Lebanon, or Syria. It would also appear to be less severe than in Cambodia, Haiti, Mozambique, and a number of other postconflict countries. Certainly, there are no other countries in the Arab world where reports as critical of the government as those produced by the PMD and PLC would be publicly released.

On the other hand, it is clear that corruption *has* adversely affected development in a number of ways. Weak institutionalization and imbalances in social power have encouraged the appearance of opportunistic and parasitic forms of criminal corruption. Members of Palestinian Preventive Security and General Intelligence, for example, have used the lack of clear VAT regulation and oversight to shake down individuals and companies for "tax payments."[86] The monopolies have tended to inhibit free private-sector development and distort market prices. Corruption within the PA also introduced policy distortions, although it has not yet fundamentally sapped confidence in public institutions.[87] Externally, press reports of corruption threatened political support for assistance in donor countries. In both the United States and Norway, for example, legislators demanded investigations into reports that aid to the territories had been diverted. Donor willingness to provide direct support for the PA budget was particularly adversely affected. As one EU report noted, the PA "has failed to honor important commitments . . . to the international community, the financial assistance of which has been the main factor in its very survival."[88]

Political Imperatives

To understand the nature and effects of Palestinian institutional constraints on aid implementation, it is essential to put them in their political context. For the Palestinian Authority, the receipt and expenditure of aid has been closely tied not only to the developmental needs of the West Bank and Gaza but also to two additional (and not always complementary) imperatives: political consolidation of the PA and the need to strengthen the PA vis-à-vis Israel.

Aid and Regime Consolidation

With regard to the internal politics of aid, public investment and public employment have provided an opportunity to reward supporters and buttress political constituencies. This approach to public policy—hardly unique to the PA—has been reinforced by Arafat's neopatrimonial style of political management, which emphasizes personalism and patronage at the expense of long-term institution building.[89] In short, much PA decision making has been driven not by concerns about economic efficiency but by considerations of political consolidation. Viewed in this light, the growth of public-sector employment becomes understandable. One Palestinian deputy minister was quoted as remarking that "the inflation of the government's bureaucracy is one of the Authority's great economic achievements. Where else would these people find work if we had not made them clerks?"[90] Similarly, Muhammad Dahlan (head of PA Preventive Security in Gaza) explained:

> We have some 50,000–60,000 employees—I cannot give a precise figure—and we only need 20,000–30,000. For example, although we only need 10,000 people in the security organ, we have over 30,000.
> We have 36,000 people of whom we only need 10,000. This huge number is a burden on the PA and a burden on the security organ. We view it as a social issue because I cannot tell a prisoner who has spent 15 years in jail that I have no job for him.[91]

Such employment of otherwise unemployed intifada-era street activists secured the loyalty of those affiliated with Arafat's Fateh organization, while co-opting others away from the opposition and the ranks of potential troublemakers. At a higher level, many senior ministry staff were drawn from former high-ranking Fateh and PLO cadres, with much of the upper ranks of the Ministry of Finance, for example, being staffed by former members of the Fateh financial department and the PLO's Palestine National Fund. One PECDAR official, himself a former senior PLO official, noted that not only was it important to reward cadres for their loyalty and commitment, but in addition such cadres often had a political sensitivity that more qualified technical experts lacked: "If someone has put in thirty years, you can't throw them away, even if they might be less efficient than a new university graduate. Palestinians who have struggled know how to protect the peace process—it is they who are politically reliable."[92] More broadly, with an average of five to six dependents per wage earner, some half a million Palestinians benefit directly from PA employment.

Political patronage by the PA has included not only public-sector hiring but also specific projects. Arafat's office has directly financed, for example, small infrastructure projects in almost every rural community in the West Bank, often in association with external donors. Local inhabitants are well aware of where these resources have come from.

It is in order to sustain such patronage that Arafat has been so careful to preserve some discretionary funds, whether through the petroleum excise account or through revenues raised by the monopolies. For this reason, too, the PA has generally encouraged donors to channel support through the PA rather than through NGOs or other alternative channels, thus allowing the PA to claim appropriate political credit. It also explains the suspicion displayed by some PA officials (and especially Arafat) with regard to donor support for (potentially rival) NGO activities.

Political consolidation underpins many of the rivalries and divisions apparent within the administrative structures of the PA. Encouraging competition among subordinates has always been a hallmark of neopatrimonial political management, serving both to inhibit the emergence of rival power centers and to strengthen the position of the leader. Unclear lines of administrative authority serve a similar purpose, allowing a leader to reallocate responsibilities among subordinates and further enhancing the primacy of political loyalty and personal relationships over institutional structures and bureaucratic procedures. The rivalry between MOPIC and PECDAR has all the hallmarks of such a situation.

Corruption too can be seen as having, at least in part, political roots. As noted in chapter 1, it is encouraged by other characteristics of war-to-peace transitions: the influx of external resources, the uncertainty of transition arrangements, and the weakness of existing institutions. The toleration of corruption is a powerful political reward and hence a tool of political manipulation. So too is the withdrawal of such toleration. Certainly, the release of the 1997 Public Monitoring

Department report—written by an Arafat appointee and first disclosed in the semiofficial newspaper *al-Hayah al-Jadidah*—seemed to have important political purposes, namely, to trim the wings of some of the most successful ministries (MOPIC) and ministers and to respond to donor concerns about corruption without fully addressing some of the most important aspects of the problem. From Arafat's point of view, subsequent pressure on the cabinet from the PLC may not have been unwelcome, since it increased the vulnerability of cabinet ministers and allowed him to claim a mandate for reform.

Because of the importance of strong counterpart agencies and the difficulty encountered by aid agencies owing to institutional weakness within the PA, donors have devoted growing resources to institution building and public-sector reform. In addition, various public-sector reform undertakings were included in the Tripartite Action Plan. Many such initiatives have seemed rather naive, however, treating the issue as one of technical competence rather than recognizing the political roots of the problem. The result is little incentive for change: although donors argued that reform would bring greater cost-effectiveness, the existing system has helped to sustain remarkably stable support despite political stalemate and economic decline. Indeed, with a personal approval rate remaining steady at around 73 percent through much of 1996–98 (compared with around 69 percent for the security services, 58 percent for the cabinet, and around 47 percent for the legislature), Arafat must have suspected that he had a firmer grip on the task of political management than did either his domestic critics or the donors.[93]

Aid and the Peace Process

With regard to external politics, the PA has—not surprisingly—attempted to use external assistance to strengthen its position in the course of continuing negotiations with Israel. As a PECDAR official noted early in the process, "In the first phase, our economic planning is completely determined by political reasoning. . . . We have to be professional from a political point of view, not an economic point of view."[94]

Several manifestations of this linkage between development and diplomacy can be seen. Some were largely symbolic: the PA fought hard to obtain its own dialing prefix from the International Telecommunications Union (ITU), rather than utilize Israel's 972 code. In November 1998 the ITU agreed to grant the PA the code of 970—a decision hailed by the PA Ministry of Communication as "one of the basic steps on the road to announcing an independent Palestinian state." Caught up as the code was with territorial issues and the realities of Israel's continued role in Palestinian telecommunications, the Palestinians admitted that "it is not yet clear however exactly what areas the new code will cover."[95]

Jerusalem has been a more substantive example of the political imperatives of development, with the PA making efforts to maximize its presence and connection to the city. The initial formation of PECDAR was delayed, for example, by reference in its original charter to Jerusalem as its headquarters.[96] Later, the PECDAR offices (and the West Bank offices of MOPIC) were deliberately sited on the very edge of the city, virtually a stone's throw from the Israeli checkpoint. In September 1994 a meeting of the Consultative Group collapsed when the PA included some Jerusalem projects among its proposals to donors. Resolution of that particular dispute required active Norwegian mediation, concluding in a joint declaration by Arafat and Peres on September 13 in which they undertook not to raise disputed issues with donor countries. When the World Bank initiated its Trust Fund for NGOs, the question of assisting Jerusalem-based NGOs was a particularly tricky one, eventually resolved by establishing a hybrid structure that met both Palestinian demands and Israeli objections.[97] In February 1999 Israel boycotted a Consultative Group meeting when it noticed that some of the maps of the West Bank presented by the PA had the city of Jerusalem marked on them.

There has also been a constant game of cat and mouse between the PA and Israel, with the establishment of PA-linked offices in East Jerusalem and periodic Israeli measures against these.[98] The Israeli press reported a variety of activities by PA security organs, ministries, and other institutions in the eastern part of the city, noting even that East Jerusalem soccer clubs played in the Palestinian football league, administered by the PA Ministry for Youth and Sport.[99] The PA has sought to promote Palestinian economic development and real estate purchases in Jerusalem as a way of countering Israeli attempts to "Judaize" the city. Since 1994 Orient House (the official Palestinian institution in the city) has operated a Private Sector and Investment Unit, including investment-generation missions in the Middle East. Palestinian officials also periodically met with foreign diplomats at Orient House. In October 1995 both members of the Israeli Knesset and members of the U.S. Congress charged that the PA was using its funds to acquire properties in East Jerusalem.[100] In December 1997 PA plans to include East Jerusalem in its census provoked a strong reaction from the Israeli government. In May 1999, during the run-up to the Israeli election, the Likud government threatened to close Orient House altogether.

Further examples of the link between development programming and negotiating positions could be seen in many of the infrastructure projects proposed by the PA. Both the proposed Gaza port and the completed Gaza airport have important economic implications to be sure, but both are also intended to reduce Palestinian dependence on Israel and enhance the symbolism of Palestinian proto-sovereignty. Similarly, Palestinian emphasis on road construction (which accounted for some 11.9 percent of proposed public investments under the

1998–2000 Palestinian Development Plan and almost one-quarter of all infrastructure investments) is justified by the PA on the grounds of poor transportation infrastructure but in some cases appears to be intended to consolidate territorial control and block the expansion of Israeli settlements.[101] The chair of the Palestinian Legislative Council's Land and Settlement Committee, Salah Ta'mari, noted the important political dimension of infrastructure projects: "Confronting settlement expansion is a clear-cut matter. It involves developing the villages that are threatened with this expansion. It does not take a genius to realize that our villages need basic services and infrastructure development." If anything, he added, the PA was paying inadequate attention to such political factors in its development policy.[102]

DONOR CONSTRAINTS

Thus far, attention has been focused on the structural, Israeli, and Palestinian constraints on the rapid delivery of assistance to the West Bank and Gaza. However, donors too were responsible for a significant share of delays and other weaknesses in the aid program. In the CPRS survey, Palestinian officials and NGOs report substantial dissatisfaction with a number of aspects of donor performance (table 5.4).

Palestinian officials also show substantial variation in their appraisals of particular donors, with the European Union and UNDP receiving generally high marks and USAID rather negative ones.[103] While this evaluation probably reflects as much *political* dissatisfaction with U.S. foreign policy as specific dissatisfaction with the performance of USAID, other measures—for example, rates of aid implementation (table 5.5)—also suggest substantial variations in donor performance.

Such variations are telling. Since most of the factors discussed earlier—the economic and political setting in the territories, the various challenges posed by Palestinian politics and institution building, and the impact of closure and other Israeli actions—have affected all donors, they cannot explain why some donors have tended to deliver on their pledges faster than others have. Rather, factors intrinsic to donors must account for these differences. The following three sets of factors are explored: the institutional responsiveness of donor agencies; the impact of differences in the sectors and channels favored by donors; and the impact of domestic (donor) politics on aid delivery.

Institutional Responsiveness of Donor Agencies

One significant constraint on rapid disbursement has been posed by the institutional structure and internal dynamics of aid agencies themselves. One EU aid

Table 5.4. Perceptions of Donor Performance in the West Bank and Gaza

	Positive	**Fair**	**Negative**
	Prioritization of Projects by Donors		
Evaluation by Donor Officials	41%	17%	14%
Evaluation by Local NGOs	17%	28%	53%
Evaluation by PA Officials	14%	35%	50%
	Donor Expediency in Processing Proposals		
Evaluation by Donor Officials	30%	36%	24%
Evaluation by Local NGOs	15%	26%	50%
Evaluation by PA Officials	12%	31%	51%
	Fulfillment of Commitments by Donors		
Evaluation by Donor Officials	47%	41%	9%
Evaluation by Local NGOs	21%	38%	36%
Evaluation by PA Officials	11%	32%	55%

Source: Center for Palestine Research and Studies, *Prevailing Perceptions on Aid Management,* Research Reports Series no. 9 (Nablus: CPRS, December 1997), 10–11.

official recounts how, when asked by Brussels to report on the extent to which Palestinian factors were limiting the aid effort, he declined to do so—arguing that donor limitations had been at least as important, and perhaps more so.[104] And, although it might be argued that EU assistance faces particular bureaucratic obstacles (box 5.4), other donors face institutional constraints of their own.

Of course, one should not underestimate the institutional challenge of rapidly expanding donor aid programs from around $200 million per year in the early 1990s to several times that amount. In some cases, small amounts of new aid did flow quickly through discretionary embassy accounts for small projects. In general, however, new staff had to be hired and new projects identified. Since most aid agencies had an existing "stable" of projects and local contacts, the initial tendency in many cases was to simply do more of the same, rather than to rethink aid priorities. UNRWA, for example, largely dusted off its wish list of capital projects and repackaged these as its Peace Implementation Program (PIP) for donors.

Yet doing more of the same could be problematic. Many earlier aid programs had often been heavily dependent on small NGO projects and could not

Table 5.5. Aid Implementation in the West Bank and Gaza (selected donors)

Donor	Aid Disbursement (% of pledges, November 1996)	Aid Disbursement (% of pledges, November 1998)
Russia	95	95
Japan	35	98
Switzerland	28	91
Denmark	25	102
Norway	20	91
Canada	23	80
European Union (including EIB)	15 (8)	71 (42)
Sweden	4	70
Saudi Arabia	15	64
United States (USAID + OPIC)	8	69
average	*16*	*60*
World Bank	2	56
Italy	15	38
Israel	9	10
European Investment Bank (EIB)	0	19
Turkey	4	7
International Finance Corporation	0	5

Sources: AHLC, *Matrix of Donor's Assistance to the West Bank and Gaza, November 1996;* MOPIC, 1998 *Third Quarter Monitoring Report of Donor Assistance* (15 November 1998).

Note: EU figures are listed separately from EIB figures on the donor matrices. However, here a combined EU + EIB figure is also given to facilitate comparison with the figure for the United States (which includes both USAID and OPIC programs).

easily be "scaled up." In the case of the United States, for example, pre-Oslo aid had been limited and largely channeled through a limited group of U.S. private voluntary organizations rather than administered directly. As a result, with the expansion of its program for the territories, USAID had to rapidly expand its infrastructure on the ground, with bureaucratic and political struggles arising over

Box 5.4. Bureaucratic Extremes

The degree of bureaucracy encumbering aid programs has varied, of course, from donor to donor. At one end of the scale is the European Union. According to one EU official, "The main delays in European aid stem from Brussels and its bureaucracy . . . due to the centralization of the system of administration. Signatures come from the Commission [and] signatures have to come from all different departments before documents get signed by the Director General." As a result of this highly devolved process, nothing takes less than twelve months to go through from proposal, to signing of member states, to signing of agreement, to mobilization, to implementation. Indeed, it can take ten weeks simply to have any financial proposal translated into each EU language. Counterbalancing this, however, have been political will and a substantial presence on the ground. As a result, overall EU disbursement rates are quite high, at around 71 percent of pledges by late 1998 (table 5.5), although this drops to only 42 percent if the European Investment Bank pledges are included.

The paradoxical combination of a sympathetic EU foreign policy and a dense donor bureaucracy was not lost on the PA. Noted one senior official, "EU is the most complicated bureaucratically, but the best politically," while the United States "can take six months to spend 1 cent, and yet in a matter of days can produce millions."

At the other extreme are a small number of donors who are themselves developing countries and for whom aid is politically symbolic. Such countries do not have an entrenched aid bureaucracy, which can both facilitate and hamper assistance. One such donor noted that his country's assistance program had largely taken the form of checks to Palestinian ministries, with little or no follow-up. Asked about accountability, he replied: "To be very frank with you, we don't really care."

such issues as staffing levels, location (East Jerusalem versus Tel Aviv), and line authority. In the case of UNRWA, PIP was successful in attracting some $180 million for 147 projects in the territories in 1993–97, but at a cost: in some cases it may have diverted some funds from UNRWA's overstretched regular budget, and continuing operating costs were poorly factored into many of the initial projects.[105]

Gradually, donors began to develop new and larger aid programs. These projects, however, were generally subject to complex and time-consuming bureaucratic processes, entailing lengthy planning, proposal, assessment, and procurement procedures, and particular evaluations required by donor priorities in such areas as the environment, gender, and private-sector development. In part, such processes reflected a decade of criticism of Western development agencies for wasteful or inappropriate aid programs—and, consequently, a desire by donors to spend funds carefully in support of long-term development. However, these same attitudes and processes often proved poorly suited to the political realities of peacebuilding in Palestine, which required the rapid delivery of assistance in such a way as to strengthen the ongoing diplomatic process. Furthermore, many initial donor agency assumptions were—in the words of one senior World Bank official—"very facile," underestimating the political and economic difficulties that lay ahead.[106]

Through 1994–95 these difficulties often expressed themselves in a cultural clash between the realpolitik of foreign ministry officials and the commitment of their aid counterparts to careful and sustainable development. In the case of the U.S. assistance program, State Department officials often complained about the slowness and inappropriateness of USAID programs in the territories, while many USAID officials complained that they were being diverted from real, sustainable development: "How do you plan, develop, and do something of quality if you are under [constant political] pressure?" (box 5.5).[107]

The delivery of international assistance was also complicated by legal restrictions. Some of these restrictions may have speeded disbursement—particularly when funds had to be expended before the end of the financial year. For example, some credited Japan's high rate of aid implementation, in part, to the need for it to fully spend its funds by March 31 or lose them to the Ministry of Finance.[108] For the most part, however, legal restrictions slowed or complicated matters. Japan found itself bound by domestic legislation that limited its assistance to international organizations and recognized states (thus excluding the Palestinian Authority). As a result, its assistance was largely delivered through multilateral agencies (notably UNDP, UNRWA, and the World Bank–administered TATF and Holst Fund). The World Bank too faced administrative complications because the PA was not a member state, and the Oslo Agreement held the PLO responsible for Palestinian external relations. As a result, the World Bank signed its agreement with PECDAR, a PA institution established under a mandate from the PLO Executive Committee.

One area where this problem of donor regulations was particularly evident was that of funding for the Palestinian police. While the establishment of a strong local police force was a critical element in establishing a stable PA, legal restrictions prevented most aid agencies from providing direct assistance. Moreover, while the Gaza-Jericho Agreement sanctioned the establishment of a single police force with four operational divisions (civil, public security, emergency, and intelligence), in practice an array of semiautonomous security bodies soon sprang

Box 5.5. Redesigning USAID

In the case of the U.S. Agency for International Development, State Department and White House pressure led to a review and substantial revamping of the program in late 1994. As a result, previous long-term institution-building projects in the health and housing sectors were cut back significantly, as was some support for private voluntary organizations; instead, more rapid job-creation projects were supported in the areas of municipal public works, micro-enterprise, and a Gaza waste- and storm-water project. As an interim measure, increased use was also made of UN agencies, particularly UNRWA with its well-developed capabilities in the West Bank and Gaza. In total, around 40 percent of all non-Holst funds were reprogrammed.

In the process, many of the usual themes of USAID assistance were downgraded to allow for a clearer focus on the most politically effective projects, and the project process sped up. Indicative of this sharper focus on political requirements were the comments of one U.S. official, noting the de-emphasis of gender equality as an aid priority in the West Bank and Gaza Strip: "It isn't that gender is unimportant, but for the moment it is the unemployed young men that we have to worry about." The new USAID field director for the West Bank and Gaza was chosen in part because of his support for timely implementation and his sensitivity to the political needs of the aid process. All of this was a painful bureaucratic process. In the words of one senior U.S. official, there was "blood on the floor" at USAID when the shift occurred: "A lot of people did not see the train coming and got smacked." Given domestic sensitivities, the USAID program also had to be designed mindful of congressional and other views.

By 1997-98, USAID's priorities had been consolidated: economic opportunities, the water sector, and democracy and good governance. The political aspects of many of these—notably support for industrial estates and the water sector—are clear. However, this can also cause complications: progress on industrial zones has been slowed by delays in the necessary Palestinian-Israeli agreements, while water projects touch on a sensitive final-status issue and require approval from a host of actors before new wells can be tapped.

up, notably Force 17 (the old Fateh-PLO executive security unit) and Palestinian Preventive Security (a large internal security apparatus, consisting largely of ex-intifada street activists). Most donors initially resisted dealing with these organizations (especially those that lay outside the Oslo framework), although this grew more difficult as Preventive Security (and its leaders) became increasingly important on the ground. As discussed in chapter 6, a variety of mechanisms were needed to overcome these constraints.

Of the various institutional factors that facilitated or constrained donor responsiveness, one key element has often been the *local presence* of donor agencies on the ground. Having sufficient field staff is part of this local presence: smaller donors have often found themselves unable to pursue project opportunities or fully participate in consultative and donor coordination mechanisms because of personnel shortages. Perhaps even more serious, overworked field staff are less likely to take risks, show substantial initiative, or assume additional responsibilities—all of these being essential characteristics of peacebuilding—when the developmental context is fluid and uncertain, and when local (in this case, Palestinian) counterpart agencies may not be in a position to fully assume their project responsibilities. However, of equal (and perhaps greater) importance than the number of aid personnel is the quality and style of those assigned to the field. In difficult aid programs such as those in the West Bank and Gaza, idiosyncratic factors can have a substantial impact on the success and dynamism of development programs. Thus, in the case of the World Bank and UNSCO, the effectiveness of both institutions rested to a substantial degree on the skills and personalities of Odin Knudsen, Joe Saba, and Terje Larsen. Management policy—whether at headquarters or in the field—has also been important, in that it must promote the appropriate work environment and professional supports for personnel working under heavy task loads and difficult political and economic conditions.

Closely related to this is the degree of decision-making authority and autonomy delegated to field personnel. Because of the complex and dynamic nature of local conditions, peacebuilding assistance cannot easily be directed from headquarters; instead, local officials need to have the authority to act. The devolution of World Bank authority to the resident representative has already been discussed; other agencies (for example, UNDP and USAID) permitted their field directors to utilize accelerated procurement procedures. As a World Bank official later noted: "As donors it took us time to adapt our procedures to such a fluid environment. Had we created an effective local coordination forum at the beginning, rather than waiting until 1995, we could have adjusted much faster. We should have decentralized our management into the field sooner than we did."[109]

Finally, the status and the physical location of aid offices have also been important. Some countries already had consulates in East Jerusalem and have operated their aid programs from these.[110] Others established representative offices to the Palestinian Authority, whether in Jericho, Gaza, or Ramallah. Symbolically and practically, this served to facilitate donor-Palestinian interaction, although the geographic fragmentation of the PA has required substantial shuttling between the West Bank and Gaza in any case.

Sectors and Channels of Assistance

Variations in aid disbursement across donors have reflected not only varying degrees of institutional responsiveness and local presence but also the sectors chosen by different donors.

On the one hand, support disbursed through the Holst Fund could be moved extremely quickly, with the transfer from donor to the World Bank to the Palestinian Authority taking as little as a few weeks. Support for multilateral programs through the bank, the UNDP, and other agencies was also relatively quick and painless for donors. In the early years in particular, these channels were often selected by small- and medium-sized donors that otherwise lacked an established bilateral program. In those sectors involving high proportions of technical assistance, it was often easier to expend donor funds.[111] Support for humanitarian aid (usually handled by the more expeditious humanitarian assistance divisions of aid agencies) or short-term emergency employment during periods of closure was deliberately structured for rapid disbursement. NGOs, by their very nature, were eager to accept donor money quickly, although the process of supporting many small NGO projects tended to be rather demanding of donor staff resources relative to the amounts disbursed.

On the other hand, assistance for some areas was much slower by virtue of the inherent scale, technical complexity, and political complications of projects in that sector. Thus, while an overall average of 60 percent of all committed funds had been disbursed by donors as of September 1997, there was substantial variation across sectors: 82 percent of committed funds for democratic development were disbursed, but only 52 percent of those for the water-sanitation sector, 43 percent of those in the energy sector, and 23 percent of those in the transportation sector had been moved. Similar variation could be found across the different types of assistance: 92 percent of transitional and budget support commitments, 73 percent of funds for NGOs, and 69 percent of technical assistance commitments had been disbursed by September 1997, but only 49 percent of funds for public investment had been disbursed by the same date.[112]

The relationship between the tied or untied nature of aid and the speed with which projects proceed is less clear. On the one hand, with tied aid procurement cannot occur until a suitable supplier is found in the donor country. Local procurement, on the other hand, may be more likely to face delays owing to supply bottlenecks, limited contractor capacity, and inadequate local standards. Although commodity donations (effectively another form of tied aid) seemed to have a generally higher rate of disbursement, this tended to mask another sort of problem: the commodities donated could often be inappropriate to Palestinian needs. Palestinian police, for example, received multiple donations of communications equipment—much of it operating on incompatible frequencies or on frequencies not cleared for use by the PA.

Finally, loans, risk insurance, and export and investment guarantees usually proved the most difficult components of aid programs to deliver: it soon became clear that, amid the political uncertainty and periodic economic closure, few projects in the territories were sound enough to meet the banking standards that ordinarily determined lending practice. The United States allocated $125 million of its support to the Overseas Private Investment Corporation, but by December 1995 only one project—a Gaza-based concrete factory—had been provided with investment guarantees. The subsequent failure of that investment hardly encouraged greater OPIC risk taking.[113] Similarly, the European Union had allocated approximately half of its assistance through the European Investment Bank ($300 million); by September 1998 only a third of this had been committed—and none disbursed.

In the United States, the failure of loan and credit funding to materialize led to growing criticism of OPIC by State Department and USAID officials, as well as NGOs.[114] OPIC officials responded that they had already "bent over backwards" for the West Bank and Gaza and that "we can't support projects for political reasons only—the project has to be viable."[115] In Europe, the EU presidency committed itself to accelerate the disbursement of EIB funds.[116] The EIB, however, complained that the World Bank could proceed with lending only if presented with "well-prepared projects with a demonstrable technical, economic and financial viability, and promoters capable of taking on and reimbursing foreign currency loans."[117] Overall, only 22.3 percent of loans had been disbursed in the territories by September 1998. The World Bank, moreover, accounted for almost all of these disbursements: if the bank's operations are excluded from consideration, the proportion of donor loans disbursed during this same period drops to 1 percent.[118]

Domestic Politics

In many donor countries, internal politics also helped to shape—or constrain—assistance to the Palestinians. In the CPRS survey, Palestinian NGOs and officials perceived this as a significant problem (table 5.6).

In Denmark, for example, reports that a Palestinian student had helped organize Hamas suicide bombings in the spring of 1996 led opposition members of the Danish parliament to call upon the government to "immediately stop the support for Palestinian terrorists" by ending aid to the UNRWA vocational training college where he had studied.[119]

Table 5.6. Perceptions of the Impact of Donor Politics on Aid

	Positive	Neutral	Negative
	Perceived Impact of Donor Politics on Aid: All Donors		
By Donor Officials	34%	34%	19%
By Local NGOs	12%	21%	60%
By PA Officials	6%	19%	75%
	Perceived Impact of Donor Politics on Aid: U.S. Assistance		
By Donor Officials	18%	9%	43%
By Local NGOs	5%	8%	84%
By PA Officials	1%	6%	92%
	Perceived Impact of Donor Politics on Aid: EU Assistance		
By Donor Officials	30%	42%	3%
By Local NGOs	38%	42%	18%
By PA Officials	33%	43%	25%

Source: CPRS, *Prevailing Perceptions on Aid Management,* 16. The question is worded so that it might refer to both domestic politics and foreign policy.

However, nowhere was the impact of donor politics more evident than in the United States, where the issue was affected by strong congressional support for Israel, suspicion of the Palestinian Authority, and a generally less-than-friendly attitude to both foreign aid and multilateralism. Thus, the requirement for congressional aid authorization rendered the USAID budget a battleground for advancing these and other political agendas.[120]

One result of this was the PLO Commitments Compliance Act of 1993 and the Middle East Peace Facilitation Acts (MEPFA) of 1994 and 1995, all of which created legislative requirements for periodic certification by the State Department of the Palestinian compliance with the Oslo Agreement and other conditions.[121] U.S. legislation also prohibited direct U.S. assistance to the Palestinian Authority and mandated USAID support for the establishment of cross-border industrial parks (despite a preexisting legislative ban on USAID projects that might result in competition with U.S. manufacturers).

In addition, some members of Congress—encouraged by right-wing pro-Israeli lobby groups—sought to tighten restrictions still further.[122] In the spring of 1994, the House International Relations Committee requested that the General Accounting Office (GAO) investigate PLO finances, in response to press reports that the PLO had retained some \$8–10 billion in assets.[123] In June 1995 the GAO issued an inconclusive—and, at times, remarkably obtuse—report on the matter.[124] In June 1995 Senator Alfonse D'Amato and Representative Michael Forbes also sought to place greater restrictions and conditions on aid to the Palestinians, following the release of documents that purported to show PA efforts to strengthen its presence in Jerusalem. The House International Relations Committee and Senate Foreign Relations Committee again asked the GAO to investigate, this time to see whether U.S. assistance to the PA could be diverted to such purposes. The GAO report, issued in January 1996, generally praised the accountability mechanisms that had been put in place for the Holst Fund and USAID.[125] However, the chairman of the House International Relations Committee, Representative Benjamin Gilman, cited the earlier report on PLO finances to justify blocking a \$10 million U.S. contribution to the PA recurrent costs.[126] In so doing, Gilman effectively terminated all U.S. support for the Holst Fund.

One member of Congress described aid to the West Bank and Gaza as "throwing bad money after good"; another noted that "the strong supporters of Israel in Congress are committed to the principle that Palestinian aid is contingent on [the Palestinians'] good word and their good deeds and we think they're very short on both right now."[127] In May 1997 Gilman and the chair of the Senate Foreign Relations Committee, Jesse Helms, threatened to block all assistance to protest PA measures prohibiting Palestinians from selling land to Israeli settlers. Questions were also raised in response to reports of Palestinian corruption and mismanagement, resulting in yet another GAO investigation. In August of that year, MEPFA was allowed to expire without renewal. Proposed amendments to the Foreign Operations Appropriations Bill for fiscal year 1998 called for restrictions on U.S. meetings with PA officials in Jerusalem, created additional conditions and limitations on assistance to the PA, and proposed a three-month suspension of assistance.[128] In 1998 congressional pressure played a significant role in the decision by USAID to terminate support for the Palestinian Broadcasting Corporation, following reports by right-wing Israeli groups (and official Israeli complaints) of "inciteful" PBC broadcasts. Later that same year, the Clinton administration extracted congressional support for increased aid to the Palestinians (as well as Israel and Jordan) only after what some congressional aides termed a "battle royal," in which the White House threatened to otherwise divert budget funds from intelligence and defense initiatives dear to the Republican majority.[129]

For the State Department and USAID, battles with Congress over aid to the Palestinians were thus a constant political headache, and one aggravated by the change of Israeli government in May 1996. Under Labor, the Israeli government had "expressed concern over the possibility of any holdup in financial assistance," while the Israeli embassy in Washington (and some Jewish American organizations) had lobbied Congress in support of U.S. assistance to the Palestinians.[130] This political support vanished, however, after Netanyahu assumed power. Somewhat disingenuously, congressional critics of the aid effort had expressed the hope that "the new Israeli government will understand [our] position." In practice, the Israeli government often highlighted cases of alleged Palestinian maladministration and quietly encouraged congressional resistance.[131] The situation shifted again following Labor's return to power. Both Israel and the American Israel Public Affairs Committee played major roles in lobbying for U.S. aid to the Palestinians.

Domestic donor politics could also have an impact on donor programs in less direct—indeed, sometimes rather arcane—ways, often unrelated to the Middle East. In the late 1995 and early 1996, for example, the congressional legislation necessary for U.S. assistance to the West Bank and Gaza was delayed not only by opposition to aid to the Palestinians by some members of Congress but also by unrelated legislative battles over issues ranging from abortion to State Department reorganization. In the case of USAID, a congressional atmosphere often hostile to foreign aid led to an institutional climate of caution that undoubtedly affected USAID's Palestinian programming. In the case of OPIC, its Palestinian program was formulated when the organization was under attack by its critics and fighting for its budgetary life. Assailed by some U.S. NGOs and potential investors for its restrictive loan conditions in Palestine, OPIC faced broader (and contrary) general criticism for unfairly subsidizing business and competing with private-sector risk insurance. In this context, OPIC chose not to adopt a bold Palestinian program.

Donor agencies in other countries were also faced with declining budgets, the possibility of legislative criticism, and the potential challenge of investigation by the press or government auditor's office. As was the case with USAID and OPIC, agencies often responded by adopting a cautious approach to the challenges of peacebuilding.

As the preceding examination has shown, the timely and effective delivery of assistance to the West Bank and Gaza has been faced with a number of substantial obstacles. Some of these have been structural in nature, arising from the inherent difficulties of spending large amounts of money in a small economy, as well as from the almost Kafkaesque constraints created by the various, complex Palestinian-Israeli interim agreements. More important still, however, have been constraints associated with the actions (or inactions) of the key players in the process. Israeli impediments—variously arising from security concerns, diplomatic maneuvering, and bureaucratic procedures—have been the most important of these, with Israel's policy of closure having particularly negative effects on the Palestinian economy. The Palestinian Authority has borne its share of responsibility for shortcomings too: initially weak institutions have grown much stronger and more efficient, but problems of corruption and financial irregularity have undercut many of these gains. It is also clear that PA economic policy has often been driven by political concerns, most notably a desire to consolidate the domestic position of the regime and create the foundations for future statehood, while strengthening the Palestinian bargaining position vis-à-vis Israel. Finally, donors themselves were initially slow in delivering assistance in the early, critical period in 1994, in large part because many established procedures and institutions were ill suited to the time-sensitive imperatives of peacebuilding. Although problems remain, they have diminished over time with the establishment of a continuing pipeline of assistance from the donor community.

The 1998 slowdown in donor funds generated new concerns. A number of different explanations were offered for this slowdown, many of them variations of earlier themes: donors were switching aid to the slower infrastructure sector; donors were concerned about PA accountability and transparency; Palestinian or Israeli bottlenecks were slowing aid implementation. All of these may have explained part of the problem, although another plausible explanation was the lack of a pressing political "emergency" in the territories in 1998, and hence reduced pressure on donors to move money quickly. Finally, idiosyncratic factors also made themselves felt: almost three-quarters of the aid slowdown was attributable to three donors, each of which faced particular problems. In the case of the European Union, political turmoil within the European Commission slowed responsiveness. In Japan, austerity measures cut the aid budget. And in the United States, congressional resistance to foreign aid continued. Still, the slowdown was a worrying indicator of possible future donor fatigue. The onset in 1999 of costly international peacebuilding missions in Kosovo and East Timor heightened concerns still further.

Despite all of these problems, by the end of the first pledging period, 1994–98, the overall record of delivering assistance was quite good. The timely disbursement of funds on the ground, however, did not guarantee that those resources were being spent in ways that promoted peace and economic reconstruction. Accordingly, the final stage in assessing the role of foreign aid in the West Bank and Gaza is to examine how aid was allocated, how these sectors were affected, and how such priorities emerged.

6

Allocating Assistance

Using Aid to Promote Peace and Reconstruction

B
Y THE END OF THE 1994–98 pledging period, a total of $3.8 billion (of $4.2 billion pledged) had been committed by donors for specific projects in the West Bank and Gaza, and $2.6 billion of this disbursed for specific projects. But to what extent have these resources helped to build peace—or, if not peace, at least the basis for a viable Palestinian economy?

One Palestinian study of the aid process suggested that the "priorities of the foreign aid effort . . . are not in line with the development aspirations and needs of the Palestinian population in the West Bank and Gaza Strip. This development initiative has not as yet contributed to filling the socioeconomic gaps left by years of military occupation; it has not been able to create the impetus required to generate sustainable forms of economic development."[1] In its own assessment, the PA argued that "while it has been successful, and within a very short period of time, in starting the task of institution-building, rehabilitating infrastructure, and setting up high quality fiscal administration . . . its efforts were constrained by severe economic hardships."[2] In a five-year review of donor programs, the World Bank and UNSCO concluded that "donor efforts to date have been successful. They have made a major impact on the ground, delivering most new and rehabilitated infrastructure . . . [although] the objective needs of the Palestinian economy for external concessional support remain high."[3]

Assessing the relevance of assistance is inherently more ambiguous and subjective than either assessing the magnitude of aid pledges or examining the speed with which they have been implemented. Significant differences exist within the Palestinian Authority, between donors, and among analysts, as to what

161

aid priorities should be. In many cases these differences reflect the bureaucratic position of the observer, the technical expertise of the specialist, and the ideological orientation of the analyst. Thus, NGOs frequently bemoan the decline of support given to the NGO sector and the importance of civil society,[4] and some scholars have argued that international aid has served to consolidate an authoritarian PA at the expense of civil society.[5] The private sector and international financial institutions, not surprisingly, emphasize the need to "rely on the private sector as much as possible."[6] UN agencies underscore their "comparative advantage . . . as a principal development partner."[7] The Palestinian Left has complained of the nefarious role of the private sector and the World Bank in "following the dictates of the new imperialist policy in the Arab homeland."[8] Similarly, water specialists tend to emphasize the importance of water, municipalities stress the need for local public works, and so forth.

For its part, the Palestinian Authority often expresses official concern that "donor assistance has been diverted from [public] investment."[9] In a survey of donor officials, "democracy," "human rights," and "gender" were all identified as sectors that had been relatively overfunded by donors, while "economic development," "physical infrastructure," and "agriculture" were seen to have been underfunded.[10]

On the street, Palestinian public assessment of the donor effort has been mixed. In one 1997 survey, 72 percent held that services and infrastructure had improved under the PA, and 76 percent of these felt that foreign aid had contributed to this improvement. Among those who did not perceive any improvement, 26 percent blamed donors—and 47 percent blamed the Palestinian Authority. Few, however, believed that aid primarily benefited either the general population (17 percent) or the neediest sectors within it (11 percent). On the contrary, most believed that assistance either benefited those who were not in need (27 percent) or was used randomly (34 percent).[11] In a 1999 survey, 37.3 percent of Palestinians described the donors' impact on local conditions as "positive" and 9 percent as "very positive." By contrast, 11.2 percent described the impact of donor programs as "poor" and 4.3 percent as "very poor."[12] The same survey asked respondents to identify the most and least important areas for donor assistance. The results showed a strong preference for investments in education, health, and water. By contrast, there was little public priority assigned to women, housing, or the security sector (figure 6.1).[13]

This chapter explores the allocation and impact of assistance by first sketching the series of broad developmental strategies for the West Bank and Gaza drawn up by donors and the Palestinian Authority. This discussion is followed by an analysis of the actual sectoral allocation of international aid, with particular attention focused on several key sectors and categories of support. Although these sectors and categories are far from representing the sum total of

Figure 6.1. Palestinian Public Attitudes on Priorities for Donor Assistance (1999)

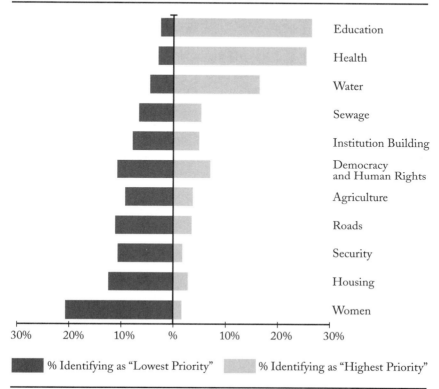

Source: CPRS, *Public Opinion Poll no. 39* (28–30 January 1999), archived at www.cprs-palestine.org/polls/99/poll39b.html.

the assistance program, they do illustrate a number of important points about the allocation of donor assistance. Thereafter, the chapter examines the agenda-setting process whereby aid priorities were identified and sectoral allocations were made—an element at the heart of any process of development assistance, but of particular relevance in the politically charged context of international peace-building efforts.

ECONOMIC STRATEGIES FOR PALESTINE

Both the PLO and the World Bank had already examined possible aid priorities in the Palestinian territories before the Oslo Agreement. Subsequently, at the time of the 1993 Washington donors conference, the World Bank was entrusted with producing a basic blueprint for Palestinian social and economic needs.

The result was the Emergency Assistance Program (EAP), which envisaged a need for $1.2 billion in donor support over three years (1994–96), in the form of public investments ($600 million), private-sector support ($300 million), start-up expenditures ($225 million), and technical assistance ($75 million). The budgetary gap between PA tax revenues and expenditures was forecast at only $158 million in 1994 and $40 million in 1995, with the PA to be self-sustaining of recurrent costs by 1996. A 1996 Core Investment Program was presented to donors at the October 1995 meeting of the Consultative Group (CG). This program was put together with UNSCO and World Bank officials largely taking the lead.

In practice, some sectoral needs proved greater than first estimated, while the PA's need for budgetary support substantially exceeded the World Bank's projections. Moreover, the imposition of extended closure in the spring of 1996 also created a need for rapid-disbursement emergency job creation, a need that had also not been anticipated by economic planners. In addition to unanticipated recurrent costs and the need for emergency employment generation, there is little evidence that donors actually utilized the EAP as a yardstick for directing their aid. In November 1996 the World Bank reported that some areas had received disbursements substantially greater than the EAP targets (education, 343 percent; health, 161 percent), while in other cases only a portion of the amounts suggested in the EAP had been delivered (power, 10 percent; agriculture, 6 percent; support to private-sector industry, 0 percent).[14]

The first medium-term economic strategy put forward by the Palestinian Authority was the $550 million Core Investment Program, presented at the October 1995 CG meeting and at the January 1996 ministerial donors conference. Although nominally presented to donors by MOPIC, the program was really a project largely assembled by the World Bank and UNSCO, with input from key donors. It included a dozen and a half "top priority" projects that lent themselves to "speedy implementation and rapid improvements in the standard of living," complemented Palestinian-Israeli cooperation (for example, in the jointly managed water sector and cross-border industrial estates), and capitalized on the political "momentum" represented by the September 1995 Interim Agreement.[15] The priority list was also shaped to fit donor predilections, with the United States having lobbied hard to make sure that its own favored projects were included.

PA institutions, led by MOPIC, played a larger role in the development of the Palestinian Public Investment Program (PPIP) for 1997, proposed to donors at the November 1996 CG meeting. This listed (but did not fully describe) some 309 projects totaling $1.3 billion.

The PPIP in turn was supplanted by the more ambitious and integrated Palestinian Development Plan. The PDP is intended to be a rolling multiyear planning exercise. The 1998–2000 version, endorsed by the PA in July 1997 and presented to donors at a CG meeting in December 1997, envisaged total investments of $3.4 billion over this period. Of this, $0.7 billion was already committed by donors, $0.2 billion to be provided by the PA, and $2.5 billion in additional support requested. The 1999–2003 version, presented to donors in February 1999, called for $4.6 billion in investment (table 6.1).[16] Reflecting concern that inadequate attention had been directed toward establishing the basis for future economic growth, the program placed heavy emphasis on the development of economic infrastructure.

Yet again, some sectors were more successful than others in attracting investment. In its presentation of the PDP to donors, the PA complained that despite its efforts at economic planning, donor investments had often seemed to ignore Palestinian priorities (table 6.2), with less funds going to infrastructure and the productive sectors of the Palestinian economy than the PA would have wished.[17]

SECTORAL DISTRIBUTION

Development strategies, of course, signal desires and intentions on the part of the framers. As can be seen from the previous discussion, actual disbursements may well differ substantially.

Although the tracking of aid flows is hampered by methodological and data limitations,[18] nonetheless some general patterns are evident. Sectoral analysis of aid disbursements over the period 1994–97 (figure 6.2) shows a peaking and then decline of support for social services (primarily health and education), a decline followed by a rise in support for state building (primarily institution building and police), and an increase in support for infrastructure (notably in water-sanitation, transportation, and energy).[19] These shifts are to be expected, given the initial start-up costs of the Palestinian Authority and its gradual institutionalization, the delays involved in larger infrastructure projects, and the initial ease of channeling funds through the functional social services ministries. Direct support for the productive sectors of the economy (including agriculture, industrial development, and private-sector support) has remained surprisingly low, although growing donor realization of the importance of private-sector activity contributed to somewhat renewed attention to this area in 1997–98.

Analysis of selected categories of assistance (figure 6.3)[20] shows the expected decline in transitional and budget support reversed by the impact of closure in 1996, which also created an unanticipated need for emergency job-creation programs. Public investments grew, although at less than the levels the PA had

Table 6.1. Palestinian Development Plan (1999–2003)

Sector	Total Sector Investment ($ millions)
Infrastructure	**2,208**
Transportation (including port and airport)	704
Environment	112
Water and Wastewater	972
Post and Telecommunications	66
Energy	110
Solid Waste	79
Housing	55
General Infrastructure	110
Institutional Capacity	**405**
Democratic Development	49
Legal and Regulatory Framework	69
Institutional Development	203
Police	85
Human Resources/Social Development	**1,126**
Education	429
Health	293
Humanitarian Assistance	23
Ex-Detainees and Returnees	23
Women	34
Human Rights and Civil Society	11
Youth	28
Culture	39
Refugee Camps	248
Productive Sectors	**767**
Agriculture	207
Industrial Development	191
Tourism	232
Other Support Projects	138
Total	**4,556**

Source: Palestinian Authority, *Palestinian Development Plan 1999–2003* (January 1999).

Table 6.2. Palestinian Investment Plans and Actual Donor Disbursements (1994–98)

	Infrastructure	Social Sectors	Productive Sectors	Institution Building
Core Investment Program (1996)	56.0%	27.3%	6.8%	7.2%
Palestinian Public Investment Program (1997)	42.0%	34.0%	16.0%	8.0%
Palestinian Development Plan (1998)	51.0%	24.2%	16.6%	6.7%
Palestinian Development Plan (1999)	47.0%	23.4%	19.6%	8.6%
Palestinian Development Plan (2000)	46.3%	25.7%	15.4%	11.8%
Average for Palestinian Investment Programs, 1996–2000	48.5%	26.9%	14.9%	8.5%
Actual Donor Disbursements, 1994–September 1998	27.5%	41.6%	8.7%	22.4%

Source: Palestinian Authority, *Palestinian Development Plan 1999–2000* (January 1999), 48.

Figure 6.2. Sectoral Disbursements of Assistance in the West Bank and Gaza

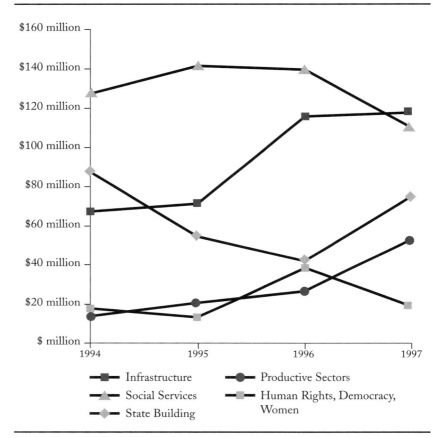

Sources: Disbursement data for 1994–96 are drawn from MOPIC, *1997 Third Quarter Monitoring Report of Donor Assistance* (28 November 1997); disbursement data for 1997 are drawn from MOPIC, *1998 First Quarter Monitoring Report of Donor Assistance* (31 March 1998).

Note: "Infrastructure" includes energy, housing, waste, telecommunications, transportation, and water; "social services" includes education, health, rehabilitation of detainees/returnees, and humanitarian assistance; "productive sectors" includes agriculture, industrial development, tourism, and private-sector development; "state building" includes police, legal affairs, and institution building. MOPIC's "undefined" and "multiple sectors" are not included.

Figure 6.3. Categories of Disbursement in the West Bank and Gaza

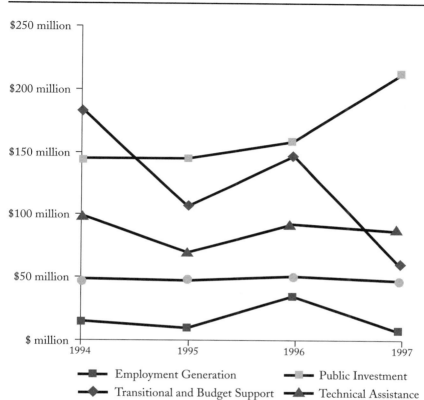

Sources: Disbursement data for 1994–96 are drawn from MOPIC, *1997 Third Quarterly Monitoring Report of Donor Assistance* (28 November 1997); disbursement data for 1997 are drawn from MOPIC, *1998 First Quarterly Monitoring Report of Donor Assistance* (31 March 1998).

Note: Equipment, in-kind, and some other categories are not included, while data on NGO disbursements overlap with the other categories (as NGOs may, for example, offer technical assistance or employment generation).

hoped for. Technical assistance fluctuated at quite high levels, and assistance channeled through NGOs remained fairly constant. Geographically, analysis of SWG sectors undertaken by UNSCO in 1996 suggested that 50 percent of donor commitments (excluding public finance and police) were directed to the West Bank and Gaza, 29 percent to Gaza alone, 18 percent to the West Bank alone, and 3 percent "unspecified."[21] Given that almost 60 percent of Palestinians reside in the West Bank (excluding East Jerusalem), this would appear to signal a disproportionate share of resources going to Gaza. However, this concentration is largely explained by the initial establishment of PA authority in Gaza, as well as the higher degree of social need there. It may also explain why surveys show stronger support for the PA, a stronger feeling that services have improved, and a more positive evaluation of donor performance among Gazans.

Behind the Figures: Sectoral Profiles

Together, social services and infrastructure sectors accounted for around two-thirds of all donor disbursements during the first five years of the aid effort. The need for investments in both areas was clear enough.

In the case of social services, a very rapid rate of population increase created an accelerating need for new clinics, schools, and other facilities. It has been estimated that between 1996 and 2005 the West Bank and Gaza will require more than 11,000 new teachers and over 9,000 new classrooms simply to maintain the current standard of education.[22] Not surprisingly, therefore, the bulk of donor resources in this area went to building, repairing, and equipping schools at all levels: between 1994 and 1998, PECDAR alone renovated more than 2,000 classrooms. With regard to health, the need to keep pace with population growth was compounded by the fragmentation of service delivery, with the Ministry of Health operating alongside a well-established private sector and an array of health-related NGOs. Between 1994 and 1998 donor support helped to increase the number of primary health care centers in the territories by 78 percent (from 207 to 369), while the number of hospital beds increased 25 percent (from 1,606 to 2,103) over the same period.[23] In a service delivery survey financed by the World Bank, 49 percent of respondents classified the health care facilities available to them as "good" or "very good," while 73 percent gave a positive rating to educational facilities.[24]

Although both social services and infrastructure sectors faced substantial challenges in taking control and managing their respective areas of responsibility, the Ministry of Education and the Ministry of Health were able to build on the nucleus of the previous Israeli civil administration. Their relatively higher degree of institutionalization, in turn, made it easier to attract donor investments: as one World Bank study noted, the "the PA's basic and secondary educational system is relatively efficient" and "appears to have a deserved reputation in Palestinian civil society and among donors for transparency."[25] The social services sector also benefited from the effective health and education programs offered by UNRWA, which represented another possible conduit for donor funding.

In the case of infrastructure investment, Palestinian need was rooted in years of neglect in this sector during the occupation. As noted in chapter 2, roads, telecommunications, electrical distribution, and other infrastructure were all weak by regional standards. Although donors found some of these areas inviting—not least because of the possible economic benefits of using technical assistance and contractors from the donor country—they also tended to be expensive, long-term projects that were further complicated by the patchwork quilt of regulatory and territorial authority assigned to the PA under the various interim agreements, as well as the ups and downs of the broader peace process. As a result, the first two major projects—the Gaza Industrial Estate and the Gaza airport—delayed their openings until the end of 1998. Smaller initiatives (notably road repairs, water, and sewage) proceeded in a more timely fashion, with PECDAR alone having completed work on fifty-nine public buildings, 784 kilometers of road, and sixty-nine water projects by the end of 1998.[26] The impact of these sorts of initiatives was particularly noticeable in Gaza, where major improvements in the road network (including traffic lights!) were evident.

Although more could be said about these broad sectors—indeed, one could easily fill several volumes with sectoral and subsectoral profiles—the best way to gain greater insight into the strengths and weaknesses of the international aid effort is to focus attention on six areas of assistance that proved unusual, controversial, or particularly difficult or important.

The first and second of these areas are important to Palestinian institution (and state) building: aid to the *security forces* and donor *budget support*. Both were essential to the establishment of the Palestinian Authority. However, assistance in these sectors has been heavily criticized for building a bloated, centralized, and authoritarian administration rather than promoting sustainable development.

The next two sections focus on donor investment in infrastructure and the productive sectors of the economy. *Emergency employment-generation programs* were first developed to deal with high unemployment rates and later expanded to meet other social and economic challenges. Critics have argued that these programs were little more than economically ineffectual make-work activities. *Agriculture*, by contrast, has received remarkably little donor support, despite the significant number of Palestinians who continue to derive their livelihood from it. The reasons for this are explored later.

The last two sections concern different types, or channels, of assistance: the need for—and failings of—*technical assistance programs* and Palestinian *nongovernmental organizations*.

Security Assistance

Assistance to the *security forces* is often of critical importance in war-to-peace transitions. The Palestinian case, however, did not involve the usual problem of demobilizing and reintegrating combatants, but rather ensuring security in the face of the challenge posed by armed rejectionist groups. Enhancing security was (as shown in chapter 2) central to all the Palestinian-Israeli agreements. Security assistance was (as discussed in chapter 4) important in the evolution of local aid coordination mechanisms. It was also (as noted in chapter 5) often legally problematic for donor countries.[27]

From the outset of the Oslo process, there appeared to be a degree of inconsistency in the international community's response to the challenge of security assistance. On the one hand, all donors recognized its importance, and Norway took an early lead in promoting discussion of how Palestinian needs might be met. On the other hand, concrete support often lagged. At the first meeting of the Coordinating Committee for International Assistance to a Palestinian Police Force in March 1994, for example, then Norwegian special ambassador Terje Larsen complained that "potential donors have not followed up" on earlier pledges of support. As a result, "the supply of assistance from the international community does not meet the urgent needs of the Palestinians."[28] Thereafter, the Committee on the Palestinian Police (COPP) set about identifying immediate (six-week, or "priority I"), short-term (four-month, or "priority II"), and longer-term requirements for the police.

The establishment and activities of COPP in and of themselves somewhat lessened the political constraints on assistance by spreading the risk more broadly and creating an intermediary mechanism to assess needs and disbursements.[29] A number of important offers of equipment followed: vehicles from Greece, Spain, and the United States; armored cars from Russia; uniforms from a number of countries. An even greater impetus, however, was provided by the signing of the Gaza-Jericho Agreement on May 4 and the first entry of Palestinian forces to these areas a week later.

As of mid-May, with Palestinian police now beginning to arrive in the territories in growing numbers, the status of donor support was a mixed one. More than 90 percent of some key equipment types had yet to be offered by the international community, and 45 percent of short-term costs remained unsupported (table 6.3).[30] Moreover, although the chair of COPP noted "a positive development regarding commitments to donate equipment," it also stressed that "the main problem is that very little has so far arrived in Gaza and Jericho."[31] Reports from the field suggested that immediately on deployment, the police were short of food, fuel, clothing, and shelter. Local families, municipalities, and NGOs scrambled to secure some of the required basic necessities. The newly deployed

Table 6.3. Donations to and Needs of the Palestinian Police

Item	Priority I: Immediate Requirement (6 weeks)	Priority II: Short-Term Requirement (4 months)	Outstanding Requirement (priorities I + II)	Unmet Requirement (% of needs)
Trucks and Jeeps	225	25	50	20
Vans and Buses	30	25	50	91
Cars and Motorcycles	95	120	165	77
Uniforms	9,000	9,000	8,000	44
Riot Equipment	1,000	1,000	1,800	90
Office Equipment (copiers, typewriters)	110	115	225	100
Construction (buildings)	$2.0 million	$15.0 million	$17.0 million	100
Operational Expenses, Fuel, Salaries, Transfer Costs	$10.8 million	$21.3 million	$14.4 million	45

Source: Committee on the Palestinian Police, *Palestinian Police Forces: Equipment* (COPP Donor Matrix, 16 May 1994). Some categories have been aggregated.

police were also without pay for weeks or even months. Noted one policeman, "I thought our life in the Palestinian police force would be an honorable one. How can they expect a soldier to remain loyal, to keep his morale high and to be upstanding when he's hungry?"[32] In Israel, the Shin Beth internal security services warned the cabinet that the PA could not be expected to maintain public order unless the situation was rectified. A violent clash between the Palestinian police and Islamists in Gaza in November 1994 increased PA, Israeli, and donor concern alike.[33]

To provide the PA with the required resources, some donors suggested that the Holst Fund be used as an intermediary mechanism for facilitating donor transfers to the police. The World Bank, however, demurred, arguing that this was outside its mandate.[34] It was then proposed that UNDP assume the role of transferring (and, in a sense, bureaucratically "laundering") donor support for police salaries. When UNDP also declined, UNRWA assumed the role from late 1994 until mid-1995, after receiving special authorization from the UN General Assembly and practical assistance from UNSCO. During this period, some $30 million was paid out in this way, financed by contributions from Denmark, the European Union, Japan, the Netherlands, Norway, Saudi Arabia, Sweden, and the United Kingdom.[35] The payment of police salaries was subject to strict audit; in one case, the PA was forced to reimburse British funds when it appeared that they had been used to pay unauthorized members of the Palestinian Preventative Security apparatus. Later, the mandate of the Holst Fund broadened, and the PA began to collect significant tax revenues, obviating the need for this mechanism. Overall, some $77 million was disbursed by donors to the police in 1994–95.

As COPP gave way to the Sectoral Working Groups, and as police financing passed from UNRWA to Holst to PA internal revenues, the context for donor assistance to the security sector changed in important ways.

First, the effective functioning of the PA in this sphere was no longer dependent on donor resources. Instead, police salaries were paid wholly through PA tax revenues, comprising some $198 million (or 23 percent of recurrent PA expenditures) in 1997.

Second, the number of security services in existence grew rapidly, from the four services (civil, public security, emergency, and intelligence) and 9,000 personnel initially authorized under the 1994 Gaza-Jericho Agreement, to ten or more agencies and around 40,000 personnel—some 10,000 more than authorized under the 1995 Interim Agreement.[36] This expansion of the security services was driven, in part, by the magnitude of internal and external security threats facing the PA (box 6.1). It was also driven by the use of the security services as a tool of political patronage, with many of those hired being former Palestine Liberation Army soldiers or other PLO cadres from the diaspora, or ex-intifada street activists from within the territories. The proliferation of different agencies was a

---

Box 6.1. When Is Big Brother Too Big?

Under Labor, the Israeli government had made little fuss about the growth of the PA security services, and privately some officials admitted turning a blind eye to the issue. Prime Minister Netanyahu, however, frequently cited excessive numbers as an example of Palestinian bad faith. Consequently the PA agreed in both the January 1997 Hebron Protocol and the November 1998 Wye River Memorandum to reduce police numbers to the levels agreed to in the Interim Agreement. Whether it would actually do this was another question, however; some PA security officials suggested that they would simply reclassify the excess numbers as civilian support personnel. Meanwhile, Palestinian and international critics of Arafat's regime often cited police numbers as an example of PA authoritarianism and bemoaned the wastage of scarce Palestinian resources.

Certainly, the PA security services exceeded their authorized number, were often repressive, and utilized funds that might otherwise have been used to meet developmental challenges. From a security point of view, however, it was not clear their size was all that disproportionate, given that they performed both internal *and* external security functions and given the possibility that collapse of the peace process could lead to direct conflict with the Israeli Defense Forces. Declared PA spending on security wages in 1997 represented around 4.8 percent of GDP, and some upper estimates of total security force spending suggested that this might be as high as $500 million, or 12 percent of GDP. Although this is far above the 4 percent average for defense expenditures in developing countries (1996), it is comparable with the 12.1 percent of GDP spent by Israel on defense (1996). A similar pattern exists with regard to personnel: whereas the PA has one security officer (*including* regular police) for every sixty-five persons, Jordan has one soldier (*excluding* police) for every fifty-five persons and Israel one soldier or police officer for every twenty-eight persons. Not surprisingly, it tended to be these sorts of security considerations—rather than concern over lost long-term investment opportunities—that drove PA decision making.

---

clear effort to create counterbalancing and rival groups that would check the emergence of any single internal challenge to Arafat's authority. Indeed, some of the agencies established seem to have had the primary task of monitoring other security organs.[37]

Third, there were growing reports of widespread irregularities and human rights abuses by the security services. These included shakedowns, protection rackets, detention without charge, beatings, torture, and even extrajudicial killings; as of December 1998, some twenty persons were reported to have died in questionable circumstances while in PA custody. The unauthorized use of firearms became more common, leading some observers to bemoan the emergence of a "gun culture" in the territories.[38] More broadly, the PA had yet to develop any solid foundation for human rights protection, judicial process, and the rule of law. Human Rights Watch noted:

> The Palestinian Authority (PA) failed to institutionalize important safeguards against human rights abuses that included patterns of arbitrary detention without charge or trial, torture and ill-treatment during interrogation, grossly unfair trials, and persecution of its critics. PA president Yasir Arafat's refusal to ratify the Basic Law, passed by the Palestinian Legislative Council in October 1997, left Palestinians without any clear statement of their rights, or of the duties and responsibilities of the executive, judicial, and legislative branches of government. Officials with specific responsibilities to safeguard human rights, like the attorney general, as well as judges, often found themselves under pressure to follow the executive's wishes, and unable to enforce their own rulings.

The report added that "lawyers reported difficulty in seeing their clients, despite receiving permits from the attorney general or court orders allowing visits" and "trials often lacked minimal due process guarantees, and judges who complained about judicial abuses sometimes faced retaliation." Furthermore, "press freedom remained restricted."[39] Even the PA justice minister, Frayh Abu Midyan, complained that the Palestinian judicial system "is in catastrophic condition," with little power and no authority over political detentions.[40]

Finally, the importance of the security dimensions of the peace process— and particularly the pressures on the PA to take countermeasures against militant Islamist groups—was underscored by periodic suicide bombings. These typically resulted in Israeli suspension of the peace process, the imposition of closure, and renewed pressure (by both Israel and the United States) for an intensification of Palestinian security measures. Widespread security measures on behalf of Israel, intended to catch the few, could serve to antagonize a much larger number of Palestinians. Arafat clearly understood this and hence alternated periodic sweeps against the opposition with periods of dialogue.

With these various developments, donor efforts tended to shift into two areas. The first was the provision of training assistance to the Palestinian police, intended to improve not only their professional skills, but also their respect for human rights and due legal process. This is the area on which the police SWG focused its attentions, and it represented over one-third of the $16 million or so publicly disbursed by donors for police purposes in 1996–97. Such assistance, and the passage of time, did result in a substantial improvement in the professionalism and behavior of the Civil Police, although not of the various paramilitary and intelligence organs.

The second area in which the United States and some European donors became involved was institutional cooperation on security and counterterrorism issues. Their cooperation was carried out, however, away from public view. It was also likely to involve intelligence-security rather than aid agencies and hence rarely showed up in donor matrices. As a result, the scope and the consequences of this institutional cooperation are much harder to assess.

Some public evidence of the importance of this area, however, was provided by the October 1998 Wye River Memorandum. This called for substantial institutionalized cooperation among the U.S. Central Intelligence Agency, the PA security services, and Israel to jointly "assess current threats, deal with any impediments to effective security cooperation and coordination and address the steps being taken to combat terror and terrorist organizations." The agreement also noted that a "U.S. [CIA]-Palestinian committee will meet biweekly to review the steps being taken to eliminate terrorist cells and the support structure that plans, finances, supplies and abets terror."[41]

A number of observers expressed grave concern at such developments, arguing that an increase in human rights abuses by the PA security forces would result. Human Rights Watch, in a letter to donor governments, stressed the responsibility of the international community in this regard:

> We write to you now to draw your attention to the many serious human rights shortcomings of the Wye River Memorandum, and to urge you to incorporate explicit human rights guarantees in all bilateral or multilateral agreements your government enters. In particular, we ask you to ensure that any aid, trade, or security agreements with Israel or the Palestinian Authority address the two greatest shortcomings of the Wye River Memorandum: its failure to include any provisions for monitoring or enforcing human rights standards, and its subordination of human rights to security concerns. Your government's actions in this regard can significantly improve the degree to which the security obligations outlined in the memorandum are met in a manner that is consistent with international human rights standards. . . .
>
> We urge your government to raise these issues in your meetings with U.S., Palestinian, and Israeli officials, to clarify your own government's understanding that the security obligations outlined in the Wye River Memorandum must be met in a manner that is consistent with international human rights standards, and to make your government's pledges of financial assistance conditional on such an understanding.[42]

Similar concern was expressed by Palestinian and Israeli human rights groups.

The paradox of (donor-supported) Palestinian NGOs criticizing (donor-encouraged) PA security measures underscored the dilemmas of this entire sector. The maintenance of security had been, and would be, a fundamental part of any Palestinian-Israeli peace process. A very small number of hard-core militants could often have a disproportionate impact through sporadic acts of extreme violence. The international community had a strong interest in that peace process, and the United States in particular pressed Arafat hard to clamp down against Hamas, Islamic Jihad, and other radical groups. Although not all security measures involve human rights abuses, it was almost inevitable that any crackdown against radicals by the PA would involve a substantial number of excesses. At the same time, donors repeatedly emphasized the importance of human rights and democratic development.

There is little evidence that donors thought through the potential contradictions: despite its very great desirability, democracy does not always resolve the problem of violent radical opposition, and political inclusion does not always defang potential political spoilers. In what directions, therefore, did the international community wish to see the PA move? Donor disbursements seemed to reflect uncertainty: whereas the police apparently received greater donor disbursements in 1994–95 ($77.0 million, compared with $19.6 million for democratic development), democracy received greater support thereafter ($44.7 million disbursed in 1996–97, compared with $16.0 million for the police).[43]

Might this paradox be resolved through a more integrated and thought-out donor assistance program? The inconsistent signals from donors were exacerbated by fragmentation among the donor institutions involved: aid agencies tended to press for human rights issues, and foreign ministries and security agencies tended to be more concerned with political stability. Substantial differences also existed among donors, with the United States pushing hardest for the security-oriented agenda. Although meaningful consensus was difficult (and probably impossible) to achieve around such a sensitive and morally ambiguous set of issues, donors could have shown greater understanding of the complexities and trade-offs involved. In the absence of such understanding, donor ambiguity served some useful purpose: support for human rights organizations helped raise the cost to the PA of the most egregious abuses, while support for the security sector addressed a real (if unpleasant) need of the peace process.

Budget Support

Budget support for the PA represented a substantial, and often controversial, aspect of international assistance during the first years of the Oslo process. For critics, such support fed an increasingly bloated, inefficient, and repressive Palestinian Authority at a time when development needs and nongovernmental organizations went underfunded. Yet it was clear from the outset of the Oslo process that the survival and effective functioning of the nascent Palestinian government was critical to the peace process and that the PA would require some initial budgetary support from donors. The World Bank's Emergency Assistance Program, for example, anticipated that the Palestinian Authority would require some $108 million in external financing in 1994 for recurrent and start-up costs, but that it would attain a balanced budget by 1995. External budget support would represent around 9 percent of donor disbursements under this plan. It also proposed some $117 million over 1994–96 to support the recurrent costs of NGO social services programs.[44]

To this end, in January 1994 the World Bank organized a special donors conference, Palestinian Authority Start-Up and Transitional Budgetary Expenditures, held in Paris. The result was the establishment of the Holst Fund as the primary conduit for donor support of the PA budget. The Holst Fund was administered by the bank, which received funds from donors and transmitted them to the PA. In turn, the PA provided an accounting of these funds, which were subject to external audit. This provided a high degree of general transparency and accountability, which was later supplemented by more general IMF monitoring of the Palestinian budget. While Holst transfers undoubtedly freed up PA cash resources that could then be used for other purposes, donors were adamant that there should be no leakage from the PA budget to directly fund either the Fateh party apparatus or the external activities of the PLO. On one occasion, such overview led to the PA having to refund monies that it had directly transferred to the PLO Martyrs' Fund to pay survivors benefits to the families of PLO fighters. Ironically, this relatively tight budget supervision may have had the unintended effect of spurring Palestinian efforts to develop supplementary, extralegal mechanisms of revenue collection, such as the various commercial monopolies.[45]

Budget support through the Holst Fund was also supplemented by other bilateral channels. The most important example was EU support for the recurrent costs of Palestinian primary and secondary education and universities. Some technical assistance programs also absorbed PA staff costs that would have otherwise been a burden on the recurrent budget.

Palestinian budgetary needs proved much greater than donors had initially anticipated, representing around two and a half times the levels the World Bank had planned. In part, this was because Palestinian start-up costs (especially for police) were higher and because of institutional disorganization within the PA. Another major problem was the delay in extending Palestinian tax authority in the West Bank, owing to delays in negotiating the Interim Agreement. During this period, most West Bank taxes leaked to Israel.[46] As a result, efforts to mobilize support to meet the immediate financing needs of the Palestinian Authority were

Table 6.4. Donor Support for PA Start-Up and Recurrent Expenditures
(1994–98)

	Holst Fund Pledges ($ millions)	Holst Fund Disbursements ($ millions)		Total Disbursements (all sources) for Transitional Costs and Budgetary Support ($ millions)
		Budget Support	Employment Generation	
1994	115.0	49.9	1.0	184.3
1995	53.7	103.6	2.7	107.2
1996	90.8	35.5	25.3	155.4
1997	14.0	23.1	5.9	59.1
1998	3.9	0.7	4.8	NA

Sources: AHLC Secretariat, *Holst Peace Fund: Status of Funding, Future Needs* (13 May 1998); MOPIC, *Quarterly Monitoring Report of Donor Assistance* (various).

a recurrent and often central aspect of donor meetings throughout 1994–95. During this period, donors were called on by the AHLC to provide at least 26 percent of their aid in the form of support for recurrent costs; in fact, the actual proportion was nearer to 29 percent of disbursements.

Periodic signs of instability—such as bombings by Palestinian rejectionists and confrontations between the PA and Hamas—underscored the importance of providing immediate resources to the PA. At the same time, donor concern with issues of transparency and accountability grew, and there remained a strong desire to dispose of the burden of budget support as soon as possible. The Understanding on Revenues, Expenditures and Donor Funding for the Palestinian Authority (November 1994) and the subsequent Tripartite Action Plan (first signed at the April 1995 AHLC meeting) reflected both of these concerns.

By 1996 it appeared as if the PA might further narrow its revenue gap for recurrent (but not investment) expenditures. At the beginning of the year, the IMF projected a deficit of $75 million. In practice, PA revenues actually exceeded initial targets, but expenditures were higher still because of new demands created by Israeli closure in the spring and due to the continued growth of the PA payroll. Although the international community—recognizing the political need to sustain the PA—met this challenge through the Holst Fund and other bilateral mechanisms (table 6.4),[47] its impatience with continuing budget support became ever more evident. Indeed, by 1997 there was little enthusiasm among donors for another round of Holst contributions. As one World Bank official noted:

> Partly . . . this is because the PA has yet to carry out the various "transparency" commitments promised in December 1996 at the Brussels AHLC, and promised by March 1—consolidating all fiscal accounts under the Ministry of Finance, clarifying all "monopoly accounts," and consolidating these too, etc. . . . In addition, there are concerns about the size of the public payroll, and questions about how tightly resources are being managed.

The World Bank official added, "The donors' assumption, which perhaps they are comfortable holding, is that Arafat does not really need their money and is able to plow back some of the 'monopoly' earnings into the budget." Of course, no donor really knew how large these off-the-books resources might be, other than from indirect indicators, such as "the Arafat decibel level." The muting of Palestinian complaints of slow aid delivery was thus seen by donors as evidence that the immediate PA's financial needs were becoming less pressing.[48] In 1997 external budget support accounted for only 4 percent of PA revenues, and the IMF suggested that a surplus PA recurrent account was possible by 1999. Although the Holst Fund was kept open as a conduit for employment-generation funds and emergency cash transfers, during 1998 little support flowed through this channel. In 1999 the World Bank recommended to donors that the Holst Fund was no longer needed and hence should be terminated.

Other channels of recurrent cost support also declined. In the case of postsecondary education, for example, EU support fell from $15 million to $17 million per year in 1994 and 1995 to $11.3 million in 1996 and $8 million in 1997. Universities were told that they would have to generate a larger share of their own revenues, notably through higher tuition fees.

There is little doubt that, though never popular with donors and criticized by many NGOs for diverting developmental resources into support for a burgeoning PA bureaucracy, international support for Palestinian start-up and recurrent costs played an absolutely critical political role. As the World Bank later noted, "Some argue that we compromised the development program by diverting so much to budget support. Obviously those grant resources are now unavailable for investment—but what choice was there? In 1994 and 1995, Palestinian recurrent expenditure far exceeded revenues."[49] In the initial stages of the Oslo process such support undergirded efforts to establish a functioning Palestinian administration, something that would not have been possible solely from local resources. The Holst Fund represented a particularly effective mechanism for this administration, as well as for dealing with unanticipated economic shocks such as the closures of

1996. Indeed, budgetary support through the Holst Fund represented one of the few effective mechanisms for rapid and flexible disbursement of donor funds, thus helping to offset the initial delays associated with other aspects of international assistance. The World Bank's own internal guidelines on postconflict reconstruction subsequently highlighted the Holst Fund as representing an "unprecedented success," and perhaps "the best example" of a successful aid mechanism in post-conflict countries.[50]

It is also important to note that, for all the attention given to the short-comings of the PA, its record of domestic revenue collection has been impressive. By 1996 domestic revenues were equal to a healthy 17 percent of GDP, rising to 21 percent by 1997.[51] In contrast, many other transitional and postconflict countries have often experienced difficulty in raising a suitable amount of domestic resources, owing to weak collection mechanisms, very high rates of tax evasion, and the political influence of entrenched economic elites. In El Salvador, for example, tax revenues have been in the range of only 11–12 percent of GDP, and in Guatemala only 8 percent of GDP.[52] The mounting challenge to the PA was thus not revenue collection (although income and corporate tax evasion was a problem), but rather expenditure control aggravated by liquidity problems. As noted in chapter 5, the growth in the public-service wage placed growing pressure on the budget, pressure that would grow more acute with the prospect of overdue civil service pay increases and eventual pension payouts. At the same time, Arafat's continued diversion of excise revenues into an account outside the control of the Ministry of Finance made it difficult to meet these expenses on a reliable basis. Clearly, in the view of donors, both of these problems were the PA's—and not the responsibility of the international community to fix through budgetary bailouts.

Emergency Job Creation

Emergency job creation became a substantial, and largely unanticipated, component of the assistance program owing to both Israeli closure of the West Bank and Gaza and the more general decline in Palestinian labor within Israel. The potentially destabilizing consequences of this situation caused growing concern, prompting various emergency employment projects.[53] Critics suggested, however, that these were ineffectual make-work projects that (like security assistance and budget support) diverted attention from the underlying developmental needs of the Palestinians.

The forerunners of these emergency projects were a number of earlier employment generation programs in the territories. In 1989 UNRWA initiated its Shelter Rehabilitation Program, which involved building shelters for poor refugee families living in refugee camps. In 1992 Save the Children Federation started another program, which provided jobs through the construction of rural infrastructure. Following the Oslo Agreement, UNRWA secured funding for continuation of its Shelter Rehabilitation Program in Gaza, while UNDP oversaw a "Gaza clean-up" program in late 1994. The latter in particular was driven by the political need to show immediate tangible benefits in the territories following the establishment of the PA. Other similar campaigns were launched in conjunction with the Sectoral Working Group on employment generation.

Following the bombings of February and March 1996 and the subsequent prolonged closures, two additional and much larger employment generation schemes were implemented by PECDAR, one sponsored by the World Bank and another by UNDP. UNRWA also continued and expanded its employment-generation programs. These programs provided up to 52,500 full-time equivalent jobs at their peak in the summer.[54] The management of funds earmarked for employment-generation programs was handled by UNDP and World Bank staff on the donor side and by PECDAR and local municipalities and village councils on the Palestinian side. Another major portion of the budget was used to cover the fees charged by implementing contractors.

The primary goal of employment-generation schemes was the alleviation of poverty resulting from a loss of jobs in Israel owing to closure. In this respect, their impact depended on how well they included the poor (and excluded the nonpoor), and the share of the wage bill in the budget. All employment generation programs in the territories required beneficiaries to work for the assistance they received. Participants were paid a basic wage that was lower than the prevailing market rate for the same kind of work, thus deterring the nonpoor from taking part. Average daily wages for workers in these programs ranged from $11.30 to $21.70, depending on the level of skill required. Beneficiaries were thus targeted by self-selection, whereby the wage level determined the attractiveness of employment to individuals. Wages were sometimes set lower than the poverty line, to ensure targeting of the poorest and to generate the largest possible number of jobs.

The total budget earmarked for all employment-generation programs during the period of October 1993 to October 1996 amounted to over $90 million. About $48 million of the total budget is estimated to have created a total of 1,216,448 job-day opportunities. The net monetary transfers to workers employed through these schemes amounted to $13.4 million, or about 28 percent of the total budget.

The impact of these programs in alleviating poverty is hard to ascertain. The total transfers of all programs to the poor in the form of wages during 1994–July 1996 amounted to $10.3 million, which is estimated to have covered less than 8 percent of the total amount needed to alleviate poverty in the West Bank and Gaza Strip during that period. The effectiveness with which programs channeled assistance to the poor varied substantially depending on administrative cost,

proportion of labor input, and wage rates. One analysis suggested that the World
Bank and UNRWA programs were particularly effective in this regard, while SWG
programs and the UNRWA Shelter Rehabilitation Program were least effective.[55] On the other hand, programs with heavy labor input generally involved
the lowest level of permanent asset creation, while the UNRWA shelter rehabilitation programs and some SWG programs fared much better in this regard.

As noted, employment generation schemes were criticized for being low-
wage, short-term make-work activities with little lasting contribution to sustainable development. In the case of the World Bank and PECDAR, their so-called
second-generation employment programs put greater emphasis on needs assessment and asset creation, albeit at the necessary lower rate of labor inputs. More
fundamentally, however, such criticism failed to recognize that such programs
have never been intended to be anything more than a temporary response to a more
fundamental problem: substantial Palestinian unemployment and the economic
shocks generated by periodic Israeli closure of the territories. Alluding to the potentially adverse political consequences of such a situation for the Palestinian Authority and peace process, one World Bank analysis noted that "it became imperative
that Bank strategy must adjust to tackle immediate needs; without some provision of relief, there might be little need to plan for the medium-term."[56] A later
AHLC paper was even more explicit, terming such programs a "stop-gap initiative, intended to alleviate economic hardship and lessen the risk of destabilizing
social unrest."[57] In this respect, employment generation programs have been
timely and well suited, signaling precisely the sort of responsiveness and political
sensitivity required by peacebuilding programs.

Agriculture

If emergency job creation has been a substantial if unanticipated component of
donor programs in Palestine, agriculture is representative of an important sector that
has been largely ignored by donors. According to MOPIC data, this sector—
which accounts for approximately one-fifth of Palestinian employment, trade, and
GDP—received only 1.7 percent of donor commitments and 0.3 percent of disbursements ($31 million) by the first quarter of 1998.[58] Among the donors, few
(Japan, Spain) have seemed willing to sink substantial funds into this sector.

There are several reasons for this reluctance. One is political: the agricultural
sector—bound up as it is with issues of both land use and water consumption—
is potentially sensitive. Although agricultural production generally increased
under occupation, development of the sector was largely ignored by the Israeli
authorities, excepting those aspects of modernization (such as greenhouse production) that used less land and water. Subsequent to the Oslo and Interim Agreements, development of this sector continued to be constrained by limits on water

usage and by the fact that much agricultural land fell within area C, beyond the administrative control of the PA.

From an economic standpoint, the World Bank's 1993 assessment of the sector indicated both strengths and weaknesses but emphasized the uncertain competitiveness of this sector. It called for some $46 million to be spent by donors in this area, representing around 3.8 percent of overall commitments.[59] The bank argued that this reflected the potential for donor-supported investment and the primacy of commercial and other conditions in determining sectoral growth; critics argued that it reflected the bank's traditional emphasis on market mechanisms.[60]

Another reason for the cool attitude of donors toward agriculture arose from perceptions that the PA itself did not view this sector as a high priority. The first PA cabinet did not have a minister of agriculture, but rather delegated the portfolio to the minister of finance, who had neither an agricultural background nor time to spare for this secondary assignment. In early 1996 a minister was appointed, although he too had little background in the area. The PA's low ranking of agriculture was also manifest in budgetary allocations: the ministry's share in the budget was only 1.7 percent of the total during 1996–97. The 1999–2003 Palestinian Development Plan redressed this somewhat, calling for investments of $206 million (or 4.5 percent of the total PDP). Still, this was less than the priority assigned to the tourism sector, and agriculture proved to be one of the less successful areas of the PDP in attracting donor funds.

On top of all this, the Ministry of Agriculture was particularly hard hit by the bureaucratic politics that afflicted many PA institutions (as discussed in box 5.3).[61] This inhibited institutional effectiveness and institutional development. Such institutional weaknesses, in turn, were carried over into the agriculture SWG, considered by many to be one of the least effective of the Sectoral Working Groups. The paucity of external support thus compounded the weakness of the sector and vice versa.

Technical Assistance

Technical assistance—that is, the transfer of knowledge (often from external experts)—is an essential tool for promoting capacity building in developing countries. It is also often a form of tied aid, with much of the funds flowing back to the donor country to consultants and technical experts. According to MOPIC data, technical assistance totaled $337 million in 1994–97, representing some 17 percent of disbursements.

Palestinian officials frequently complained about technical assistance and in particular about the excessive volume and low quality of assistance that was provided.[62] Some external assessments echoed these complaints.[63] In many cases, the external experts provided could not speak Arabic and had a poor understanding of local conditions (and politics), producing reports that languish on shelves. Moreover, foreign experts are almost invariably paid at rates several times greater than that of their Palestinian counterparts, creating additional tensions. Initiatives such as UNDP's TOKTEN program and the World Bank's Palestinian Expatriate Professional Fund attempted to alleviate some of these weaknesses by making greater use of expatriate Palestinian expertise financed through a centralized mechanism but continued to face the dilemma of having to offer higher financial incentives to attract expertise while ensuring their smooth integration into local institutions where salaries were substantially lower. Moreover, TOKTEN assignments tended to be of short duration, usually three months. This left little time for orientation and productive impact and led some local staff to resent external compatriots for their perceived lack of commitment. As a result, "there seemed to be few cases where TOKTEN assignments have been considered worthwhile by the receiving agency."[64]

More broadly, the institutional weaknesses of the PA also meant that the provision of technical assistance was often supply- and donor-driven, rather than arising from clearly identified, prioritized, and expressed Palestinian needs. In turn, the availability of technical assistance in some sectors and not in others tended to distort strategic institution building. Poor internal tracking of externally funded staff positions also tended to disguise the long-term recurrent costs of certain PA activities and projects.

Poor donor coordination (or donor competition) also created problems. Not infrequently, Palestinian agencies were offered multiple technical experts from different sources, sometimes each offering differing advice or training. Wide variation among donors in salary and other policies for consultants and contracted staff could also be problematic.

Finally, Palestinian officials report substantial frustration when experts have been proffered instead of the required equipment or financial resources— particularly when local expertise is available, but other resources are not. According to senior MOPIC officials, technical assistance and related auxiliary components can compose up to half of donor support for any given (capital) project. Indeed, there is a widespread perception among many Palestinian aid officials that the potential ability of donors to insert their own national technical experts into a project is a major factor in shaping donor priority setting.

One external assessment noted, "Both the PA and MOPIC itself are displaying all the unsettling attributes of [technical assistance]," including support for "activities which are unlikely to be sustainable, either because of the PA's overall inability to afford them without donor support, or because skill transfer is not taking place, or, even if it is, because the PA is unlikely to retain the services of those trained."[65] None of this is to suggest, of course, that technical assistance is unimportant: as one UNDP official noted, "All the negative things [said] about technical assistance are true—but they still need technical assistance."[66] However, it is to suggest that donors need to pay greater attention to when and where such support is really required, and in what form it can best be provided.

The NGO Sector

The focus of post-Oslo international aid efforts, together with the establishment of the Palestinian Authority, put a severe squeeze on both Palestinian NGOs (of which some 850–1,200 operate in the West Bank and Gaza) and international NGOs (INGOs, of which approximately 200 are active).[67] In the early 1990s, the NGO sector received approximately $170–240 million from the PLO, international donors, and private benefactors and was—in the absence of a state apparatus—responsible for a significant portion of the health, education, and social welfare sector, as well as development and other activities. As a consequence of first the Gulf War and later the redirection of aid funds to the PA following the Declaration of Principles, this amount fell to roughly $60–90 million per year. Overall, only about one-tenth of post-Oslo aid disbursements were through NGO channels. One survey of Palestinian NGOs found that health and education projects were those that received the largest shares of donor support. It also found that NGOs in the West Bank, and especially in the Jerusalem-Ramallah-Bethlehem area, tended to receive a disproportionate amount of support. The northern West Bank and southern Gaza Strip—areas with far fewer NGOs active—were particularly disadvantaged.[68]

There were several reasons for the shift away from NGO channels. Many post-Oslo development projects were simply too large for local NGOs to effectively bid on or participate in. Moreover, although NGOs are often quite cost-effective and disburse funds "on the ground" more quickly than other channels, they can also be more difficult to deal with from a donor perspective. In particular, grants to NGOs typically involve a relatively small disbursement and may require more staff time (per dollar disbursed) for preparation, follow-up, and oversight. NGOs themselves showed poor coordination and never found an effective formula for representation within the donor coordination framework. Above and beyond this, however, the reduction of donor support to the NGO sector reflected the political imperative and realities of the post-Oslo era. Unlike in the earlier period of Israeli occupation, there were now nascent Palestinian official institutions that could be, and had to be, supported. In many cases, these new bureaucratic structures were assuming responsibilities that had once been the purview of NGOs, and it was only appropriate that an increasing share of donor support in such areas as health, education, and social services be directed toward them.

While post-Oslo support for the NGO sector declined, external funds still represented a very important resource for local NGOs, with the United States and the European Union the single largest sources of NGO funding. In the EU case, however, this represented a small proportion of its overall aid disbursements (around 8 percent), declining as the aid program progressed. American assistance, by contrast, was a quite large proportion (around 22 percent), reflecting congressional prohibition of direct assistance to the PA as well as the legacy of the pre-Oslo pattern of U.S. aid. Other donors, like Canada (34 percent), Switzerland (18 percent), and the Netherlands (18 percent), also allocated a relatively high proportion of aid to NGO channels and partnerships.[69]

There was wide variation too in the types of NGO funding provided. Many countries placed heavy emphasis on North-South partnerships, channeling support for Palestinian NGOs through organizations in the donor country. Some countries funded a wide range of NGO projects on the basis of opportunity and merit, while others stressed compatibility with their bilateral programs: sectoral economic development activities; social services sectors; human rights and democratic development. Some donors—Norway and Canada, among others—emphasized "people-to-people" or dialogue activities intended to promote Palestinian-Israeli reconciliation. Many of the mid-range donors developed particularly flexible mechanisms for NGO support. The Canadian government's embassy-based Canada Fund was one example, allowing small-project funding to be provided with only minimal delays. The number of Palestinian NGO office photocopiers bearing a CIDA sticker was one indicator of the success of this approach.

In many cases, continued NGO reliance on donor funding shaped the extent to which NGO priorities were driven by donor priorities rather than local need. Typically, donor support was most easily available for new programs in sectors relating to the contemporary thematic concerns or bilateral programming of agencies—human rights, democratic development, gender, the environment, and so forth. By contrast, funds were rarely available to support less popular areas (such as agricultural development) or to support the recurrent costs of regular operations. As a result, NGOs were often forced to fund their regular activities and operating costs by securing a series of special project grants from donors and international NGOs. To do so, many responded to the thematic priorities of funders less out of conviction than out of the imperatives of fund-raising.

For its part, the PA attempted to bring Palestinian NGOs under an increasing degree of control. The words of one senior PECDAR official reflected this approach: "Money should be centralized in the PA, then distributed to the NGOs. . . . The PA needs to be supported instead of the NGOs because they signed agreements. . . . No one wants to block NGO work; we just want to promote their work."[70] In part, PA efforts to subordinate the NGO sector were part of a natural process of extending state authority into various social policy sectors. However, such efforts were also aimed at strengthening the PA's political sway. The disproportionate support among many NGO activists for non-Fateh opposition groups and the historic connections between grassroots organization and factional competition in the territories both heightened the potential for PA-NGO conflict still further.[71] In an apparent effort to intimidate, some NGOs received visits from either the security services or an NGO "monitoring committee" established by Arafat. Islamist NGOs and those associated with the (independent) Palestinian NGO Network (PNGO) appeared to be a particular focus of PA interest.

Greater pressure on some Palestinian NGOs came in late 1998 and 1999, following the signing of the Wye River Memorandum. In this the PA had pledged to clamp down on not only paramilitary groups, but also their "support structure"—a reference to Islamist charitable organizations, which Israel had long charged were a front for Hamas and Islamic Jihad and which the PA had accused of laundering donations from foreign supporters and governments. Shortly thereafter, more than a dozen Islamist NGOs were ordered closed by the PA.

Another set of challenges arose from the PA's periodic budgetary problems. In the spring of 1999, PA wage restraint led to waves of labor unrest among teachers, health workers, and others. In response, Arafat reportedly pushed for the formation of a unified trade union movement—under Fateh control.

Later that same year, the release of an UNSCO report, *Rule of Law Development in the West Bank and Gaza Strip*, had interesting—if unintended—effects.[72] Annoyed by subsequent comments by the international press and Palestinian human rights NGOs, a number of pro-PA figures and newspapers launched attacks against the alleged financial and other irregularities of the NGO community. These attacks were clearly meant to intimidate, although some members of the NGO community did have a somewhat murky record in this regard.

Given all of these indications, it was hardly surprising that the PA's initial Draft Law Concerning Charitable Societies, Social Bodies and Private Institutions also envisaged an extensive system of state registration and supervision, apparently based on the most restrictive elements of Egyptian and Jordanian NGO law. Adoption was delayed, however, by NGO and donor criticism, as well as by bureaucratic infighting among Palestinian ministries. In this process, MOPIC emerged as pushing a more liberal version of the legislation, while NGO activists strongly pressed for legal protections of rights and a registration system under the auspices of the Ministry of Justice rather than the (more internal security–oriented) Ministry of the Interior. Effective lobbying of the PLC seemed to result in a partial NGO victory in the summer of 1998, with the legislature endorsing a version that reflected NGO concerns.[73] This was finally signed by Arafat in 1999—but not before he revised it to reassign responsibility for NGO registration to the Ministry of the Interior. One positive sign, however, was the appointment in July 1999 of a current PA minister, Hasan Asfour, to open better lines of communication with the NGOs.

As with other security issues, donor attitudes to the role of Palestinian civil society were often ambiguous or contradictory. For all donors, an overriding concern was to strengthen the PA, and hence the peace process. NGOs were not always seen as essential in this process: in the blunt words of one U.S. State Department official, "we don't care about NGOs . . . you have to have [political] institutions in place."[74] Most USAID and other aid officials had a rather different view—once more reflecting the differences of institutional culture within donor countries. Thus, whereas many Western donor agencies expressed concern at PA efforts to subordinate the NGO sector, the United States and other members of the international community urged the PA to assume more robust measures against Islamist organizations, including Islamist NGOs.

Yet the links between Islamist charitable groups and Islamist militants were often fuzzy, consisting more of overlapping membership than operational control of the former by the latter. In many cases—in part because of their ideological determination—Islamist charity groups were particularly effective in the health, education, and social welfare areas, and in many cases they had even won support from Western aid agencies for precisely that reason. (The same was also true on the Palestinian Left, with at least one very well known PFLP-linked NGO receiving much of its funding from Western donors, despite the PFLP's opposition to the Oslo process.) Further complicating the picture, "Islamists" themselves embraced a diverse array of views and supporters, not all of them hostile to the peace process. It was also not clear to what extent Islamist charitable organizations had an effect on Palestinian political attitudes,[75] although it was clear that Hamas and Islamic Jihad activists did make use of some for fund-raising and recruiting purposes. It also was not clear whether donor support encouraged moderation or indirectly financed violence, and whether the banning of such groups suppressed terrorism or radicalized the opposition. Most probably all of these effects were at work.

In any event, and leaving aside the issue of PA policy toward groups suspected of having links to Hamas and Islamic Jihad, the overall NGO sector has often shown cost-efficiency, flexibility, and innovation. It has also made a broader contribution to the pluralism of Palestinian society. Consequently, its broader weakening has been a source of concern for many observers.[76] Unusually, the World Bank—which, as an institution, has historically been suspicious of NGO activity—proposed the establishment of a Palestinian NGO Trust Fund to supplement existing funding sources. Such a fund might not only strengthen NGO activities, but also enable the bank to tap new donor resources.

The proposal faced serious challenges. While some Palestinian officials supported the idea—and even went so far as to suggest that it was proposed by the PA[77]—many others were less than enthusiastic about the existence of an independent pipeline of resources to local NGOs. Indeed, Arafat once described it as a "fatal mistake," complaining to one donor official that local NGO activists were "all communists." Differences also arose between MOPIC and PECDAR over the issue.

For their part, many local NGOs were concerned at the possible role of the World Bank and PA in allocating grants, and there were questions over how the fund would deal with NGOs based in Jerusalem. Fears were also expressed that the existence of such a central fund would increase the weight of donors in setting NGO agendas.[78] The development of any local consensus on these issues, however, was inhibited by the functional and geographic fragmentation of the NGO sector, as well as political differences among NGOs. Instead, as soon as the project was proposed, a number of new NGO coordinating groups suddenly appeared in the territories, some closely tied to the PA and others clearly hoping to get a piece of any new funding pie.

Finally, many donors were unwilling to contribute to the project. The problem here was largely one of profile: why support an indirect World Bank funding mechanism when greater political credit could be obtained by directly financing nongovernmental groups? In the end, however, sufficient funds were received to launch the project, with $14.5 million in financial support coming from the World Bank, Italy (which earmarked its contribution for Italian NGOs), and Saudi Arabia.[79] Management of the project was contracted to a consortium composed of the (Palestinian) Welfare Association along with the British Council and Charities Aid Foundation. The first call for submissions in 1998 attracted a large number of applications, and the first disbursements were made later that same year.

SETTING THE AGENDA: SHAPING MENUS, MAKING CHOICES

Another way of getting at the relevance of international assistance for peacebuilding and reconstruction is to shift focus from sectoral and distributional issues to examining the process of agenda setting and the extent to which agreed-upon sets of developmental and peacebuilding priorities emerge and are accepted by the various actors concerned. As is evident from both the World Bank's EAP and the PA's subsequent PPIP and PDP, agenda setting has been a far more complex process than simply identifying sectoral "needs" or "priorities" based on some abstract technical criteria. Rather, developmental and political objectives interact with a range of other considerations, many of them seemingly extraneous to the tasks of peacebuilding and reconstruction.

One sample of PA officials, asked about the determinants of donor aid programs, generally ranked "Palestinian preferences" (along with "Israeli preferences") as relatively unimportant, along with the "sectoral expertise of donors." With the exception of the World Bank, aid coordination mechanisms (UNSCO and the LACC) were not seen as important in agenda setting. Instead, "donors' desire for enhanced political profile," "the economic interests of donors," and "the World Bank" are identified as having the strongest effect on the targeting of international assistance, followed by "domestic lobby groups," "the desire to produce immediate local benefits," and "the desire to politically strengthen the Palestinian Authority."[80]

It might be argued that, in emphasizing the self-interested actions of donors, such a view overstates the rationality of donor programs. As with any large bureaucracy, decisions are in large part driven by institutional and idiosyncratic factors, as well as a substantial degree of serendipity: the need to move money out of a budget before the end of a financial year, the appearance of fleeting project opportunities, the outcome of particular meetings or high-level contacts, or the sectoral preferences of senior aid officials. In short, policy is often not so much *made;* it *happens.* Asked to explain the emergence of water as an area of concentration for USAID, for example, one American official simply noted that "a couple of the people who managed the program were water resource people."[81] Similarly, the development of the World Bank's innovative Palestinian NGO Project was largely driven by the bank's dynamic principal country officer at the time, Nigel Roberts, who himself came from an NGO background.

Yet with this important caveat firmly in mind, it is nonetheless clear that donor agenda setting *has* been driven by political and economic calculations. As one World Bank spokesperson noted, "if we are honest, we have to admit we still place too much emphasis on visibility and commercial self-interest, which interferes with cooperation among ourselves and with our Palestinian colleagues."[82]

This comment must be seen in appropriate context, however. Donors themselves work in an environment in which the general sustainability of assistance depends on demonstrating to their governments and populations that aid serves that national interest, whether in terms of advancing foreign policy, securing new trade and investment opportunities, or upholding a broader set of values. Of course, the relative mix of motives varies from donor to donor. USAID often appears particularly defensive, with its Web site proudly proclaiming, "Close to 80 percent of USAID's grants and contracts go directly to American firms and non-governmental organizations" and "Foreign assistance fosters an enabling environment for U.S. trade and investment in developing nations."[83] By contrast, in the Nordic countries, there is much greater public support for aid and generally less tying of assistance to national procurements.

The result can be emphasis on sectors with trade or investment potential and the tying of assistance (including the provision of donor technical assistance). Another result is emphasis on projects with high political visibility: in the blunt words of one senior Western foreign ministry official, "it isn't much good to us if we can't announce it."[84] Similarly, trendy themes (such as democratization) may be emphasized, while important but less "sexy" sectors (such as agriculture) are ignored. One manifestation of this is the "showcase" project, driven overwhelmingly by political rationales. At times, the results can be spectacularly expensive and unsuccessful. The USAID-funded Karameh Towers housing project (box 6.2) is one case in point; another is the EU-funded Gaza European Hospital (box 6.3).[85]

Another common result was the educational exchange, in which Palestinian academics or experts were invited to spend time in a donor country, ostensibly to acquire new skills but also to establish hopefully lasting connections. One typical program saw two dozen Israeli, Palestinian, and Jordanian social workers brought over to study in a university in a donor country. It was not clear, however, whether the training was appropriate for Palestinian needs, and the students themselves were removed from productive work in their own countries for a year. The total cost—$2 million, plus privately raised donations—would have endowed a permanent faculty of social work at an existing Palestinian university, but instead was largely spent in the West. The project did, however, generate plenty of photo opportunities and sympathetic press coverage.

Other cases were more ambiguous. Norway's provision of $10 million through UNDP for neighborhood improvements, green spaces, and children's playgrounds in Gaza, for example, certainly didn't fall within the confines of traditional development programming and was criticized by some as a cosmetic, nonproductive make-work scheme. Yet the parks it created did provide a symbolic public indicator of the changed atmosphere brought on by self-rule and the peace process.

The importance of political profile in shaping donor programs in the territories has a number of other implications. Specifically, donors may be reluctant to support multilateral aid projects that do not highlight their own particular contribution. The Holst Fund and some other programs run by UN agencies or the World Bank have encountered this problem: recipients may be unaware who is providing the support, and it may be more difficult to "hang a flag" on the resulting outcome if multiple donors contributed varying amounts. As a result, if projects are to be effective they must have built into them some capacity for enhancing donor profile. The World Bank's NGO Trust Fund, for example, was able to attract Italian money by allowing much of it to be earmarked for Italian NGOs. PECDAR was effective at signposting its various projects and offered potential

Box 6.2. White Elephants in Gaza?

Not everyone agrees that the Karameh Towers housing project in Gaza can be classified as a "white elephant," since the completed towers are now largely inhabited. However, with the average price of a four-bedroom flat at $30,000—while Gazan annual per capita income fluctuates at around $1,200 and the poverty line has been drawn at $600 per annum—the incongruity between the intention to provide low-income housing and the reality of Karameh becomes obvious.

Karameh Towers was built as a political showcase project. It was negotiated by the United States with the PLO in Tunis following the signing of the Declaration of Principles in 1993 and was intended to represent a donor commitment to the peace process. USAID provided $10 million in funding and supervised the construction, with a U.S. construction management company and local contractors hired to undertake the actual building. The Palestinian Housing Council (PHC)—USAID's counterpart organization—was responsible for the design, which comprised 192 apartments in six buildings that were to provide affordable housing for low- and middle-income groups.

It wasn't until the construction was finally completed in August 1996 that the problems began to emerge. Cost was the main issue. Although the finishing and the design of the flats were of high quality, construction was expensive and completely overran its initial financial framework. The cost of an apartment (excluding the fees of the management company) was finally set at $42,000 for a large apartment (110 square meters) and $35,000 for a small one (90 square meters)—the same price as for a private development. Thus, beautiful California-engineered, earthquake-proof apartments graced the Gazan skyline but fell well short of meeting the needs of the initial target group (families with an income of $200-$700 per month).

USAID negotiated with the PHC to raise the ceiling of eligibility or else offer the option of longer-term sale. However, just as they were about to receive a list of potential tenants for approval from the PHC, USAID found that tenants were already moving in, even without water and electricity. All six buildings were fully occupied soon after. In some cases, individual tenants acquired more than one apartment, sometimes an entire floor, and in many cases only paid a first installment. Left with few other options, USAID considered how to use the "reflows"—the installments that the tenants pay, if and when they are paid—to secure the future maintenance of the area. This revenue (held in accounts by the PHC) had to

Box 6.2. *(cont.)*

be used with the approval of USAID, which had only limited recourse (other than to threaten to curb future aid) to pursue the issue further.

Palestinian commentators identified a number of reasons for these problems. Some say that the initial project concept was ill thought through, the design should have been much simpler, and the costing structure of the apartments was wrong from the start. There was poor monitoring and supervision of the project, with political tensions further fueling problems and much pressure on the Palestinians to make the flats available. The lack of an enforcement mechanism in the original memo of understanding was also a deficiency. Finally, closure measures taken by the Israeli authorities delayed the shipment of materials and created additional costs. At the outset of the project, USAID was to provide technical assistance to the PHC (which was expected to become the Ministry of Housing) and initiate a home improvement program. But as USAID priorities changed with the political dynamics of the State Department (which insisted on more visible projects), these two supportive components were abandoned.

Meanwhile, a similar EU low-cost housing project in Gaza encountered similar problems. An auditor's report on the $20 million project found that the apartments had been designed with "elegance and luxury," at an average of over $60,000 each—some 80 percent more than planned. Purchasers paid little in the way of a down payment, and many subsequently failed to pay their mortgages. Palestinian sources suggested that more than 80 percent of the units were taken by returnees, security officials, and other Arafat loyalists. The PA disputed this, arguing that most of the purchasers were low-income families and asserting that the improvements cited in the EU report (including satellite dishes and granite kitchen surfaces) had often been paid for directly by tenants.

Most important of all, neither the USAID nor EU projects really addressed the major problems facing low-income families in Palestine. Together, the two projects provided housing to perhaps 3,000 persons— or less than a month's population growth in Gaza. Housing shortages arose from the weakness of Palestinian mortgage lending, the lack of clear land title (notably for refugee camp inhabitants), and the absence of any coherent PA program to either spur residential/rental construction or encourage lending to low-income families. More fundamentally, poor housing conditions in Gaza reflected both poor economic conditions and the lack of mobility between Gaza and the West Bank.

Box 6.3. In Need of Chronic Care: European Hospital, Gaza

The initial project concept in the late 1980s was to construct a $45 million hospital in Khan Yunis that would provide for the primary and secondary health care of some 400,000 Gazans in the surrounding area—and a visible symbol of European support for the Palestinians. The 232-bed hospital would help meet the projected needs of the Gaza Strip as a whole and was to serve as a model for the entire Palestinian health sector. Since it would be inappropriate for the European Union to provide the money to the Israeli occupation authorities, and since no Palestinian administration existed at the time, UNRWA was chosen to implement the project. Several years later, the hospital was still far from being operational, and many questioned its viability.

Most visitors are impressed with the physical state of the hospital, carved to completion by the same Irish firm responsible for regilding the Dome of the Rock in Jerusalem and surrounded by $750,000 worth of landscaping. However, design problems emerged during construction that were not tackled by specialists but by architects, engineers, and administrators, further compounding the flaws: the hospital morgue was located next to the kitchen; ambulance access to the emergency room was awkward; patient and visitor access was poorly thought through, with the chances of visitors walking inadvertently into isolation areas very high; the hospital kitchen was undersized; there was a shortage of elevators; telecommunications systems were inadequate; plans to create a computerized system were canceled, despite the eventual need to administer over 600 staff and support 200 inpatients and 100 outpatients; utilities had no management system to control their usage, resulting in potentially hugely costly bills; there was no confirmation that the air conditioning could cater for the isolation rooms; there was no security on the premises; and the blue and primary yellow paintwork was attractive but rendered evaluation of a patient's pallor virtually impossible. Even the location of the hospital was problematic. The site itself was chosen after Israel refused to allow construction in the north of the Gaza Strip, as originally planned. Over half an hour away from the main supply point of electricity, water, and sewage, the hospital necessitated the construction of an independent power plant and sewage and water-storage facilities.

Incremental solutions to these shortcomings were ineffective because of the lack of technical expertise and effective project management. Instead,

Box 6.3. *(cont.)*

the project progressively exceeded its capital budget. By the time the European Union undertook comprehensive investigations into the matter, costs had climbed to over $52 million (resulting in a high per-bed cost of over $200,000), and UNRWA had already dug into $9–$10 million of its core refugee services budget. The root problems in this project stemmed in part from the complexity and multifaceted nature of hospital construction. Hospitals are unlike many other capital projects, requiring highly sophisticated design and management techniques. UNRWA had never built a hospital before in Gaza, much less one that was to meet accepted international standards of best practice. Even if the expertise had been available, constructing such a hospital in the heart of occupied Gaza was not likely to have been a straightforward task. Several observers had long emphasized the incongruity between Gaza's health needs and the complexity of the hospital being proposed to meet them. Many also suggested that the upgrading of Gaza's existing hospitals would have provided a better, faster solution. However, at the time, hospitals were under the control of the Israeli Civil Administration and this was not an option.

In addition to design problems, the hospital faced severe long-term financing problems. As one 1998 EU auditor's report noted, "The cost of maintaining and using this hospital will be well over the financial means of this country." Faced with a limited budget and other pressing needs, the PA simply couldn't afford to operate the expensive new facility. As a consequence, once completed the hospital sat empty, with the EU, UNRWA, and the PA paying up to $10,000 per month to simply maintain the building. In a telling statement, sewage had to be trucked to the empty facility to prevent a breakdown in its otherwise idle waste-processing equipment.

The European Hospital was, moreover, not the only case of this. In Jericho, a new hospital financed by the Japanese was also regarded by many as excessively lavish and inappropriate to regional health needs. Here too the costs of operations stretched the already heavily burdened budget of the Ministry of Health.

In early 1999, the EU, UNRWA, and PA Ministry of Health did sign a Memorandum of Understanding that was intended to enable the hospital to open its doors at some time in the year 2000. It remained to be seen, however, whether what was intended to be a blessing for Gaza's health sector could be saved from being a nightmare.

donors a menu of small- and medium-scale activities that their support could be directed to.

The problem of profile is particularly acute for small- and medium-scale donors, who face the threat of being "crowded out" by the European Union, Japan, and the United States. Some opted to enhance their visibility (and perhaps their effectiveness) by identifying clearly defined niches: Switzerland, for example, has focused much of its program on detainees/returnees, vocational training, and education; Australia has won recognition all out of proportion to the size of its small program by concentrating on legal reform and facilitating the SWG subgroup on this theme. However, a narrow focus is not the only answer: Sweden was successful by energetically pursuing opportunities as they arose, while Denmark's effective program lay somewhere between these two poles. Canada's comparably sized program, however, was less well recognized on the ground, despite a high rate of disbursement—perhaps because an unusually large proportion (some 30 percent of its 1994–96 disbursements) was initially channeled through the Holst Fund. As a consequence, a review of Canadian aid was undertaken in 1997. This resulted in a closer integration of aid and foreign policy (in particular, a greater emphasis on refugees to complement Canada's work as gavel holder of the multilateral Refugee Working Group), as well as the opening of a new Canadian representative office in Ramallah.

Interestingly, it is unclear whether showcase projects and an emphasis on political profile always have the desired effect. In one 1999 public opinion survey, Palestinians were asked to identify the donor that had made the largest contribution to the Palestinian economy. When compared with the relative level of donor disbursement, the data provide interesting insight into which actors have derived the most (political) "bangs" for their (developmental) "bucks" (figure 6.4).

In general, the public recognition of donors mirrored the relative level of donor disbursements, suggesting that bangs and bucks are closely linked—in other words, that public profile is largely a product of the extent of resources delivered on the ground. Interestingly, however, Japan's approval ratings outstripped even its already large aid effort, despite its relatively low-key political engagement and the fact that a large proportion of its program had been delivered through UNDP, UNRWA, the World Bank, and other multilateral intermediaries. This suggests that donor misgivings about obscuring their contributions through reliance on multilateral mechanisms may be misplaced. Also of interest were the relatively high profile of France relative to the size of its program and the relatively low profile of Germany relative to its. Here, the most likely explanation is that public perceptions of active French sympathy for Palestinian aspirations, and contrasting views of Germany as having a traditionally pro-Israeli orientation, may have colored public attitudes.

Figure 6.4. Palestinian Public Recognition of Donor Performance

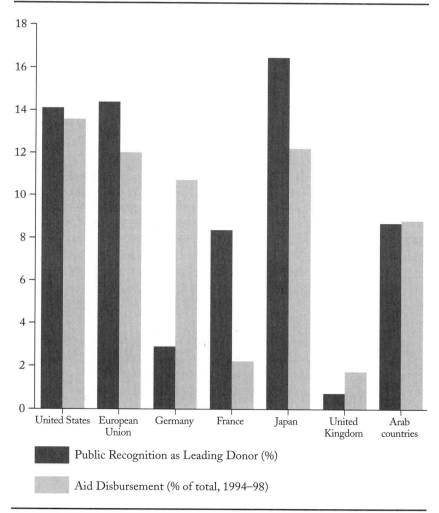

Source: CPRS, *Public Opinion Poll no. 39* (28–30 January 1999), archived at www.cprs-palestine.org/polls/99/poll39b.html.

As donors note, the mismatches that can occur between donor and Palestinian priorities can also be a function of weak internal agenda setting by the Palestinian Authority, which results in a multiplicity of programs and projects being proposed to donors without any clear sense of prioritization. Some observers suggested that some senior PA policymakers were inattentive to the planning process and indeed had a poor sense of what it was intended to achieve. There also remained problems with internal PA structures and mechanisms, despite the establishment of a PDP ministerial Steering Committee. This organizational confusion could find expression in a lack of coordination between senior MOPIC officials, between MOPIC's Gaza and West Bank offices, between MOPIC and the sectoral ministries, and between MOPIC and the Ministry of Finance. The result could be an extended list of projects compiled from among "wish lists" submitted by various PA ministries, rather than a cohesive, integrated, and clearly prioritized national plan.

The process also remained highly, and perhaps inevitably, politicized. The sometimes contentious issue of whether planning took place on a sectoral or ministry-by-ministry basis, for example, not only was a question of planning efficacy, but also had important implications for the relative resources and influence of bureaucracies and ministers. Preparation of the first PDP, for example, took place largely apart from the established budgetary planning process within the Finance Ministry. Conflict between the PA cabinet and the Palestinian Legislative Council over agenda setting—aggravated by such incidents as delays in submitting the PA budget and MOPIC's failure to consult the PLC before submitting the first PDP to donors—also reflected broader political and institutional struggles.

Finally, there was also Palestinian criticism of excessive interference by the World Bank in Palestinian priority setting. Some PA and donor officials accused the bank of being "heavy-handed" and even of writing documents in MOPIC's name. Bank officials frankly admitted, "The criticism for previous years that we were too involved is correct, though the PA had very limited capacity at that stage." In the case of the PDP, however, "in no way did we push priorities, project selection criteria, or other material issues" but instead helped organize donor input and assist the stylistic preparation of the final document and presentation.[86] The bank may have also been a convenient political target for some, and at least one MOPIC official sought to divert PLC criticism of his ministry in that alternate direction.

The complex process of both donor and PA agenda setting has occurred, moreover, against the backdrop of the perceived political needs of the peace process, most notably the need to stabilize the Palestinian Authority. Perhaps the clearest evidence of this is donor support for the Holst Fund through 1994–96, as well as support for emergency job creation in 1996–97. Neither of these activities fitted into the traditional framework of development assistance, and indeed from the perspective of most aid agencies they ordinarily would have been seen as wasteful or ineffective expenditures that encouraged dependency and did little to encourage sustainable growth. In the West Bank and Gaza, however, the more pressing imperative of political and social stability prevailed. In many ways, this tended to reflect the triumph of foreign ministry officials over their aid agency colleagues, particularly in the early and politically crucial years of the program. Of course, for the PA too a parallel process was at work, with projects driven not only by economic needs but also by political imperatives and the PA's desire to boost its domestic and international profile. A case in point was the PA's Bethlehem 2000 project (box 6.4).[87]

Yet as the aid program continued, a modus vivendi of sorts developed. Palestinian development planning continued to strengthen in many key regards, with the 1999–2003 Palestinian Development Plan a substantial improvement over the 1998–2001 version. And despite periodic irritations, tensions, and lack of coordination, both the PA and donors seem to have settled on a course with which all are fairly comfortable.

✦   ✦   ✦

What conclusions can be drawn about the impact of all this on the Palestinian economy and economic development? External assistance has not established a viable economic system for Palestine, which remains geographically fragmented and heavily dependent on Israel for trade, labor export, and many other things. The Palestinian economy has yet to develop clear areas of comparative advantage and remains highly vulnerable to external shocks. There have been serious problems of institutional development. The PA's large public-sector payroll, irregularities in its fiscal regime, and problems of corruption and off-the-books financing (through the monopolies) have all arisen, in part, for political reasons. But whatever their short-term political utility to the regime, they all represent legacies that will weaken future economic development efforts.

However, it is important also to recognize that the West Bank and Gaza have acquired what one UNSCO report referred to as the "pieces" of the economic and social development "mosaic."[88] Transportation, communications, waste, and water infrastructures have improved. Some PA ministries have achieved very credible levels of institutionalization and efficiency. Most social services have generally kept pace with the very rapid rate of population growth and in some cases have even shown modest improvement in service delivery. Other capacities have been built or strengthened. Although these modest successes were generally obscured by the very negative economic impact of closure and political maneuvering, they were evident in other ways. With the reduction in Israeli use of closure, the Palestinian economy did show real growth in 1998, above and beyond the rate of population increase. The PA itself estimated that annual growth of 2.2 percent in GNP per capita could be achieved under conditions of improved mobility for goods and labor.[89] Among the public, there were also some slight signs of economic

Box 6.4. Build It and They Shall Come? Bethlehem 2000

The Bethlehem 2000 Project always had an important economic purpose: to put in place a tourist infrastructure that would allow the Palestinians to reap substantial gain from the millennial celebrations of up to 2 million Christian tourists in the Holy Land in the year 2000. Simultaneously, the project has a clear political appeal to the Palestinians, drawing international attention to their situation and offsetting earlier Israeli celebrations of Jerusalem's 3,000th year.

To this end, around $130 million was allocated to the project by the PA, together with a comparable amount of private-sector investment. The enormous task, however, was complicated by substantial infrastructure needs, political rivalries, a weak Ministry of Tourism, and a very complex local political environment. The latter included no fewer than thirty-seven local authorities (plus three refugee camps) serving a population of fewer than 150,000 in the Bethlehem district, as well as sometimes rival religious authorities and delicate relationships between predominately Christian and Muslim population centers. Inefficiencies and infighting also plagued aspects of the project. In late 1999, one PA official noted that "except for meetings and pledges, virtually nothing has been completed."

Moreover, as with other Palestinian development initiatives, two other potential challenges hovered over the project: the threat of closure interrupting the movement of tourists and competition from the Israeli tourist industry (which reportedly invested some $650 million in its already much better developed tourist infrastructure in anticipation of the tourist boom). Officially, Israel welcomed the arrival of Christian pilgrims—but it also expressed disquiet at the political symbolism involved, complaining that a "purely religious occasion has been cynically manipulated in order to advance a narrow political interest." The political sensitivities around the issue could also be seen in a resolution adopted by the UN General Assembly in support of the project in November 1998. This called on Israel to ensure "freedom of movement" around the "Palestinian city of Bethlehem"—a compromise wording accepted after Israeli objections to "Bethlehem, Palestine" in the original resolution.

Politics made itself felt in a more comical way too. When U.S. president Bill Clinton briefly visited Bethlehem in December 1998, local officials prepared by quickly repaving many of the streets in the city center that had earlier been ripped up during construction. As soon as the president left, the new pavement was ripped up again so that work could continue.

improvement and greater optimism: in one January 1999 opinion survey, 38.9 percent of Palestinians reported that their economic condition had improved in the past three years (23.1 percent said it had worsened), while 56.3 percent were optimistic about their economic futures (26.2 percent were pessimistic).[90] In the longer term, however, sustainable development in Palestine ultimately depends on the outcome of the peace process itself and the shape of any future Palestinian state.

As the preceding discussion has shown, the allocation of development assistance in Palestine across various sectors has been a complex and dynamic process. It has been shaped by economic conditions, but economic conditions themselves that have often been closely linked to a highly changeable—and even unstable—political environment. The establishment of the PA (and hence the shift from transitional support to long-term investment) took longer than expected, both because of delays in negotiating the interim agreements and because of internal problems of Palestinian institution building. The economic crisis in 1996–97, caused by closure, also caused a diversion of donor funds away from public investment and into such areas as budget support and emergency employment. In short, development planners have been asked to make allocation decisions in a planning context in which uncertainty has been the norm.

On top of all this, the allocation of external assistance has also been driven by a complex array of factors, many of them unrelated to either peacebuilding or economic development. For donors, considerations of political profile and economic interest have often loomed large. For the PA, bureaucratic politics and the sorts of diplomatic and regime imperatives identified in chapter 5 have been prominent considerations. In many sectors, a vicious circle of sorts developed, where the most efficient ministries secured outside aid, while those most in need of assistance were least able to get it. In other cases, donors sent mixed messages: for example, the tensions between counterterrorism measures and human rights in the security sector, or the attitude of donors to the role of NGOs and Palestinian civil society. In the latter case, the local NGO community, under pressure from diminished funding and the threat of PA hegemony, searched for its niche within the broader context of Palestinian state building and social development. Finally, development planning was often serendipitous and idiosyncratic, shaped by the right (or wrong) people being in the right (or wrong) places at the right (or wrong) time.

For some, this may present a shocking picture of inefficiency. For those with field experience in conflict and postconflict settings, it probably looks familiar. As has been emphasized throughout this study, the trick is to search not for a *perfect* system—which does not exist or perhaps exists only in perfect contexts—but for *better* ways of undertaking development assistance in war-to-peace transitions. Recognition of the underlying dynamics at work, of the sorts identified here in the Palestinian case, is an essential and fundamental element in doing so. Consequently, and by way of conclusion, it is to the broader lessons of the Palestinian case that this study now turns.

7

Conclusion

Strengthening Peacebuilding

M AY 1999 WOULD PROVE a critical month for the Middle East peace process. On May 4 the Oslo Agreement expired, and the crucial permanent-status negotiations between Israel and the Palestinians had yet to take place. On May 17 Israeli voters decisively elected a new Labor-led government, headed by Ehud Barak. Because large differences remained between the Israeli and Palestinian positions on borders, settlements, Jerusalem, refugees, and other contentious issues, any negotiations would prove very difficult. However, with the change in government, the negotiating process itself had been revived.

Some months earlier, in November 1998, ministerial and other senior representatives of the international donor community had met in Washington to pledge support for another five years of transitional assistance for the West Bank and Gaza. Their comments spoke volumes on the difficulties and delays that had been encountered, just as their very presence underscored the important role that aid had to play in supporting the search for peace. As U.S. president Bill Clinton noted:

> Despite our best efforts since 1993, an honest assessment would lead us to the conclusion that we have not realized all our intentions. There has been too little tangible improvement in the lives of the Palestinian people. Per capita income is down. Unemployment is too high. Living conditions are extremely difficult.
>
> At the outset of the next phase of the peace process, we must candidly acknowledge that we have to change these circumstances. No peace stands a chance of lasting if it does not deliver real results to ordinary people. Our challenge today, therefore, is to do more to deliver these results and to do it sooner rather than later.

U.S. secretary of state Madeleine Albright also noted that "progress to date has not been sufficient. Despite all the efforts of nations represented in this room, the lives of most Palestinians continue to be uncertain and difficult." This, she warned, "has made peace and security harder to achieve. For hardship and hopelessness are parents to extremism and violence." Arafat, not surprisingly, directly blamed Israel's policy of closure for the deterioration of economic circumstances.[1]

As noted at the outset of this volume, the importance of the donor effort in Palestine makes it a valuable case to study. The donors themselves have periodically recognized the importance of reflecting on their efforts, so as to avoid past mistakes and build on success. However, the sensitivity of the task tended to inhibit this. Individually, internal evaluations of previous efforts tend to soft-pedal weaknesses and in any event have rarely been circulated in public. Collectively, it was—and will be—difficult for either multilateral agencies or the collective structures of donor coordination to broach many of the politically sensitive issues surrounding the aid effort with full candor. This has made external assessment all the more important.

As also noted at the outset, learning lessons is important for comparative purposes too. International assistance to the West Bank and Gaza stands out as one of the largest, and most complex, cases of post–Cold War peacebuilding. Although the context for this assistance has been unique—indeed, one of the recurrent themes throughout this study has been the fundamental ways in which the particular dynamics of the peace process, regional politics, and Palestinian socioeconomic realities affected donor efforts—it is no more "unique" than any other case. Contextual factors will inevitably loom large in any war-to-peace transition. Yet all of the underlying challenges—mobilizing adequate levels of assistance, coordinating such assistance in effective ways, delivering assistance in a timely fashion, and allocating assistance in useful ways—also remain (box 7.1).[2]

MOBILIZING ASSISTANCE

The Palestinian case reveals the unsurprising finding that donor mobilization is a function of political, strategic, and economic interests. It also underscores, however, the importance of broader ideological attitudes toward aid on the part of donor governments and their societies. As a result, there can be wide variation in the relative "generosity" of different members of the international community. The Nordic (or "like-minded") donors stand out as particularly generous contributors to reconstruction in the West Bank and Gaza, whereas the United States has provided a surprisingly small share of assistance in view of its economic size and global leadership.

However, while these may represent the major factors determining how much aid is offered by whom, the Palestinian case also suggests that *periodic donor meetings* can be very useful in mobilizing resources (box 7.2).[3]

Box 7.1. Learning Lessons

In learning lessons from the Palestinian case, it is important not to do so in isolation. Recent years have spawned a growing number of studies intended to improve the provision of international assistance to war-torn and transitional countries. It is striking, however, how often reviews of specific programs or cases do not attempt to explicitly refine previous work, whether by confirming, modifying, qualifying, or rejecting previous guidelines. Not to do so, of course, is to risk constantly reinventing the wheel (or local aid coordination committee).

For the purpose of this study, the most important points of comparison are the *DAC Guidelines on Conflict, Peace, and Development Cooperation* (1997) and the World Bank's *Post-Conflict Reconstruction: The Role of the World Bank* (1997). The former, drawn up by the Development Assistance Committee of the OECD, comprises the collective wisdom and assembled "best practices" of bilateral Western donors. The *DAC Guidelines* make no explicit use of lessons learned from the Palestinian case. The latter (a restatement of the bank's earlier "Framework for World Bank Involvement in Post-Conflict Reconstruction") does draw heavily from the Palestinian and Bosnian cases.

Other useful points of comparison include the Overseas Development Council's study *Making Peace Work* (1996), the UN Research Institute for Social Development's War-Torn Societies Project (1998), and the ongoing work of the Humanitarianism and War Project (Brown University), the Pledges of Aid project at the Center on International Cooperation (New York University), the Peace Implementation Network (Fafo), and the International Development Research Centre (Ottawa), many of which were cited in the first chapter of this volume.

Learning lessons, of course, is not solely a function of teaching them: organizations and individuals must internalize them too and modify their future behavior appropriately. The available evidence suggests that this does not always occur: as Larry Minear of the Humanitarianism and War Project has noted, agencies have often revealed "lackluster learning curves." Institutional inertia, the absence of incentives for constructive criticism, inappropriate mechanisms of accountability, staff rotation, budget cutbacks, the pressures of events, and changing priorities all represent barriers—barriers beyond the scope of this study, but very important nonetheless.

Such conferences are useful in several respects. First, they facilitate donor-recipient contact and do so in a less labor-intensive and time-consuming manner than multiple bilateral consultations. At donor meetings, recipients can mount their

---

Box 7.2. Fund-Raising

The issue of mobilizing assistance for war-to-peace transitions has thus far received surprisingly little attention. In general, existing analyses tend to focus on delays in implementing aid or imbalances in sectoral distribution, rather than on mobilization of funds.

The *DAC Guidelines,* for example, suggest in passing that the establishment of an International Committee on Reconstruction of Cambodia "played a catalytic role" in generating resources for that country's transition but provide no sense of how or why it played this role or what broader lessons should be learned. Bilateral agencies, of course, might be reluctant to address such issues—after all, the funds for peacebuilding come from their own pockets, often diverted from either more pressing humanitarian assistance or more sustainable economic development.

There has been more attention to the issue by multilateral agencies, in the context of mobilizing resources for humanitarian emergencies (including war) through consolidated appeals and other mechanisms. Yet the World Bank too devotes little attention to the issue, despite the very substantial fund-raising role played by bank staff in the West Bank and Gaza.

Some of the most useful work in this regard has emerged from academic studies. The Humanitarianism and War Project has explored the complex relationship between donor mobilization and media coverage, suggesting that intensive early media coverage increases the pressure to be seen to be doing something in a high-profile case, while later coverage is less frequent and often more critical, perhaps eroding support for aid programs. In the Palestinian case, both effects of the media can be seen, although the phases are often indistinct and overlapping.

The Pledges of Aid project has focused specifically on donor mobilization. With regard to the role of donor conferences, it suggests that some recipients (such as South Africa) decry these as "begging bowl excursions," while others (such as Bosnia and Cambodia) find them to be useful. The difference appears to hinge on the relative need for assistance. The government of South Africa has exerted substantial control over incoming assistance, declining that which does not fall within its area of priority and requiring donors to engage in bilateral consultations with the government. By contrast, where there is greater desire for assistance (as in Palestine and Bosnia), recipients seem more likely to value donor conferences.

best possible appeal for assistance to multiple representatives simultaneously. Second, conferences generate a certain degree of internal and external pressure on donors to mobilize resources. Officials are reluctant to arrive at such meetings with nothing to offer, and political competition may actually create incentives for greater mobilization (thus offsetting the danger of "free riding"). Finally, conferences provide a useful opportunity for what can best be termed "political theater," enabling donors to advertise their support for the peace process both at home and in the region. The close connection between high-level donor conferences and critical events in the peace process (for example, the October 1993 pledging conference, immediately after the Oslo Agreement; the January 1996 ministerial conference, after the Interim Agreement and before Palestinian elections; and the November 1998 pledging conference, after the Wye River Memorandum) is evident in the Palestinian case.

One drawback of large, well-publicized donor conferences is that they can exacerbate *problems of pledge inflation,* in which donors—eager to maximize the political "bang" for their financial "buck"—exaggerate their generosity (through double counting, the rollover of uncommitted funds in subsequent pledges, and a general overselling of what aid can achieve). This in turn generates excessive or unrealistic local expectations on the part of recipient governments and populations, who believe that they have been promised more than donors are really willing to provide. Certainly, the Palestinians felt that they were initially led to expect more assistance, more quickly delivered, and more directly and flexibly allocated. This created political tensions and suspicions. Unrealistic expectations were fed not only by donors but also by the Palestinian Authority, which has sometimes exaggerated aid or unfairly blamed donors for its own political purposes.

Because of this, it is important that once pledges have been made, processes are put in place to ensure *close monitoring of aid pledges, commitments, and disbursements.* This reduces the level of donor/recipient misperception and contributes to greater donor compliance. Aid monitoring also provides an opportunity for a periodic "status report" or "reality check" by the donor community. With regard to assistance to the Palestinians, a combination of effective tracking of aid (first by the AHLC–World Bank, later by MOPIC), coupled with a clear five-year pledge period, facilitated measurement, monitoring, and comparison of donor pledges.

Certainly, the data collected in the Palestinian case were never fully complete nor fully accurate. Moreover, donors continued to try to inflate pledges, notably again at the November 1998 Washington pledging conference. There, some countries included non–West Bank/Gaza UNRWA budget contributions to increase their totals, and others undoubtedly included uncommitted funds from 1994–98. Such was the confusion that, a month after the meeting, MOPIC officials admitted that they still were "not too confident about the additional figures of pledges that have come out from that conference" because "information remains sketchy."[4]

Still, MOPIC's overall reporting compares favorably with aid management in many transitional developing countries and represents a substantial achievement given the size and complexity of the donor effort. In many other cases of transitional assistance, where data are lacking, the pressures on donors to deliver are correspondingly reduced.

Finally, in the Palestinian case there has been mixed evidence of donor fatigue. While the (apparent) magnitude of pledges made at the November 1998 Washington donors conference was quite high, actual disbursements in 1998–99 were down. Here, however, one should be careful about drawing too many conclusions: the Arab-Israeli conflict has continued to rate high in both strategic importance and media attention, both of which are powerful spurs to mobilization. Were either of these factors to wane, it is likely that donor interest would wane too.

Burden Sharing

One of the most interesting sets of findings to emerge from the Palestinian case concerns the issue of burden sharing. The substantial variation of donor generosity has already been noted. Obviously, this variation has implications for the total level of resources available to support a war-to-peace transition. However, it also has other, secondary effects. In particular, *inequitable burden sharing among donors can inhibit donor coordination* by creating tensions over "leadership" of the aid effort. Although adequately managed for most of the period since 1993, such tensions periodically surfaced in the Palestinian case between the United States and the European Union and have sometimes hampered the effectiveness of donor coordination mechanisms. They were particularly evident once more in the run-up to the November 1998 donors conference. EU diplomats, who had declared their intention to assume a "leading role" at the meeting,[5] were disappointed to learn that it would be chaired by the formal cosponsors of the Madrid peace process: namely, the United States and Russia. In view of Russia's marginal political role and financial insolvency, this decision was undoubtedly galling to the Europeans. To smooth ruffled EU feathers, Washington offered a number of secondary procedural concessions, including a larger-than-normal EU delegation and a place at the end-of-meeting press conference.

Can strong aid monitoring reduce the scope of donor inequalities? Certainly, such monitoring increases transparency, and that in itself can make "free riding" more difficult. However, to date monitoring has almost invariably tracked the absolute amounts of aid provided by donors, not their relative generosity. As a result, donors (and recipients) themselves can have very different perceptions of the relative burdens assumed, as well as the proportion of aid that has actually been delivered—despite everyone having access to precisely the same numbers on donor pledges, commitments, and disbursements. U.S. officials, for example, tended to underestimate the gap separating U.S. generosity from that of the European Union. Western officials tended to underestimate the relative degree of Arab commitment. The Palestinians tended (for political reasons) to hold a more positive assessment of EU aid delivery—despite the fact that, when the European Investment Bank was included in the European totals, there was little difference between EU and U.S. rates of aid implementation.

Could this problem be alleviated, in Palestine or elsewhere, by the adoption of some explicit burden-sharing formula? It is doubtful. The existence of an agreed-upon burden-sharing formula in the levying of United Nations general dues, for example, has not prevented major disputes over this issue, including the large U.S. arrears. Given the variation in national interests and in national aid policy, it is difficult to imagine donors agreeing on such a formula in connection with any case.

Could this problem be reduced by explicit attention to burden-sharing indicators, in the context of more stringent aid monitoring? In this case it is questionable whether such efforts would secure the cooperation of the less generous donors. Indeed, in the early years of the Palestinian aid effort, even the summary donor matrices themselves were officially not available to reporters or the public. In some other contexts, notably that of Cambodia, donors have explicitly blocked the distribution of aid monitoring reports so as to avoid embarrassment. Multilateral agencies and recipient governments—the two sets of actors most involved in aid monitoring—are in no position to antagonize current or potential donors by highlighting their shortcomings.

NGOs, academics, and journalists are somewhat better placed to do this. So too is a lead donor that combines leadership with diplomatic clout. The dynamics of Cold War defense expenditures neatly illustrates the point: within NATO, smaller countries with lower rates of military spending often came under political pressure from the United States, Germany, and Britain to assume a larger share of the alliance's military costs. This pressure was possible because of the diplomatic weight of these countries, as well as their leading military roles. In the case of contemporary aid, however, the obvious lead donor—the United States—may lack the required credibility when its own share of the peacebuilding effort lags behind that of others. In the Palestinian case, constant implicit and explicit European criticism of U.S. efforts may well have played a significant role in the subsequent U.S. decision to substantially increase its aid in 1999.

COORDINATING ASSISTANCE

The conventional aid coordination mechanism in many developing countries is the World Bank Consultative Group, meeting periodically to harmonize assistance efforts. International aid to the West Bank and Gaza, however, spawned a

Box 7.3. Local Ownership

Both the *DAC Guidelines* ("local ownership should be given the maximum effect possible") and the War-Torn Societies Project *Summary Report* ("the promotion of national and local ownership of external assistance projects can, at times, become an objective in itself since it contributes in important ways to building local capacities") recognize that recipients must play a leading role in shaping aid coordination, priorities, and implementation. However—and this was clearly an important issue to arise in the Palestinian case, as noted—none of the existing recommendations on peacebuilding really addresses the trade-offs between local ownership and rapid implementation in contexts of weak local capacity. These must be faced up to explicitly, rather than swept away under the conceptual carpet of "host country ownership."

In Palestine, a more participatory coordination mechanism in 1994–95 would undoubtedly have slowed the delivery of aid. Thus, although the PA may have grown to resent the perceived imperialism of donors, UNSCO, and the World Bank, it was perhaps for the best. At the same time, international donors should have been clearer on how the transition could be made from these emergency circumstances to the more desirable situation of a leading PA role. In other words, the important lesson from the Palestinian case appears to be that donor coordination mechanisms should have, from the outset, processes built into them for greater devolution of planning and coordination functions. Moreover, it is important to *enhance the capacity of recipients to participate in, learn from, and ultimately manage coordination mechanisms,* a "common learning process" noted

host of coordination mechanisms: the AHLC, JLC, LACC, and Sectoral Working Groups, as well as the coordinating roles assumed by the World Bank, UNSCO, and MOPIC. The effectiveness of these was mixed.

Many of the findings in this study echo lessons that have been pointed to elsewhere. The *DAC Guidelines,* the World Bank, and the War-Torn Societies Project (WSP) have all emphasized the importance of timely access to flexible resources. The *DAC Guidelines* stress the importance of leadership by one or more respected international actors in donor coordination and the need to provide adequate resources for coordination mechanisms; the bank has now given considerable thought to its potential role in this regard. All three highlight the importance of mechanisms for field-level consultation. In other regards, however, the Palestinian case suggests the need to expand on, or qualify, certain prior policy recommendations (boxes 7.3, 7.4).

Box 7.3. *(cont.)*

by the WSP but not by the World Bank or DAC. This wasn't really done in conjunction with the initial LACC-SWG structure, thus fostering growing Palestinian doubts about the value of these.

   Another problem to arise from the concept of "host country ownership" of the coordination and developmental processes arises from the inherently political character of development assistance. This is true in all circumstances, but especially in contexts of peacebuilding. As the WSP notes, this can turn "the most trivial administrative task into a political act." To the extent that hosts play larger roles in donor coordination and priority setting, they are likely to increasingly assert their political priorities (regime consolidation, shaping ongoing negotiations, and so forth) in place of those of donors and alongside other economic and social objectives. There is little way to avoid this—but it is possible to recognize and be prepared for its inevitability. As will be noted, the Palestinian case also underscores that the politics of aid coordination exists not only among donors and between donors and recipients, but also within recipients themselves. In this regard, the *DAC Guidelines* fail to devote adequate attention to these issues; in contexts of bureaucratic and political fragmentation or rivalry, "host countries" cannot be thought of as a single entity with which "coordination" is undertaken. On the contrary, local actors may compete fiercely (as did PECDAR and MOPIC for a while) for pride of place in coordination mechanisms. Yet again, to be forewarned is to be prepared for the possible consequences of all this.

What (More or Less) Worked . . .

On the positive side, the Palestinian experience suggests that *coordination mechanisms need to be at both top/external and local/sectoral levels.* High-level coordination (the AHLC and the CG) was important to provide some overall sense of direction and to address fundamental constraints. Conversely, local meetings (the LACC and the SWGs) had the advantage of involving those local aid officials who actually knew what was happening on the ground, as opposed to the sometimes less well informed diplomats and senior aid officials who attended high-level meetings. The Palestinian experience also suggests that *both inclusive and exclusive mechanisms are useful.* Inclusive mechanisms—such as the CG and LACC—give all donors some sense of participation in the process and allow a broad airing of analyses and views. More limited groups—such as the AHLC and JLC—bring

Box 7.4. Donor Coordination and "Strategic Frameworks"

In discussing donor coordination, both the *DAC Guidelines* and the World Bank's *Framework* stress the need for "shared coherent policies" and "delineated roles" (World Bank) or a "common strategic framework" that "defines the underlying political, economic and social determinants and provides the context and logic for a rational allocation of resources" (DAC).

In Palestine there was a profusion of analytical paperwork from the AHLC, the LACC, the World Bank, UNSCO, and MOPIC. None of this, however, really constituted any sort of "strategic framework." The World Bank's Emergency Assistance Program was intended as such a framework, and it (and its supporting six volumes) represented an impressive contribution. However, there is little evidence that it was a major determining factor in donor programming. The subsequent PPIP and PDP were somewhat more effective as priority-setting exercises but actually offered much less in the way of systematic analysis. A number of individual reports offered perceptive insights into Palestinian needs and potentialities, but few donor officials read most of them. Indeed, only a small handful of those involved in the aid effort in late 1998 had read more than one-tenth of the analytical, agenda-setting "framework" and similar strategic material that had been produced over the preceding five years. Instead, the aid effort was characterized by a broad donor consensus on some aspects of assistance (for example, budgetary support, as represented by the Tripartite Action Plan), an increasing semblance of priority setting in some respects, common concern at common points in time about common issues (for example, mitigating closure in 1996–97, a growing emphasis on private-sector growth in 1997–99), and a far more complex (and perhaps much less "rational") process of agenda setting for other dimensions and at other times.

Would a common strategic framework have helped? Perhaps. Would it have been possible? Probably not—or at least not in any very meaningful sense.

The Palestinian-Israeli case was highly politicized, both internationally and domestically within donor countries. It is difficult to imagine donor countries agreeing on any substantial "situation analysis" and "program response" in the sense called for in the *DAC Guidelines*. It is even more difficult imagining them doing so within a time frame appropriate to rapidly changing circumstances on the ground. To the extent that something

Box 7.4. *(cont.)*

called a "strategic plan" might have been developed and agreed to, it would necessarily have been a lowest-common-denominator exercise, so vague as to shape donor behavior only marginally.

Instead, best efforts were probably directed toward preparing analytical materials for those who would utilize them, minimizing the consequences of weaker coordination, responding to particular needs (for example, periodic situation analyses by UNSCO and the World Bank), fund-raising for emergency circumstances, and filling gaps. Terje Larsen's tenure at UNSCO (and his effective presentations at donor meetings) represented this sort of "real-time" strategizing at its best. In the longer term, the consolidation of MOPIC, the PDP, and other institutions of Palestinian aid coordination were the most valuable contributions toward a more regularized process.

None of this is to say that clarity of purpose is unimportant. On the contrary, in humanitarian crises it is essential for saving lives, and in more stable environments it is an important component of "doing development right." Moreover, the *DAC Guidelines* themselves recognize that a strategic framework ought to be "a dynamic instrument mapping out the transition from relief to longer-term development" rather than a static list of projects. However, the Palestinian case indicates that such a "framework" might sometimes be less a function of an agreed, written document than of putting in place the appropriate set of institutions and individuals and forging the most productive possible interaction among them.

For the World Bank, the appropriate structures were trust funds and multilateral projects, into which donor resources could flow to support joint objectives. These worked well in the case of the Holst Fund, but less well in other cases, largely because such projects seemed less politically attractive to donors than bilateral initiatives. This further suggests that the political incentives to coordinate or cofinance need to be deliberately built into projects and structures, so as to encourage donors to use these mechanisms. In other words, it is not simply enough to identify "best practices" and hope that subsequent initiatives will borrow from them. Rather, opportunities must be structured in such a way that "best practices" also tend to be the "best choices," selected by aid participants regardless of the degree of selflessness (or selfishness) exhibited by their aid programs.

together the key actors in smaller fora more suited to effective decision making. In short, designing an architecture for aid coordination involves identifying the critical stakeholders, deciding which kinds of actors and decision makers are needed for different kinds of coordination functions, and determining the optimal size, frequency, and format of meetings. Coordination is also a hugely political task and deeply affected by political context—a theme that runs throughout this assessment of peacebuilding in Palestine.

Architecture and political sensitivity are not enough, however. In the background to the Palestinian aid effort was implicit U.S. leadership of both the diplomatic/peace process and aid coordination. Many aspects of this leadership caused grumbling from fellow donors and the Palestinians alike, and it was certainly the case that the United States could be insensitive at times to the interests and concerns of others. It is not clear, however, that there was any real alternative. Moreover, for all its shortcomings, the United States' dual role did at least ensure that both political and economic activity would proceed at a similar pace.

The Norwegian role is also noteworthy. Although Norway cannot be said to have offered enough diplomatic muscle to have truly "led" the process, its tireless work was essential, particularly amid the uncertainties of 1994. Norway's example is one that should be studied by similar states seeking to make a "soft power" contribution out of proportion to their size.

Both the World Bank and UNSCO have been moderately successful in promoting a coherent international aid effort, but they have also demonstrated shortcomings. The bank was initially slow to respond, although its responsiveness was greatly enhanced by the devolution of authority into the field (a point that both the *DAC Guidelines* and the World Bank note). Indeed, this latter aspect of its operations provides a strong lesson about the importance of providing local agency officials with the power, flexibility, and resources necessary to do their jobs. UNSCO suffered from a lack of any meaningful line authority over the UN agencies it was meant to "coordinate" and from its small size and weight relative to UNRWA and UNDP. This was a problem bound up with the relative autonomy of agencies within the broader UN system, which continues to bedevil interagency cooperation.

It is also clear that the *quality of donor coordination mechanisms depends a great deal on the quality of the coordinators.* In UNSCO, in the World Bank, among donors, and within the Palestinian Authority, key individuals have been hugely important.

. . . And What Didn't

On the negative side, it is not clear that coordinating mechanisms in Palestine *gave the recipients sufficient influence in the coordination process* (box 7.3). In the

West Bank and Gaza, donors often found it more expeditious to act unilaterally than to await the development of Palestinian capacity in aid management. Although unilateral action may have been justified at the outset of the aid effort by the urgency of the situation, it became increasingly less appropriate as time went on. Overall, the entire coordinating structure was probably too slow to react to and accommodate the growth of Palestinian institutional capacity. The Palestinian experience also underscores that *donor and recipient coordination structures should be in harmony.* This may seem self-evident, but coordination institutions can easily take on a life and momentum (or inertia) of their own. In the case of Palestine, the LACC-SWG structure was increasingly out of sync with the emerging Palestinian Authority planning mechanisms for the Palestinian Development Plan. Indeed, it wasn't until 1998–99 that the required changes in donor coordination mechanisms were considered, by which point these mechanisms themselves had largely been reduced to a role of limited information sharing.

Another problem in the West Bank and Gaza was *the unfortunate tendency of donor coordination meetings to become information-sharing meetings,* rather than either planning-coordination structures or venues for real sustained dialogue on developmental directions and obstacles. This problem arose from both the framework for meetings and competition or unilateralism among donors. Of course, even information sharing has a role and is an essential part of organizing assistance. Yet it is striking that one senior and very experienced donor official declared that a long group dinner in Ramallah—held to discuss a draft version of this study—represented a fuller dialogue on development issues than had occurred at any official donor meeting he had attended.[6]

All of these shortcomings were identified by MOPIC itself in an internal review of the first five years of the aid effort. This review called for a greater role for MOPIC in managing the external aid program and greater effort to avoid ad hoc project identification; it also urged the international donor community to refer to the PDP as its primary reference for development programming in Palestine.[7]

Not all of the responsibility for weakness in coordination could be laid at the door of donors; at times, the Palestinian Authority could have done more to make use of, and reform, the institutions of donor coordination. Moreover, poor coordination and turf wars within the Palestinian Authority—notably between PECDAR and MOPIC, but also between central and line/sectoral ministries, among different divisions (or bureaucrats) of the same ministry, and between Gaza- and West Bank–based offices—have hampered interaction with donors as well as effective internal PA policymaking. Competition between local NGOs and the Palestinian Authority has been another unfortunate feature of aid management. Some Palestinian officials clearly favored tighter controls on NGO activity, whether in the interest of efficiency or because the NGOs were seen as political rivals. Conversely, many NGOs showed little desire to cooperate with the Palestinian Authority, either because they feared government expansion into formerly NGO-dominated policy sectors or because of political differences with the Fateh-dominated Palestinian Authority. Donors tended to support the position of NGOs, but inconsistently and unevenly.

Finally, it is clear that in Palestine *donor conditionality has generally proved ineffectual.* Although some conditionality may have blunted the Palestinian Authority's tendency to adopt a sometimes domineering role in local economy through expanding bureaucracy and semipublic monopolies, the Palestinians have usually been seen by donors as too vulnerable to be punished for noncompliance. Moreover, there is a potential contradiction between conditionality and host country ownership of the development process (although in the Palestinian case, neither has been implemented well). Conversely, Israeli actions—a major factor in the weakness of the Palestinian economy—have not been subject to sanction or conditionality because the Israeli position is too strong. The latter, of course, can also be seen as a failure of political will, notably in the continuing pro-Israeli tilt in U.S. Middle East policy. One should be careful in drawing too many general conclusions from this, however. In less sensitive regions and less salient transitions, donors may well wield conditionality with greater frequency and to greater effect.

DELIVERING ASSISTANCE

Analytically, the case of the West Bank and Gaza illustrates the methodological problems involved in tracking disbursements and suggests the difficulty of comparing the delivery of assistance across cases. In general, however, it can be concluded that—despite a slow start—*the record in Palestine is comparatively good.* By the end of 1998 a large portion of 1994–98 aid had been disbursed or committed.

One reason for this was the Holst Fund, which proved to be an extremely effective mechanism for disbursing funds to the Palestinian Authority in a timely fashion and for supporting the critical task of Palestinian institution building. Indeed, it is a mechanism that deserves emulation in other comparable cases, as the World Bank itself has recognized. This success is in some ways ironic, given the general unpopularity of the Holst Fund among donors who would have preferred to support visible long-term development projects rather than to facilitate less visible short-term budget assistance. The unusual role of UNRWA and UNSCO in the payment of police salaries during the initial establishment of the Palestinian Authority also represents precisely the right sort of adaptability needed to meet the challenges of transition.

Conversely, other mechanisms have been less successful. *Loans and investment guarantees have proved particularly ineffectual,* especially when granted through agencies (OPIC, the European Investment Bank, the IFC) whose regulations and operating procedures are ill suited to the unstable and time-sensitive imperatives of peacebuilding. Although some funds are probably better than none, such support should not be seen as a substitute for much more useful and effective grant and soft loan assistance and can in fact aggravate the problem of unmet host country expectations. Many *multilateral initiatives were also less effective than they might have been,* despite the inherent desirability of single coherent programs. Part of the problem here was the initially slow pace of action by the World Bank, which both slowed implementation and deterred some donor interest. However, much of the problem was also one of marketing this mechanism to donors in such a way as to offset the competing attractions of high-profile bilateral donor initiatives.

With regard to those factors that have slowed or otherwise constrained the delivery of assistance, *Israeli policies stand out as having a particularly negative effect,* equaling or exceeding the combined benefits of all donor assistance. Closure has been the most evident and costly of these, but other actions (such as slow port clearances and permit delays) have also had a debilitating effect on the flow of assistance. Moreover, at no point did donors develop any coherent strategy for addressing such policies and actions other than through bilateral representations and occasional (carefully worded) joint statements. If there is a striking failure in peacebuilding in Palestine, this is it. It is a failure, moreover, rooted in a lack of political will, as well as in the lack of leverage by all donors over Israeli policy. More generally, this issue, among others, highlights the fact that *domestic politics within donor countries can have effects on the timely and effective delivery of donor assistance.* This effect varies from donor to donor and probably from case to case. However, the United States seems peculiarly vulnerable to this, which raises larger questions about the capacity of the United States to undertake economic peacebuilding.

It is also evident that *problems of Palestinian institution building also slowed the delivery of assistance.* Some of these were perhaps unavoidable, given the nature of the transition; others might have been averted. In assessing these problems, it is important to understand the political dynamics (such as the neopatrimonial strategies of political management) that may underlie them. This is not to recommend that donors blithely accept whatever political machinations recipient governments may produce. It is, however, to emphasize yet again that *for transitional assistance, the context is always inherently political.* Donors should not be naive. Rather, they should try to understand and anticipate such factors and to help *foster the process of institution and capacity building,* even when it goes outside the traditional job descriptions of aid agencies and officials. Indeed, responding effectively to the complexities of host country politics and the weaknesses of host country institutions is a fundamental element of effective reconstruction and peacebuilding.

Finally, as in virtually all aspects of the aid process, in the timely delivery of assistance *the quality of key individuals and the flexibility of institutions were critical* (box 7.5).

ALLOCATING ASSISTANCE

The experience of the West Bank and Gaza demonstrates that *a variety of factors shape the allocation of donor assistance,* with the donors' desire to raise their political profile and advance their economic interests ranking high among these. While this may be unavoidable, it is also important to maintain focus on *the fundamentals of transitional assistance: political stabilization and economic reconstruction and development.* Given the uncertain environment that they face, donors must build flexibility into their programs and even then "expect the unexpected."

Examination of the Palestinian case also underscores *the need for common donor-recipient agenda setting.* The value of such agenda setting has already been highlighted in previous discussions of donor coordination, but it is worth reiterating that the recipient is by far the most important element. Accordingly, donor assistance must aim at *developing the agenda-setting capacity of host countries.* In the absence of such capacity, donor efforts become even more uncoordinated and potentially mismatched to local needs and circumstances.

As noted earlier, there has been substantial criticism of the short-term nature of much international assistance to Palestine, with its focus on budget support and emergency employment generation rather than on long-term productive investment. This study, however, suggests that both the Holst Fund and the emergency employment programs were politically necessary stopgap measures. Security assistance was also very important, although donors tended to exhibit a schizophrenic concern for both counterterrorism and human rights with little thought on how the two might best be accomplished in tandem. The NGO sector has suffered substantially, and perhaps excessively, from a post-Oslo reallocation of donor resources. The World Bank's efforts to counteract some of this reallocation were unusual and praiseworthy, even if they generated some suspicion on the ground. It is clear that technical assistance is needed, but it must be more carefully provided. To date, the provision of technical assistance has been donor driven and often ill suited to local circumstances.

As the political and economic situation stabilizes, more resources must be directed toward investment. Unfortunately, stabilization of the situation was largely beyond the control of donors (or, for that matter, the Palestinian Authority). Moreover, the provision of foreign aid is only part of the picture: a vibrant private

Box 7.5. People and Structures

The lessons of international aid to the West Bank and Gaza confirm the recommendations made in the *DAC Guidelines* regarding the need for streamlined, flexible, and decentralized aid operations. They also underscore some of the most insightful findings of the War-Torn Societies Project. Here, two particular aspects should be underlined. The first is WSP's observation that "to be effective, external assistance must be carefully timed to local dynamics"—with the accompanying observation that "there are important differences between the anthropological/political time in which reality in the field evolves, and the chronological/bureaucratic time that governs international assistance agencies." No one who has spent any time engaged with both Palestinian realities and headquarters procedures could doubt the significance of this observation.

The WSP also stresses that peacebuilding requires "specially trained and exceptionally qualified field staff to cope and succeed in such difficult and unstable circumstances," staff who have the "ability to take and manage risk, the analytical capacity to understand complex situations in a holistic way, political acumen and maturity, pragmatism and creativity and exceptional commitment." In Palestine, some donor and agency officials exhibited these characteristics. Others did not, and it showed.

The WSP also underscores, as this study has too, that agencies must provide appropriate supports if they are to expect staff to rise to and maintain these standards under dynamic and often stressful conditions. The present study has not addressed these managerial issues in great detail. However, the Palestinian case suggests that examination of the human resource processes within agencies—the processes whereby individuals are hired, trained, assigned, and assessed—may be one of the most important aspects of international peacebuilding to be addressed in subsequent analyses and evaluations.

sector has a fundamental role to play in Palestinian sustainable development. Through most of the interim period, conditions—some of them self-inflicted by the Palestinian Authority, many of them imposed by factors beyond Palestinian control—rendered this very difficult. As one World Bank official noted:

To attain the high growth rates of 8–10 percent of GNP which are needed to make a real dent in unemployment and poverty and to recapitalize WBGS infrastructure and social sectors, a far higher degree of political certainty will be required than exists at present. This will only be provided by significant progress towards a stable final settlement.[8]

As noted in the conclusion of chapter 6, the international aid effort did help to establish some important elements of the development "mosaic" in Palestine.[9] By 1998–99 these had helped to arrest the decline of the Palestinian economy and could (backed with continuing foreign aid) sustain modest economic growth. However, as with a mosaic, many of these developmental pieces were irregular and disconnected and themselves composed only part of an incomplete picture. They did not represent the firm basis for a vibrant Palestinian economy, although they did contribute to that eventual goal. Truly sustainable development in Palestine can come only with peace.

The challenges of all this were, and are, substantial. Under any set of circumstances, Palestine faces the problems associated with limited natural resources (notably land and water) and an explosive rate of population growth. Its economic dependency on Israel, while possibly lessened by alternative economic and political arrangements, will always be substantial. It also faces negative, as well as positive, legacies from the interim period. In particular, problems associated with deep-seated political patronage, corruption, and public-sector weaknesses are likely to sap the effectiveness of any future economic policy. As a consequence, any future Palestine will also be afflicted by the legacy of large public-sector employment and the consequent challenge of maintaining a sound fiscal regime. These problems are not unsolvable. But given the way they have become rooted in the understandable imperatives of regime maintenance, they will be very difficult to reform.

Donors and Institutional Development

Such weaknesses underscored the extent to which, as aid efforts continued, "institutional development" represented one of the most serious challenges facing donors and Palestinians alike. In 1998 the World Bank noted that both donors and the Palestinian Authority had concentrated on the establishment of structures without adequate attention to the ways in which the institutional and political setting affected policy processes. Establishing the right "rules of the game"—that is, focusing on processes and underlying dynamics rather than simply on structures —was essential.[10] In May 1999 the UNSCO report *Rule of Law Development in the West Bank and Gaza Strip* noted that, despite significant progress and even allowing for the uncertain political environment, much work still needed to be done in this area.[11] In June 1999 an international task force organized by the (U.S.) Council on Foreign Relations underscored this point in a major report on the weaknesses of, and priorities for, Palestinian institution building. The report —after stressing that "the Palestinian Authority has achieved levels of service delivery, revenue mobilization, financial accountability, and utilization of international assistance that are at least commensurate with, and in some aspects exceed, those in countries of comparable development and income"—emphasized that "much remains to be done." Specifically, it suggested that the Palestinian Authority "suffers shortcomings that range from insufficient institutionalization of citizens' rights and the concentration of executive power, through the use of large-scale public-sector hiring to ease unemployment and to reward political loyalty, to instances of police violence and flawed financial management." A lengthy series of detailed recommendations were included.[12]

Substantial amounts of donor resources were spent on many aspects of institution development. The 1999 UNSCO report alone detailed some $100.7 million in past, current, or planned donor activities related to the rule of law. Yet many donor efforts in this area had also been naive (box 7.6).[13] On one level, the mere establishment of offices—through the provision of office equipment, expertise, and project funding—had often been seen as sufficient to develop Palestinian capacities in needed areas. Administrative shortcomings and the need for civil service reform, on the other hand, had tended to be seen as a technical issue: if the Palestinian Authority could just be shown how to operate a rational-bureaucratic public sector, the necessary adjustments would then follow. Similarly, legal reform was seen as requiring the right laws, with little attention to what their actual (rather than theoretical) impact might be. Reflecting their technocratic expertise, external consultants penned reports that tended to be catalogs of inefficiencies and weaknesses, current and possible organizational schema, and accepted international "best practices" in the sector concerned. Rarely were underlying, often informal dynamics taken into account. Yet, as has been seen—in the difficulties of the environmental and agricultural sectors, the growth of public-sector employment, the development of commercial monopolies, and the subordination of economic planning to the imperatives of the peace process—many outcomes were inexplicable *without* reference to the context within which Palestinian development has occurred. In short, in a situation where administrative inefficiencies often served real political purposes, they could hardly be addressed from a narrowly technical point of view.

Moreover, donor policies sometimes aggravated the very problems that donor programs sought to address. As has been seen in the environmental sector, donor support could reinforce the fragmentation of the Palestinian Authority, with different donor agencies each supporting competing institutions. As evidenced in the agricultural sector, a vicious cycle could easily develop whereby donors avoided problematic sectors, thus compounding the weakness of those sectors by starving them of needed resources. In turn, this weakness tended only to further deter donor support. Conversely, other areas might be the beneficiaries of support precisely because they were already strong; this was certainly true of education and social services and probably true of MOPIC too. Much the same effect

Box 7.6. Governance

Virtually all reviews of international peacebuilding—not to mention the broader policy frameworks for most donor and multilateral agencies—point to the importance of good governance. But what does this mean?

The *DAC Guidelines* offer a fairly typical formula: good governance involves respect for human rights, participation, democratization, "transparent and accountable" governments, and vibrant civil societies. If present, these things increase the possibilities for peace. Conversely, their absence generates the potential for conflict.

But is this true? The linkage is often rather more complex than the *DAC Guidelines* or many other reviews suggest. Take, for example, the issue of corruption. Certainly, as the *Guidelines* suggest, "partiality and corruption in the public institutions responsible for managing public resources and social services directly undermines the credibility of the state [and] can encourage marginalised groups to resort to violent means to effect change." Equally, corruption may be (as in the West Bank and Gaza, and indeed many other places) a mechanism of neopatrimonial political management, used to consolidate regimes and *maintain* political stability (and perhaps even peace). Which is it? Or—since in most cases both delegitimization and coalition building may be at work at the same time—how does one deal with the many negative features without destabilizing the broader political setting? Indeed, how does one deal with governance issues at all, given entrenched financial and political interests within the state? On these questions, the *Guidelines* are largely silent.

In part, these issues reflect the inherent challenges of institutional development discussed below. The failure of the *DAC Guidelines* to highlight them, however, also points to two weaknesses within many donor agencies and multilateral agencies.

could be found within ministries as well, with bureaucratic development occurring in those areas where donor resources were forthcoming, but not in others. The frequent provision of technical assistance and external support for staff salaries compounded this problem. Collectively, there seemed little explicit recognition on the donor side that (justified) appeals to the Palestinian Authority to put its administrative house in order ought to be combined with greater awareness of what donors could do to help (rather than hinder) this process.[14]

The result of all this could be a series of imbalances in the development of PA institutions. Donor policies also created a strong incentive to engage in administrative rent-seeking behavior, with Palestinian agencies pursuing project initiatives

Box 7.6. *(cont.)*

The first of these is a problem of disciplinary blinders. Dealing with governance issues, promoting institutional development, or undertaking a host of other peacebuilding tasks requires that program staff bring the right array of analytical skills to the table. As James Boyce has argued with regard to international financial institutions, the present knowledge base may not be optimal: "Today, the ratio of economists to other social scientists— including political scientists, sociologists, anthropologists—on IFI staffs is roughly 20 to 1. At the risk of offending my fellow economists, I must say that it is not obvious that this is an efficient mix. . . . Lifting the curtain between the economic and political dimensions of peacebuilding thus may have implications for the composition of IFI staffs" ("Reconstruction and Democratization: The International Financial Institutions and Post-Conflict Transition" [paper presented to the Latin American Studies Association Annual Congress, Chicago, September 1998]). Boyce's comments could equally be applied to sectoral specialists and other technocratic personnel. (Conversely, of course, aid workers may justifiably complain that the politically oriented members of foreign ministries fail to appreciate the technical complexities and economic underpinnings of reconstruction.)

A second problem is one of wishful thinking. It would be nice to believe that the various justifiably important dimensions of peace, development, and social justice—social reconciliation, environmentally sustainable development, socioeconomic and gender equity, democracy, and so forth—all contributed to one another in a self-reinforcing virtuous circle. In the long run, perhaps they do. However, as noted in chapter 1—and as highlighted in the discussion of the Palestinian security sector—the short-term realities may be far more complex and morally ambiguous. Recognizing this is an essential first step to dealing with such dilemmas.

because they seemed likely to attract external support, rather than because they were most needed.

Addressing such issues would require a multisectoral approach, in which regulatory reform, bureaucratic reorganization, and incoming project support are all harnessed to clear and coordinated institution-building objectives. To be successful, such an approach must be designed to harmonize (or at least reconcile) administrative function and political imperatives, seeking to overcome inertia or entrenched resistance by constructing winning coalitions for reform. Finally, it must anticipate probable obstacles to implementation. These include the difficulty of mobilizing adequate bilateral or multilateral resources for the multiple components of a program, the inherent complexity of multisectoral initiatives, and the consequent risk that problems with one element will have an undesirable ripple effect on other, linked components.

Donors and Political Stabilization

As is evident from this discussion, donor efforts to build viable and effective Palestinian institutions have had mixed effects. What of their success in stabilizing the political situation in the West Bank and Gaza—and thereby creating the space under which the peace process might (or might not) move forward?

Fairly consistently, public opinion surveys show that around two-thirds of all Palestinians in the West Bank and Gaza believe that the peace process has harmed the Palestinian economy. Although this might be seen as a major indictment of the economic dimension of the peace process, it is actually rather difficult to show any correlation between economic circumstances and political views. Support for the peace process, for example, slowly grew through 1994–96, at a time when the economy was in its sharpest rate of decline. Conversely, support for negotiations subsequently declined through 1997–98, at a time when deterioration of the economy had actually slowed. Similarly, support for armed attacks against Israel dropped from more than half in 1994 to less than a quarter in the spring of 1996 (at the height of closure). As Israel's position hardened under Netanyahu and settlement activity continued, support for attacks grew, briefly exceeding 50 percent again in the fall of 1998. Further complicating the picture, about one-quarter of those who opposed the peace process also opposed armed attacks against Israelis, and up to one-third of those who supported the process also supported such attacks.[15]

Although opposition to negotiations and support for militant action do correlate somewhat with age and education (with youth and the most educated strata most inclined to radicalism), they do not vary substantially with unemployment or economic condition. In fact, surveys show that perceptions of improved or declining economic fortunes have absolutely no discernible impact on Palestinian attitudes to the peace process.[16] There does exist a slight relationship between a positive view of the impact of donor programs and support for the peace process. However, it is doubtful that the quality of donor programs is the major reason for this. Rather, those (for example, Hamas supporters) who oppose negotiations are also likely to view Western donors suspiciously.

The overall picture, then, is that support for the peace process is largely determined by the state of the peace process rather than by economic incentives or standard of living. This, however, is only part of the picture: the continuation of the peace process has depended not only on public attitudes to negotiations (and, conversely, to violent opposition) but also on the political survival of the Palestinian

Authority. Clearly, a catastrophic collapse of the Palestinian Authority would neg-atively affect the search for durable peace. Conversely, the survival of the Pales-tinian Authority kept the process alive, albeit with uncertain results. Here a much more direct linkage exists between donor efforts and political outcomes.

As noted earlier, it is difficult to see how the Palestinian Authority might have established itself at all in the absence of donor support. Beyond this, a mix of public policy, periodic repression, and political patronage has been used by the Palestinian leadership to cement its political position and marginalize that of the opposition. Certainly, there is ample evidence of Fateh's declining fortunes over time: its support slipped from around 47 percent in March 1996 (when support for the peace process was high) to around 38 percent in September 1998 (when support for negotiations was at a low point), before rebounding slightly in early 1999. During the same time, support for the main militant opposition groups (Hamas, Islamic Jihad, the PFLP) roughly doubled to around 19 percent.[17] Never-theless, Fateh's leading position was maintained over a period when Palestinian per capita incomes dropped sharply and unemployment rates sometimes reached peaks of 40 percent. Approval rates of Arafat also remained fairly high, although they showed signs of significant decline in the latter part of 1998. Significantly, sup-port for the Palestinian Authority tended to be somewhat higher in Gaza, where PA and donor resources tended to be disproportionately focused. More ominously, the Palestinian Authority's handling of economic policy issues was generally rated quite low in most surveys, suggesting that in the longer term this might be a source of substantial discontent.

In addition to facilitating the political consolidation of the Palestinian Authority, donor support also fueled the establishment of statelike Palestinian in-stitutions, which in turn created further political momentum toward the eventual attainment of Palestinian self-determination and sovereignty. The Israeli Labor Party dropped its objections to a Palestinian state before the 1996 elections, and increasing numbers of Israeli politicians spoke of it as a natural outcome of the peace process. Surveys showed that by 1998 around half of all Israeli Jews accepted the establishment of a Palestinian state, and around two-thirds felt that such a state would in fact be established.[18] All of this was a striking contrast to the pre-Oslo period, when support for Palestinian statehood had been confined to the dovish margins of the Israeli Left.

Externally, the international community also increasingly spoke of Palestin-ian statehood as a desirable outcome. This too represented a marked change: when the PLO's Palestine National Council had previously declared "independence" in 1988, recognition had largely been confined to its Arab and Third World allies. A decade later, EU diplomats argued that "donors should start helping the Pales-tinians to prepare for full statehood," while even First Lady Hilary Clinton of the

United States felt free to declare support for eventual Palestinian independence.[19] In April 1999 President Clinton, in a letter to Arafat, declared: "We support the aspirations of the Palestinian people to determine their own future on their own land."[20] The State Department, pressed on the issue, refused to rule out Palestinian statehood. The European Union went a step further, with a joint statement noting that member states "reaffirm the continuing and unqualified Palestinian right to self-determination including the option of a state; look forward to the early fulfillment of this right; appeal to the parties to strive in good faith for a negotiated solution on the basis of this right, which is not subject to any veto."[21] This shift reflected new realities on the ground in the region—and, in particular, the post-Oslo construction (with donor resources) of a Palestinian proto-state in the West Bank and Gaza.

PUTTING IT ALL IN CONTEXT

The steady deterioration of the peace process during 1996–98 and the broader decline of the Palestinian economy in the 1990s underscore that development assistance can neither create peace in the absence of political will among all of the local parties nor single-handedly create prosperity in the face of multiple economic shocks and structural constraints. In the case of Palestine, the policies of Israel's Likud-led government and the periodic imposition of closure on the West Bank and Gaza meant that neither political will nor economic stability was present during much of the interim period envisaged by the framers of the Oslo Agreement.

Yet, this having been said, the increase in post-1993 international assistance has played an important and perhaps critical role. Without such assistance, Palestinian GNP would have likely declined a further 6–11 percent.[22] According to a public opinion survey commissioned by the World Bank in the summer of 1999, there are signs of real progress in many local services and infrastructure thanks to the aid effort. A large majority of Palestinians noted significant improvements in schools, the quality of education, and roads since the start of the peace process. Most people surveyed also thought that health facilities and sewage facilities have improved. Only in the case of PA institutions, the legal system, drinking water, and the status of democracy did most people hold negative opinions.[23]

It is unlikely that the Palestinian Authority could have established itself as a functional bureaucratic entity without outside support. And—although much more difficult to assess—the provision of such assistance has undoubtedly strengthened the political stability of the Palestinian Authority, whether by bolstering policy performance or buttressing political patronage.

In a retrospective discussion of the aid effort in Palestine, Odin Knudsen, the first World Bank resident representative to the West Bank and Gaza, once commented that his job had been about "creating options." In an influential paper, Mary B. Anderson once enjoined aid agencies and others to seek to "do no harm" in their efforts to promote peace and development.[24] These are both fitting tests for the aid effort in Palestine, and for peacebuilding more broadly.

Some critics of the aid effort have argued that Palestine is a "foreign aid sinkhole."[25] Donors, some suggest, have supported the establishment of "an obesity of a bureaucracy," a "nasty, thuggish little kleptocracy run by and for the benefit of President Arafat and his bureaucrats and gunsels and cronies, without benefit of law or semblance of order," in which "bribery is endemic, services are nil, connections are everything, and might is the only right there is."[26] Yet, although waste, authoritarianism, and corruption are substantial and very real problems, such an assessment widely overstates the situation. War-to-peace transitions are invariably difficult—especially when aspects of the "war" continue and full "peace" remains elusive. Maladministration is commonplace, indeed almost ubiquitous, under such conditions. On balance, the record in Palestine was, given the context, better than many.

Others pointed to the poor state of the economy as an indictment of the peace process, and the poor state of both as an indictment of Palestinian and international development efforts. Such criticism, however, rests on an unreasonable expectation of what economic peacebuilding can achieve. Donor money *cannot* buy peace or purchase the requisite political will. The international community *can* try to foster conditions more, rather than less, conducive to political reconciliation.

Certainly, aid efforts could be faulted in many respects. Yet on balance—given economic challenges, treacherous political currents, and limited tools—the contribution was invaluable. In Palestine, aid built capacities and offset economic decline. It was especially critical in offsetting the devastating effects of closure in 1996–97. It sustained space for continued negotiation amid political uncertainty. And aid facilitated the political survival of the Palestinian Authority amid diplomatic stalemate, especially when the Netanyahu government appeared committed to unraveling the Oslo Agreement.

The election of a new Israeli government in May 1999 ushered in a renewal of meaningful negotiations. Without international assistance it is doubtful whether the Palestinian Authority—or the peace process—would have been around to see the day.

Notes

Note that many references cite documents issued by institutions of one kind or another. These documents vary widely in terms of format (printed books, photocopied reports, electronic files, e-mail bulletins, etc.) and distribution (some were circulated internally, others distributed more widely). Unless otherwise noted in the reference, the publisher is the issuing institution and the place of publication is that institution's headquarters.

In some cases, versions of these documents or updated information may be available online. Interested readers are urged to consult the links at www.arts.mcgill.ca/mepp/meppnet.html *or the following Web sites:*

Center for Palestine Research and Studies: www.cprs-palestine.org

Israel (Ministry of Foreign Affairs): www.israel-mfa.gov.il/peace

Palestine Economic Forum: www.palecon.org *(includes links to MAS and Palestine Economic Pulse)*

Palestine Trade Center: www.paltrade.org

Palestinian Authority: www.pna.org *(includes links to MOPIC, PECDAR, and PCBS)*

Palestinian Development Plan: www.palestine-PDP.org

Palestinian Refugee ResearchNet: www.prrn.org

World Bank: www.worldbank.org

UNRWA: www.unrwa.org

UNSCO: www.unsco.org

1. INTRODUCTION

1. For the full text of the agreement, see the *Journal of Palestine Studies* 23, no. 1 (fall 1993): 116–121, or the Israel Information Service at www.israel-mfa.gov.il/peace/dop.html.

2. "Co-sponsors' Summary" (paper presented at the Conference to Support Middle East Peace, Washington, D.C., 1 October 1993).

3. Lewis Preston, "The International Effort to Invest in Peace in the Occupied Territories—and the Role of the World Bank" (paper presented at the Conference to Support Middle East Peace, Washington, D.C., 1 October 1993).

4. Abdallah Bouhabib, interview, "The World Bank and International Aid to Palestine," *Journal of Palestine Studies* 23, no. 2 (winter 1994): 66.

5. Center for Palestine Research and Studies (CPRS), *Public Opinion Poll no. 10* (30 June 1994), archived at www.cprs-palestine.org/polls/94/poll10b.html; *Public Opinion Poll no. 16* (16–18 March 1995), archived at www.cprs-palestine.org/polls/95/poll16b.html#econsit.

6. Jerusalem Media and Communications Center (JMCC), public opinion survey, *Palestine Report* (11 April 1997): 7; Ministry of Planning and International Cooperation (MOPIC), *First Quarterly Monitoring Report of Donor Assistance: Tables* (5 June 1997), table 1.

7. "The Donor Experience, and the Way Ahead" (statement by the World Bank to the Fifth Consultative Group Meeting for the West Bank and Gaza, Paris, 14–15 December 1997).

8. Development Assistance Committee (DAC) of the Organization for Economic Cooperation and Development (OECD), *Development Cooperation: 1996 Report* (Paris: OECD, 1997), 99.

9. Calculated from DAC, *ODA Receipts and Selected Indicators for Developing Countries and Territories* (8 February 1999), accessed at www.oecd.org/dac/htm/Tab25e.HTM on 4 April 1999.

10. Data for 1996–97, from DAC, *Major Recipients of Individual DAC Members' Aid* (8 February 1999), accessed at www.oecd.org/dac/htm/us.HTM on 4 April 1999.

11. World Bank, *The World Bank's Experience with Post-Conflict Reconstruction* (Washington, D.C.: World Bank Operations Evaluation Division, 1998), table 3.2.

12. World Bank, *World Bank 1998 Annual Report*, appendices, accessed at www.worldbank.org/html/extpb/annrep98/pdf/apnd.pdf on 4 April 1999.

13. Boutros Boutros-Ghali, *An Agenda for Peace: Preventive Diplomacy, Peacemaking, and Peace-keeping* (New York: United Nations, 1992), A/47/277-S/24111, 17 June 1992, paras. 15, 21, 55.

14. *Postconflict reconstruction* is often (but not exclusively) used by those emphasizing the economic and social components of postwar rebuilding. *Transitional assistance* is used to refer to aid in support of a broader range of wrenching political and economic reorientations—a category that includes shifts from command to market economies, democratization, and war-to-peace transitions. In many cases, countries may be engaged in a double or even triple transition. *Complex humanitarian emergencies* is a concept that has grown up within the humanitarian relief community to describe the complications that arise from relief activities amid political strife. Similarly, terminology such as *peace operations* or *peace maintenance* has arisen from analysts of *second-generation* or *multidimensional peacekeeping operations*, involving a complex array of military/security, humanitarian, and developmental tasks. The notion of *peace implementation* has been used to focus attention on the challenges presented by the implementation of written peace agreements rather than on peacebuilding in the (earlier) negotiations phase or the (later) consolidation phase. By contrast, literature on *early warning* and *preventive diplomacy* focuses on how best to avoid the initial outbreak of violence. All of these concepts, needless to add, overlap substantially.

15. Steven Holtzman, "Post-Conflict Reconstruction," Environment Department Work in Progress (Washington, D.C.: World Bank, Social Policy Division, 1996), 28.

16. Michael W. Doyle, *Peacebuilding in Cambodia,* IPA Policy Briefing Series (New York: International Peace Academy, December 1996), 3.

17. Lloyd Axworthy, "Building Peace to Last: Establishing a Canadian Peacebuilding Initiative" (address given at York University, 30 October 1996), accessed at www.dfait-maeci.gc.ca/english/news/statem~1/96_state/96_046e.htm.

18. On the role of the media, see Warren Strobel, *Late-Breaking Foreign Policy: The News Media's Impact on Peace Operations* (Washington, D.C.: United States Institute of Peace Press, 1997); Larry Minear, Colin Scott, and Thomas G. Weiss, *The News Media, Civil War, and Humanitarian Action* (Boulder, Colo.: Lynne Rienner, 1996).

19. World Bank, *Post-Conflict Reconstruction*, 21.

20. Ibid., 20–21.

21. Alvaro de Soto and Graciana del Castillo, "Obstacles to Peace-Building," *Foreign Affairs* 94 (spring 1994): 74.

22. Mark Taylor, "Coordination and International Institutions in Post-Conflict Situations," *Leiden Journal of International Law* 10 (1997): 266.

23. Antonio Donini, *The Policies of Mercy: UN Coordination in Afghanistan, Mozambique, and Rwanda,* Watson Institute Occasional Paper no. 22 (Providence, R.I.: Brown University, Thomas J. Watson Jr. Institute for International Studies, 1996). For details of the reform initiatives proposed by Kofi Annan in July 1997, see www.un.org/reform/.

24. Andrew Natsios, "NGOs and the UN System in Complex Humanitarian Emergencies: Conflict or Cooperation?" *Third World Quarterly* 16, no. 3 (1995).

25. Stewart Patrick, "Pledges of Aid: Multilateral Donors and Support for Postwar Reconstruction and Systemic Transformation" (discussion paper presented at the Social Science Research Council/Center on International Cooperation, New York University, 27 August 1997); Herman Rosa and Michael Foley, "El Salvador: Draft Report" (paper presented at the Pledges of Aid workshop, Center on International Cooperation, New York University, May 1998).

26. Kenji Yamada, "Pledge Gaps in Cambodia: Preliminary Report" (paper presented at the Pledges of Aid workshop, Center on International Cooperation, New York University, May 1998), table 1.

27. In Mozambique, for example, close coordination between the UN secretary-general's special representative, Aldo Ajello, and the international donor community was particularly important in keeping the process on track. For an assessment, see Dennis C. Jett, "Lessons Unlearned—Or Why Mozambique's Successful Peacekeeping Operation Might Not Be Replicated Elsewhere," *Journal of Humanitarian Assistance* (19 July 1997), accessed at www-jha.sps.cam.ac.uk/a/a075.htm.

28. World Bank, *Post-Conflict Reconstruction: The Role of the World Bank* (Washington, D.C.: World Bank, 1998), 6–9.

29. On the impact of the media on both peacemaking and aid activities, see Strobel, *Late-Breaking Foreign Policy.*

30. OECD, "Aid and Other Financial Flows in 1996," press release (19 June 1997), table 2, accessed at www.oecd.org/news_and_events/release/aida.pdf.

31. James Boyce, "External Assistance and the Peace Process in El Salvador," *World Development* 23, no. 12 (December 1995): 2102–2105.

32. James Boyce, "Adjustment toward Peace: An Introduction," *World Development* 23, no. 12 (December 1995); de Soto and del Castillo, "Obstacles to Peace-Building."

33. John Prendergast, *Frontline Diplomacy: Humanitarian Aid and Conflict in Africa* (Boulder, Colo.: Lynne Rienner, 1996), 7–8.

34. The Web site of USAID fully reflects this defensiveness, variously stressing that "close to 80 percent of USAID's grants and contracts go directly to American firms and non-governmental organizations"; noting that "foreign assistance fosters an enabling environment for U.S. trade and investment in developing nations"; and complaining that "despite the good work America's foreign assistance programs do around the globe, these programs have often been misunderstood by the American public" (www.info.usaid.gov/about/y4naid.html, version of 6 September 1997). For sharp (conservative) criticism of USAID, see the Heritage Foundation, "Inspector General's Verdict: Fraud, Waste, and Abuse at USAID" (25 March 1997), www.mediaresearch.org/heritage/library/categories/forpol/fyi134.html.

35. Donald Brandt, "Relief as Development, but Development as Relief?" *Journal of Humanitarian Assistance* (4 July 1997), www-jha.sps.cam.ac.uk/a/a005.htm.

36. International Federation of Red Cross and Red Crescent Societies, *World Disaster Report 1995*, chap. 16, www.ifrc.org/pubs/wdr/95/ch16.htm. The code was agreed to in 1994 by Caritas Internationalis, Catholic Relief Services, the International Federation of Red Cross and Red Crescent Societies, International Save the Children Alliance, Lutheran World Federation, Oxfam, the World Council of Churches, and the International Committee of the Red Cross. In the context of civil conflict, such principles may be difficult to maintain, since the provision of scarce resources in such an environment has inevitable political consequences. At the same time, "nonpartisanship," "independence," and "humanitarian space" are not only moral responses to human suffering but operational requirements too. Without them, effective humanitarian action in times of war is difficult: access and logistics are likely to be impeded and relief workers targeted as combatants. For more information on the need for these principles, see Larry Minear and Thomas Weiss, *Humanitarian Action in Times of War: A Handbook for Practitioners* (Boulder, Colo.: Lynne Rienner, 1993), 23–28.

37. DAC, *Cooperation for Sustainable Development*, DAC Progress Assessment (May 1997), www.oecd.org/dac/pdf/esd.pdf.

38. For a useful discussion, see Ian Smillie, *Relief and Development: The Struggle for Synergy*, Watson Institute Occasional Paper no. 33 (Providence, R.I.: Brown University, Thomas J. Watson Jr. Institute for International Studies, 1998).

39. DAC, *Conflict, Peace, and Development Co-operation on the Threshold of the Twenty-First Century*, DAC Policy Statement (May 1997), www.oecd.org/dac/pdf/epcdc.pdf.

40. Mats Karlsson, "Relief and Development: A False Dichotomy?" *Challenge of Peace* 5 (July 1997): 5.

41. Kenneth D. Bush, "Fitting the Pieces Together: Canadian Contributions to the Challenge of Rebuilding Wartorn Societies" (paper prepared for the International Development Research Centre, Ottawa, July 1995), 5.

42. Boyce, "External Assistance and the Peace Process in El Salvador," 2108.

43. Ibid.

44. Interview, February 1999.

45. World Bank, *Post-Conflict Reconstruction*.

46. Roland Paris, for example, argues that the guiding donor paradigm of liberal internationalism, with its emphasis on markets and democracy, "has not been a particularly effective method of establishing stable peace." See Roland Paris, "Peacebuilding and the Limits of Liberal Internationalism," *International Security* 22, no. 2 (fall 1997): 56. A more detailed analysis is offered by Timothy Sisk (who suggests that "the international community often places too much emphasis on democratic elections without considering their potentially adverse impact in situations of severe ethnic conflict") and Marina Ottaway (who notes that "democracy as a stable state is highly desirable, but democratization . . . can trigger highly undesirable side effects"). See Timothy Sisk, *Power Sharing and International Mediation in Ethnic Conflicts* (Washington, D.C.: United States Institute of Peace Press, 1996), xii; Marina Ottaway, "Democratization in Collapsed States," in *Collapsed States: The Disintegration and Restoration of Legitimate Authority,* ed. I. William Zartman (Boulder, Colo.: Lynne Rienner, 1995), 236.

47. Pauline Baker, "Conflict Resolution versus Democratic Governance: Divergent Paths of Peace?" in *Managing Global Chaos: Sources of and Responses to International Conflict,* ed. Chester Crocker and Fen Osler Hampson with Pamela Aall (Washington, D.C.: United States Institute of Peace Press, 1996), 570.

48. DAC, *DAC Guidelines on Conflict, Peace, and Development Cooperation* (Paris: OECD, 1997).

49. Nicole Ball with Tammy Halevy, *Making Peace Work: The Role of the International Development Community,* ODC Policy Essay no. 18 (Washington, D.C.: Overseas Development Council, 1996), 29 (summary at www.odc.org/peace.htm). See also the sequence of stages envisaged by the World Bank, presented in table 1.1.

50. As previously noted, donor resources were a major incentive for cooperation in Mozambique. In Cambodia, humanitarian assistance was an essential part of the UNTAC mission. Reconstruction assistance, however, lagged, thus severely constraining its effective use by UNTAC during the transitional period. Michael Doyle, *UN Peacekeeping in Cambodia: UNTAC's Civil Mandate* (Boulder, Colo.: Lynne Rienner, 1995), 50–51.

51. On UNTAC, see Doyle, *UN Peacekeeping in Cambodia.*

52. Ibid., 18.

53. Ball with Halevy, *Making Peace Work,* 88.

54. On the broader question of "peace conditionality," see Nicole Ball, *Pressing for Peace: Can Aid Induce Reform?* ODC Policy Essay no. 6 (Washington, D.C.: Overseas Development Council, 1992); Boyce, "External Assistance and the Peace Process in El Salvador."

55. There have been very few studies of civil war termination in Lebanon, in part because the process is such an undesirable one: extensive violence and quasi occupation by an external actor (Syria) that frequently used punitive force against civilian targets; little fundamental reconciliation and no investigation of wartime atrocities; the establishment of a severely constrained and fundamentally sectarian semi-democracy; human rights abuses; little state effort to address basic social inequalities; little significant peacebuilding role for external donors. At the time of this writing, however, Lebanon's future would appear much more tranquil than that of Angola, Bosnia, Cambodia, Haiti, or Mozambique—all of which have received much greater analytical attention.

56. The work of Joel Migdal on "strong societies" and "weak states," although not written to address postconflict situations, is particularly insightful in this regard. See Joel Migdal, *Strong Societies and Weak States: State-Society Relations and State Capabilities in the Third World* (Princeton, N.J.: Princeton University Press, 1988); Joel Migdal, Atul Kohli, and Vivienne Shue, eds., *State Power and Social Forces: Domination and Transformation in the Third World* (Cambridge: Cambridge University Press, 1994), especially the introduction and chapter 1.

57. See, for example, Sisk, *Power Sharing and International Mediation in Ethnic Conflicts*; Neil Kritz, ed., *Transitional Justice: How Emerging Democracies Reckon with Former Regimes,* vol. 1, *General Considerations* (Washington, D.C.: United States Institute of Peace Press, 1995).

58. Holtzman, "Post-Conflict Reconstruction," 24.

59. For a discussion, see Joan Nelson and Stephanie Eglington, *Global Goals, Contentious Means: Issues of Multiple Aid Conditionality,* ODC Policy Essay no. 10 (Washington, D.C.: Overseas Development Council, 1993).

60. For a discussion of this, see Prendergast, *Frontline Diplomacy.*

61. International Monetary Fund (IMF), *Cambodia Public Expenditure Review,* vol. 2, *Main Report* (Washington, D.C.: IMF, 1999), 61.

62. Susan Rose-Ackerman, "Which Bureaucracies Are Less Corruptible?" in *Political Corruption: A Handbook,* ed. Arnold Heidenheimer, Michael Johnston, and Victor T. LeVine (New Brunswick, N.J.: Transaction Publishers, 1989), 815.

63. John Waterbury "Corruption, Political Stability, and Development: Comparative Evidence from Egypt and Morocco," *Government and Opposition* 11, no. 4 (fall 1976).

64. "I'm shocked, shocked to find gambling is going on in here . . . ," Louie to Rick in *Casablanca* (1942).

65. I. William Zartman, "Putting Things Back Together," in *Collapsed States.*

66. Hillel Frisch and Menachem Hofnung, "State Formation and International Aid: The Emergence of the Palestinian Authority," *World Development* 25, no. 8 (August 1997): 1244.

67. Ibid., 1246.

68. Glenn Robinson, *Building a Palestinian State: The Incomplete Revolution* (Bloomington: Indiana University Press, 1997), 198, quoting a speech given by Shibley Telhami to the United Nations Conference on Palestine, Paris, 30 June 1995.

69. John Maynard Keynes, *A Tract on Monetary Reform* (London: Macmillan, 1924).

2. THE CONTEXT

1. Useful general historical overviews of the conflict are provided by Baruch Kimmerling and Joel Migdal, *Palestinians: The Making of a People* (New York: Free Press, 1993); Mark Tessler, *A History of the Israeli–Palestinian Conflict* (Bloomington: Indiana University Press, 1994); Charles D. Smith, *Palestine and the Arab-Israeli Conflict,* 3d ed. (New York: St. Martin's Press, 1996).

2. On this transitional period, see Paul Noble, "The PLO in Regional Politics," in *Echoes of the Intifada: Regional Repercussions of the Palestinian-Israeli Conflict,* ed. Rex Brynen (Boulder, Colo.: Westview Press, 1991); Rex Brynen and Paul Noble, "The Gulf Crisis and the Arab State System: A New Regional Order?" *Arab Studies Quarterly* 13, nos. 1–2 (winter-spring 1991); Rex Brynen, "Adjusting to a New World Order: The PLO and the Twilight of the Soviet Union," in *The Decline of the USSR and the Transformation of the Middle East,* ed. David Goldberg and Paul Marantz (Boulder, Colo.: Westview Press, 1994).

3. Based on data from the Palestinian Central Bureau of Statistics (PCBS), archived at www.pcbs.org/english.

4. Abdelfattah Abu Shokor finds a Gini coefficient of 0.423 for the West Bank and 0.445 for Gaza. See "Income Distribution and Its Social Impact in the Occupied

Territories," in *Income Distribution in Jordan,* ed. Kamel Abu Jaber, Matthes Buhbe, and Mohammed Smadi (Boulder, Colo.: Westview Press, 1990). Radwan A. Shaban calculates a Gini coefficient of 0.378 for expenditures. See "Living Standards in the West Bank and Gaza Strip" (Ramallah: MAS, 1977), archived at www.palecon.org/masdir/publications/livingstandards.html.

5. World Bank, *Developing the Occupied Territories,* vol. 6, *Human Resources and Social Policy* (Washington, D.C.: World Bank, 1993), table 2.3. Of these migrants, more than half were employed in technical or managerial positions.

6. World Bank, *Developing the Occupied Territories,* vol. 2, *The Economy* (Washington, D.C.: World Bank, 1993), 11–16 and table 17.

7. World Bank, *Developing the Occupied Territories,* vol. 3, *Private Sector Development* (Washington, D.C.: World Bank, 1993), 85–86.

8. Ibid., 30–31. The single largest group of these, representing around one-third of all establishments, was in the textile sector.

9. World Bank, *Developing the Occupied Territories,* vol. 2, tables 26–32; World Bank and the Palestinian Economic Policy Research Institute (MAS), *Development under Adversity? The Palestinian Economy in Transition,* discussion draft (30 October 1997), appendix table 11.

10. Palestinian Economic Council for Development and Reconstruction (PEC-DAR), *Rehabilitation and Re-integration of Ex-detainees in the Occupied Palestinian Territories* (PECDAR, June 1994), 6.

11. Data drawn from Peace Now, "The Real Map," November 1992, in *Journal of Palestine Studies* 23, no. 3 (spring 1993): 148–154 ; "Settlement Report," May 1994, in *Journal of Palestine Studies* 23, no. 4 (summer 1994): 98–99. According to the Israeli government's own admission, settlement activity continued after the start of the peace process, with the settler population increasing 50 percent between 1992 and 1996. Prime Minister's Office (Israel), *Prime Minister's Report* 1, no. 13 (2 December 1997).

12. World Bank, *Developing the Occupied Territories,* vol. 2, 48–56; Water Resources Action Program, *Palestinian Water Resources* (Jerusalem/Gaza: WRAP, October 1994). Estimates of annual renewable water supplies range from 600 to 800 million cubic meters.

13. World Bank, *Developing the Occupied Territories,* vol. 2, table 3.

14. Sara Roy, *The Gaza Strip: The Political Economy of De-development* (Washington, D.C.: Institute for Palestine Studies, 1995), 192–198. Indeed, a number of analysts suggested that, before the intifada, total Israeli revenues from the territories (through local taxes, deductions from the wages of Palestinians employed in Israel, and indirect taxes) actually exceeded total civil expenditures, thus resulting in a net gain to the Israeli treasury. Raja Shehadeh, "Israel and the Palestinians: Human Rights in the Occupied Territories," in Brynen, *Echoes of the Intifada,* 37.

15. Meron Benvenisti, *U.S. Government Funded Projects in the West Bank and Gaza, 1977–83,* West Bank Data Project Working Paper no. 13 (Jerusalem: West Bank Data Project, 1984), table 12.

16. World Bank, *Developing the Occupied Territories,* vol. 1, *Overview,* 8–11; World Bank, *Developing the Occupied Territories,* vol. 5, *Infrastructure,* 3–9; United Nations Development Program (UNDP), *World Development Report 1996* (New York: Oxford University Press, 1996), table 15.

17. World Bank, *Developing the Occupied Territories,* vol. 6, 23, 26.

18. Calculated from ibid., 37; World Bank, *Developing the Occupied Territories,* vol. 1, table 2; and UNDP, *World Development Report 1996,* table 14. Data for Jordan are for 1992.

19. World Bank, *Palestinian NGO Project,* Project Appraisal Document 16696 GZ (19 June 1997), annex 4.

20. For a discussion by one deported mayor, see Abdul Jawad Saleh, *Israel's Policy of De-institutionalization* (London: Jerusalem Centre for Development Studies, 1987). See also Moshe Ma'oz, *Palestinian Leadership on the West Bank: The Changing Role of the Mayors under Jordan and Israel* (London: Frank Cass, 1984).

21. World Bank, *Developing the Occupied Territories,* vol. 5, 19–23. The allocation of funds was clearly used to encourage "good behavior" on the part of local officials.

22. Institute for Social and Economic Policy in the Middle East, *Securing Peace in the Middle East: Project on Economic Transition* (Cambridge, Mass.: Harvard University, John F. Kennedy School of Government, June 1993), 102.

23. World Bank, *Developing the Occupied Territories,* vol. 3, 70–80.

24. Shehadeh, "Israel and the Palestinians," 42.

25. For example, Military Order 1262 of 1988 required approval of up to six different departments for industrial and import/export licenses, or for registering companies; high-yield chickens and cows sometimes became the subject of search missions by the IDF. See Shehadeh, "Israel and the Palestinians," 42, as well as the detailed discussion in Robinson, *Building a Palestinian State,* 52–65.

26. United Nations Special Coordinator for the Occupied Territories (UNSCO), *The West Bank and Gaza Strip Private Economy: Conditions and Prospects* (February 1998), archived at www.arts.mcgill.ca/MEPP/unsco/private/report.html. Roy, *The Gaza Strip.*

27. UNDP, *Compendium of Ongoing and Planned Projects* (Jerusalem: UNDP, March 1992); interview with senior UNDP official, August 1994.

28. Data drawn from UNDP, *1993 Compendium of External Assistance to the Occupied Palestinian Territories* (Jerusalem: UNDP, July 1993); UNDP, *1994 Compendium of External Assistance to the Occupied Palestinian Territories* (Jerusalem: UNDP, August 1994). Sectoral data are for 1993; the distribution for 1992 is similar. OECD data are from DAC, *Development Cooperation: 1996 DAC Report* (Paris: OECD, 1997), table 33.

29. The main U.S. NGOs (or private voluntary organizations [PVOs]) involved over the years have been CARE, Catholic Relief Services, Cooperative Development Foundation, Holy Land Christian Mission, YMCA, Save the Children, AMIDEAST, and American Near East Refugee Aid (ANERA). The Society for the Care of the Handicapped—a Palestinian NGO—has also been supported. Sara Roy, "U.S. Economic Aid to the West Bank and Gaza Strip: The Politics of Peace," *Middle East Policy* 4, no. 4 (October 1996): 556. See also Benvenisti, *U.S. Government Funded Projects in the West Bank and Gaza, 1977–83*; Leopold Yehuda Laufer, *U.S. Aid to the West Bank and Gaza: Policy Dilemmas,* Leonard Davis Institute for International Relations Policy Studies 12 (Jerusalem: Hebrew University of Jerusalem, May 1985).

30. Denis Sullivan, "NGOs in Palestine: Agents of Development and Foundations of Civil Society," *Journal of Palestine Studies* 25, no. 3 (spring 1996): 94.

31. For a useful history of UNRWA, see Benjamin N. Schiff, *Refugees unto the Third Generation: UN Aid to Palestinians* (Syracuse, N.Y.: Syracuse University Press, 1995).

32. United Nations Relief and Works Agency (UNRWA), *UNRWA's Financial Situation: Briefing Paper Prepared for the Informal Meeting of Major Donors and Host Governments* (Amman: UNRWA, 10–11 June 1997), 8.

33. Ze'ev Schiff and Ehud Ya'ari, *Intifada: The Palestinian Uprising—Israel's Third Front* (New York: Simon and Schuster, 1990), 203. The PLO's Palestine National Fund itself reported expenditures in the territories of $487 million between 1979 and 1987, with education being the largest component. Neil Livingstone and David Halevy, *Inside the PLO* (New York: William Morrow, 1990), 169.

34. United Nations Conference on Trade and Development, *The Palestinian Financial Sector under Israeli Occupation* (New York: UNCTAD, 1987), cited by Salim Tamari, "The Palestinian Movement in Transition: Historical Reversals and the Uprising," in Brynen, *Echoes of the Intifada,* 19.

35. World Bank, *Developing the Occupied Territories,* vol. 2, 28.

36. John Clark and Barbara Balaj, *NGOs in the West Bank and Gaza* (Washington, D.C.: World Bank, February 1996), 3; Joachim Zauker with Andrew Giffel and Peter Gubser, *Toward Middle East Peace and Development: International Assistance to Palestinians and the Role of NGOs during the Transition to Civil Society* (Washington, D.C.: InterAction West Bank/Gaza NGO Support Project, December 1995), 20.

37. *U.S. News and World Report,* 26 April 1993, 50.

38. Clark and Balaj, *NGOs in the West Bank and Gaza,* 1.

39. *U.S. News and World Report,* 51; *al-Quds,* Jerusalem (20 October 1997), Internet edition (via *Foreign Broadcast Information Service* [FBIS]).

40. Samir Hulayla, in *Jerusalem Post,* 25 August 1993.

41. *Reuters World Report,* 0609 GMT, 22 August 1993; 1245 GMT, 23 August 1993.

42. Tamari, "Palestinian Movement in Transition," 17–18.

43. Roy, *The Gaza Strip,* 151.

44. Denis Sullivan, "NGOs in Palestine: Agents of Development and Foundations of Civil Society," *Journal of Palestine Studies* 25, no. 3 (spring 1996): 94.

45. In 1991, there were 188 registered charitable associations in the West Bank and 51 in Gaza; the Union of Charitable Societies had some 350 member organizations. Clark and Balaj, *NGOs in the West Bank and Gaza*, 1, 18.

46. In the early 1990s, 330 cooperatives were registered, only nine of them in Gaza. Ibid., 1.

47. Six universities were established in the West Bank and two in Gaza. None received funding from the occupation authorities.

48. World Bank, *The Palestinian NGO Project: A Discussion Paper for the Public* (1 April 1997), accessed at www.arts.mcgill.ca/MEPP/PDIN/docs/wbngos2.html.

49. Rita Giacaman and Penny Johnson, "Palestinian Women: Building Barricades and Breaking Barriers," in *Intifada: The Palestinian Uprising against Israeli Occupation*, ed. Zachary Lockman and Joel Benin (Toronto: Between the Lines, 1989).

50. Palestinian female labor force participation, for example, stood at 11–12 percent in the mid-1990s, compared with rates of 18 percent in Jordan, 23 percent in Syria, 27 percent in Egypt, and 39 percent in the developing world as a whole. UNSCO, *Economic and Social Conditions in the West Bank and Gaza Strip* (fall 1996): 30; UNDP, *World Development Report 1996*, table 16. Survey results suggest that Palestinians were somewhat *less* likely to support the principle of women voting in legislative elections (87.9 percent, compared with 97.8 percent in Jordan) or running for legislative office (71.8 percent, compared with 75.5 percent in Jordan), although the differences fall within the studies' margin of error. CPRS, *Public Opinion Poll no. 12* (29–30 September 1994), archived at www.cprs-palestine.org/polls/94/poll12b.html#women; Mousa Shteiwi and Amal Daghestani, *A Field Survey on Jordanian Women's Participation in Political Life* (Amman: University of Jordan, Center for Strategic Studies, September 1993).

51. On this period and subsequently, see Emile Sahliyeh, *In Search of Leadership: West Bank Politics since 1967* (Washington, D.C.: Brookings Institution, 1988).

52. Clark and Balaj, *NGOs in the West Bank and Gaza*, 1, 4.

53. Tamari, "Palestinian Movement in Transition," 20–25. For a detailed assessment, see Joost Hiltermann, *Behind the Intifada: Labor and Women's Movements in the Occupied Territories* (Princeton, N.J.: Princeton University Press, 1991); Robinson, *Building a Palestinian State*.

54. Interview with DFLP Politburo member, Amman, August 1991.

55. Islamist groups were sometimes accused of receiving funds from Iran, although donations also came from Kuwait and other conservative Arab states, particularly after they became alienated from the PLO during the 1990–91 Gulf War.

56. Because Islamist health clinics and other social institutions were often highly effective, they also attracted some Western donor assistance, particularly in Gaza. An employee of one Western aid agency noted that when Israel deported 415 prominent members of Hamas in December 1992, instructions were received from headquarters to determine whether any aid funds had gone to organizations linked with these

individuals. Sure enough, several of the deportees were members of the boards of directors of several health and social welfare projects that the aid agency had supported. Interview with Western aid agency employee, Ramallah, May 1997.

57. It is important to note that many Palestinians have supported Islamist movements as an expression of their support for social Islam, rather than as a full endorsement of particular political views. Similarly, it should be noted that Fateh itself enjoys significant support among those who describe themselves as highly religious, especially those who are older and more conservative.

58. Data of political support are an approximation based on the findings of CPRS, *Public Opinion Poll no. 2*, 5–10 October 1993, archived at www.cprs-palestine.org/polls/94/poll2a.html. It should be noted, however, that public opinion can be volatile; a survey taken before Oslo, for example, would have shown less support for Fateh and greater support for its opponents. It is also likely that survey research underestimates support for radical and rejectionist groups. However, opinion polls do provide a good indication of the rough levels of support for various parties and were by and large vindicated by the Palestinian election results of January 1996.

59. For details, see Hiltermann, *Behind the Intifada*, 134.

60. Clark and Balaj, *NGOs in the West Bank and Gaza*, 1; Graham Usher, "Palestinian Trade Unions and the Struggle for Independence," *Middle East Report* 194, no. 5 (June/July–August 1995): 22.

61. Tamari, "Palestinian Movement in Transition," 19.

62. Majdi al-Malki, "Clans et partis politiques dans trois villages palestiniens," *Revue d'études palestiniennes* 52 (summer 1994): 201. A report by *U.S. News and World Report* (26 April 1993) suggests that, at the PLO's heyday, as many as 150,000 persons inside or outside the territories received either PLO welfare payments or payments to the families of those killed, wounded, or arrested in the struggle. For discussion of corruption in PLO funding, see Said K. Aburish, *Cry Palestine: Inside the West Bank* (Boulder, Colo.: Westview Press, 1993), 181–190.

63. For a more detailed analysis of neopatrimonial politics in Palestine (from which the present discussion derives), see Rex Brynen, "The Neopatrimonial Dimension of Palestinian Politics," *Journal of Palestine Studies* 25, no. 1 (fall 1995).

64. Many liberation and revolutionary movements organize along democratic centralist lines, crushing internal opposition and suppressing external rivals. By contrast, Fateh has often used patronage to manipulate dissidents and dampen dissent. A corollary is that when Arafat finds himself unable (because of external constraints or lack of funds) to engage in neopatrimonial politics, the prospects of repression increase.

65. Rex Brynen, *Sanctuary and Survival: The PLO in Lebanon* (Boulder, Colo.: Westview Press, 1990), 174. In Lebanon before 1982, the PLO employed up to 10,000 civilian and 15,000 military personnel. Arafat exercised increasingly tight control over resources (including even requisitions by military units for new boots), in what Yezid Sayigh describes as a "straightforward system of patronage." Sayigh,

Armed Struggle and the Search for State: The Palestinian National Movement, 1949–93 (Oxford: Clarendon Press, 1997).

66. For information on the activities of the Refugee Working Group, the various Middle East and North Africa (MENA) economic summits, and the Middle East Development Bank, consult the various resources available at the Palestinian Refugee ResearchNet/Palestinian Development InfoNet Web site at www.arts.mcgill.ca/ mepp/mepp.html. For an overview of the multilaterals, see Joel Peters, *Pathways to Peace: The Multilateral Arab-Israeli Peace Talks* (London: Royal Institute for International Affairs, 1996).

67. Declaration of Principles on Interim Self-Government Arrangements, 13 September 1993, archived at www.israel-mfa.gov.il/peace/dop.html.

68. Agreement on the Gaza Strip and Jericho Area, 4 May 1994, archived at www.israel-mfa.gov.il/peace/gazajer.html.

69. Annex IV: Protocol on Economic Relations, 29 April 1994, archived at www.israel-mfa.gov.il/peace/gjannex4.html.

70. Protocol on Further Transfer of Powers and Responsibilities, 29 August 1995, archived at www.israel-mfa.gov.il/peace/further.html.

71. Graham Usher, "The Politics of Internal Security: The PA's New Intelligence Services," *Journal of Palestine Studies* 25, no. 2 (winter 1996): 22–23.

72. Israeli-Palestinian Interim Agreement on the West Bank and Gaza Strip, 28 September 1995, archived at www.israel-mfa.gov.il/peace/interim.html.

73. Haim Gvirtzman, *Maps of Israeli Interests in Judea and Samaria*, BESA Security and Policy Studies no. 34 (Ramat Gan, Israel: Bar-Ilan University, Begin-Sadat Center for Strategic Studies, December 1997), 5.

74. Election results can be found at the Web site of the Palestinian Central Election Commission at www.planet.edu/cec/.

75. Protocol Concerning the Redeployment in Hebron, 17 January 1997, archived at www.israel-mfa.gov.il/peace/hebprot.html.

76. CPRS, *Public Opinion Poll no. 10* (30 June 1994), archived at www.cprs-palestine.org/polls/94/poll10b.html; *Public Opinion Poll no. 16* (16–18 March 1995), archived at www.cprs-palestine.org/polls/95/poll16b.html#econsit.

77. Jerusalem Media and Communications Centre public opinion surveys, reported in *Palestine Report* (11 April 1997 and 25 April 1997). According to the latter, most felt that services had improved "a lot" (20.2 percent) or "a little" (51.8 percent).

78. UNSCO, *The Economy of the West Bank and Gaza Strip: A Retrospective on the 1990s and Future Challenges* (January 1999), 6.

79. UNSCO, *Quarterly Report* (April 1997), tables 9–10; UNSCO, *Report on Economic and Social Conditions in the West Bank and Gaza Strip* (spring 1999).

80. UNSCO, *Quarterly Report* (October 1997), section II.2–3; UNSCO, *Report on Economic and Social Conditions in the West Bank and Gaza* (spring 1998), section

II.2, both archived on the UNSCO Web site at www.arts.mcgill.ca/mepp/unsco/unqr.html.

81. A breakpoint of $650 per annum was used. Palestine Economic Policy Research Institute (MAS), *MAS Economic Monitor* (June 1997); summary at www.palecon.org/masdir/monitor/monitor.html.

82. UNSCO, *Quarterly Report* (October 1997).

83. UNSCO, *Quarterly Report* (April 1997), table 23; UNSCO, *The Economy of the West Bank and Gaza Strip* (spring 1999), 9.

84. *Independent* (London), 10 December 1998.

85. B'tselem, *Divide and Rule: Prohibition on Passage between the Gaza Strip and the West Bank* (Jerusalem: B'tselem, May 1998), 11, 18.

86. This discussion of closure relies heavily on UNSCO, *Economic and Social Conditions in the West Bank and Gaza Strip: Quarterly Report, Winter–Spring 1997* (1 April 1997); World Bank and MAS, *Development under Adversity?* chap. 3.

87. UNSCO and World Bank, *Closure on the West Bank and Gaza: Fact Sheet* (6 October 1997); UNSCO, *Quarterly Report* (October 1997), table 21.

88. UNSCO and World Bank, *Closure on the West Bank and Gaza: Fact Sheet* (6 October 1997).

89. Data drawn from UNSCO, *Quarterly Report* (October 1996), 12; UNSCO, *Quarterly Report* (April 1997), table 22; UNSCO, *Quarterly Report* (October 1997), table 1; UNSCO, *Report on Economic and Social Conditions in the West Bank and Gaza* (spring 1998), table 1. Figures include Palestinians working in Israeli settlements.

90. Crops sensitive to delay or damage caused by intrusive security inspection accounted for approximately 78 percent of Gaza's daily agricultural exports prior to the sustained closure of February–March 1996, worth over half a million dollars per day. When affected by closure, such crops had to be dumped on local markets at reduced prices, had to be sold at lower value to Israeli food processing industries, or were refused by purchasers altogether. UNSCO, "Costs of Closure: Some Preliminary Indicators on Costs of Closure in the Gaza Strip" (draft of a paper presented to the Ad-Hoc Liaison Committee, 12 April 1996), 8.

91. UNSCO, *Economic and Social Conditions in the West Bank and Gaza Strip, Winter–Spring 1997*, 6, 17, 19.

92. For a discussion, see Samir Abdullah and Clare Woodcraft, "Israeli Closure Policy: Sabotaging Sustainable Development," in *The Economics of Middle East Peace: A Reassessment*, ed. Sara Roy (Stamford, Conn.: JAI Press, 1999).

93. World Bank and MAS, *Development under Adversity?* table 3.1.

94. UNSCO and World Bank, *Closure on the West Bank and Gaza: Fact Sheet;* MOPIC, *First Quarterly Monitoring Report of Donor Assistance* (5 June 1997).

95. Israeli Government Press Office (11 September 1998), archived at www.pmo.gov.il/english/policy/oslo5.html.

96. *Prime Minister's Report* (e-mail bulletin), 25 November 1998.

97. Palestinian Center for Human Rights (PCHR), *Submission of the Palestinian Center for Human Rights to the United Nations Human Rights Committee* (e-mail bulletin), July 1998.

98. Ibid.

99. Associated Press, 20 October 1994.

100. Israeli cabinet communiqué, 30 November 1997.

101. In a further twist, Israel later withheld some funds and blocked some automobile imports, demanding that the Palestinian Authority halt car theft by criminals as well as acts of terrorism. Israel Internet News Service (11 November 1997).

102. The proportion of Palestinians who blamed Palestinian suicide bombers for closure dropped from 31 percent in March 1996 to only 18 percent in September 1997. CPRS, *Public Opinion Survey no. 29* (18–20 September 1997), archived at www.cprs-palestine.org/polls/97/poll29a.html.

103. CPRS, *Public Opinion Survey no. 29;* CPRS, *Public Opinion Survey no. 34* (25–27 June 1998), archived at www.cprs-palestine.org/polls/98/poll34b.html; CPRS, *Public Opinion Survey no. 36* (8–10 October 1998) (via e-mail, from CPRS).

104. Wye River Memorandum (23 October 1998).

105. Sharm el-Sheikh Memorandum on Implementation Timeline of Outstanding Commitments of Agreements Signed and the Resumption of Permanent Status (4 September 1999), archived at www.israel-mfa.gov.il/mfa/go.asp?MFAH0fo30.

3. MOBILIZING ASSISTANCE

1. Address by Warren Christopher at Columbia University, New York, 20 September 1993.

2. "Cosponsors' Statement," Conference to Support Middle East Peace, 1 October 1993, in *Journal of Palestine Studies* 23, no. 2 (winter 1994): 128–129.

3. This analysis has benefited greatly from participation in the Pledges of Aid project, conducted by a comparative international team under the auspices of the Center on International Cooperation at New York University and the Social Science Research Council.

4. The Development Assistance Committee of the OECD defines "commitments" as "a firm obligation, expressed in writing and backed by the necessary funds, undertaken by an official donor to provide specified assistance to a recipient country or multilateral organization," while "disbursements" are defined as "the release of funds to, or the purchase of goods or services for a recipient . . . the actual international transfer of financial resources. . . ." By contrast, "pledges" is a more nebulous political term, marking a general promise of assistance for commitment and disbursement to unspecified future projects. DAC, *Development Cooperation: 1996 DAC Report* (Paris: OECD, 1997), 175.

5. In November 1996 the World Bank reported that loans and guarantees made up $760 million of the $2,996 million (25 percent) then pledged by donors. Using a somewhat different procedure, MOPIC calculated that loans represented 22.6 percent of donor commitments by November 1997. Secretariat of the Ad-Hoc Liaison Committee (AHLC), *Matrix of Donors' Assistance to the West Bank and Gaza*, 5th revision (November 1996); MOPIC, *Third Quarterly Monitoring Report of Donor Assistance: Tables* (28 November 1997).

6. Although no detailed statistics are available on the composition of these loan amounts, DAC data suggest that most Western ODA loans are concessional, containing an effective grant component of around 63 percent. DAC, *Development Cooperation: 1996 DAC Report*, table 27. Unlike most countries in transition, Palestine started from a "debt-free beginning," a status that many advisers (including some at the World Bank) urged them to preserve. I am grateful to Jim Boyce for his comments on this issue.

7. Again, no detailed data are available for the Palestinian case. Typically, around one-third of Western bilateral aid is tied, with the proportion highest in the area of technical assistance. DAC, *Development Cooperation: 1996 DAC Report*, table 31.

8. World Bank, *Pledges to the Core Investment Program* (10 January 1996). Indeed, one World Bank official later acknowledged that "the figure had to total over $1 billion because of the [Palestinian] elections." Interviews, February 1996.

9. MOPIC, *First Quarterly Monitoring Report of Donor Assistance: Tables* (5 June 1997).

10. After 1998, some Palestinian officials expressed concern that a shift to annual pledging might facilitate some aid slippage among donors. Discussion with MOPIC official, July 1998.

11. Stewart Patrick, meeting summary for Pledges of Aid: Multilateral Support for Reconstruction and Transition project, Center on International Cooperation (8–9 May 1998), via *PALDEV Digest* listserv, 4–5 June 1998; "The Check Is in the Mail: Pledges of Aid and Multilateral Coordination of Post-Conflict Reconstruction" (paper presented to the annual meeting of the Academic Council on the United Nations System, Cornwallis, Canada, June 1998).

12. Preston, "The International Effort to Invest in Peace in the Occupied Territories—and the Role of the World Bank"; World Bank, *Developing the Occupied Territories: An Investment in Peace*, vol. 1, 24–25; Abdallah Bouhabib, interview, "The World Bank and International Aid to Palestine," 65.

13. Bouhabib, interview, "The World Bank and International Aid to Palestine," 68.

14. PLO, Department of Economic Affairs and Planning, *Programme for Development of the Palestinian National Economy for the Years 1994–2000*, Executive Summary (Tunis: PLO, July 1993), 38, 41. The $14.4 billion figure is adjusted to 1994 prices, including contingencies.

15. For an analysis, see Senator Robert Byrd's comments to the Senate Appropriations Committee, 1 April 1992, in *Journal of Palestine Studies* 21, no. 4 (summer

1992). U.S. assistance to Israel since 1949 is approximately equal to U.S. aid to sub-Saharan Africa and Latin America combined.

16. *Al-Ra'y* (Amman), 20 October 1996 (via FBIS).

17. Discussion with senior Palestinian diplomat, January 1995.

18. Calculated from DAC, *ODA Receipts and Selected Indicators for Developing Countries and Territories* (8 February 1999), accessed at www.oecd.org/dac/htm/Tab25e.HTM. The DAC data exaggerate Palestinian per capita receipts by using low population figures. Accordingly, a figure is also calculated from data on disbursements and population provided by MOPIC and the PCBS.

19. Interviews with Danish and Norwegian officials, May 1997 and January 1998.

20. John Stackhouse, "Palestinian Culture Shock," *Globe and Mail* (Toronto), 15 March 1999.

21. Donor contributions to UNRWA's general budget were $245.2 million (1992), $233.8 million (1993), $239.3 million (1994), $243.0 million (1995), $247.5 million (1996), and $251.7 million (1997). In absolute terms, the largest donors to the UNRWA budget were the European Union, Japan, and the United States. The most *generous* donors, however, were Kuwait, Norway, and Sweden (measured using contributions as a proportion of donor GNP, as in figure 3.1). "1997 UNRWA Donor Generosity Index," *FOFOGNET Digest* listserv (31 December 1998), also archived on Palestinian Refugee ResearchNet at www.arts.mcgill.ca/mepp/prrn/prfront.html.

22. *Jordan Times*, 10 September 1998.

23. UNRWA, *Report of the Commissioner-General of the United Nations Relief and Works Agency for Palestine Refugees in the Near East, 1 July 1996–30 June 1997*, UN General Assembly Official Records, Fifty-Second Session, Supplement no. 13 (A/52/13), para. 13, at www.un.org/Depts/dpa/qpal/A_52_13.htm.

24. UNHCR, "UNHCR in Numbers (July 1997)" at www.unhcr.ch/un&ref/numbers/numbers.htm; UNRWA, *Report of the Commissioner-General of the United Nations Relief and Works Agency for Palestine Refugees in the Near East, 1 July 1996–30 June 1997* (A/52/13), para. 8.

25. Interview with senior Western aid official, June 1997.

26. Gerhard Pulfer and Ingrid Jaradat Gassner, *UNRWA: Between Refugee Aid and Power Politics* (Bethlehem: BADIL, January 1998), archived at www.badil.org/Refugee/ref1.htm.

27. Discussion with UNRWA official, March 1998.

28. Leaflet issued by the Union of Youth Activity Centers/West Bank, Qalandia Refugee Camp, 28 August 1997. Text carried by *FOFOGNET Digest* listserv, 2–3 September 1997.

29. *Daily Star* (Beirut), 15 September 1998.

30. In turn, UNRWA used these protests to strengthen its fund-raising position in meetings with the donor community.

31. In September 1993, the European Community consisted of Belgium, Denmark, France, Germany, Greece, Ireland, Italy, Luxembourg, the Netherlands, Portugal, Spain, and the United Kingdom. The European Community technically became the European Union on 1 November 1993. Austria, Finland, and Sweden joined the European Union on 1 January 1995. The full membership of fifteen states is used for the calculations herein.

32. MOPIC, *1998 Third Quarterly Monitoring Report of Donor Assistance: Tables* (15 November 1998).

33. Comments by senior U.S. official, June 1996.

34. *Ha'aretz* (Internet edition), 20 May 1998, 22 November 1998.

35. Spain's relatively good showing is explained in large part by the substantial loan (about 40 percent) component of its aid program, which reduces the effective value of such assistance significantly. EU and U.S. support also includes substantial loan components (around 42 percent and 25 percent, respectively).

36. Discussion with three U.S. State Department officials, December 1997.

4. Coordinating Assistance

1. Coordinating Committee for International Assistance to a Palestinian Police Force, *Term of Reference* (25 March 1994).

2. On the evolution of donor coordination mechanisms in support of the Palestinian police, see Lia Brynjar, *Implementing the Oslo Peace Accords: A Case Study of the Palestinian-Israeli Peace Process and International Assistance for the Enhancement of Security*, FFI/Rapport-98/01711 (Kjellar, Norway: Norwegian Defense Research Establishment, June 1998), 111–128.

3. The terms of reference of the LACC and JLC are set forth in the "Chairman's Summing-Up," Third Meeting of the AHLC, Brussels, 29–30 November 1994. The thinking behind establishing both sectoral groups (the SWGs) and a cross-sectoral one (the LACC) was set forth in World Bank, *Discussion Note on Local Aid Coordination* (24 June 1994).

4. The transport and communications SWG was reconstituted as two subgroups within the infrastructure SWG, in addition to subgroups on water/waste, energy, and housing/public buildings/strategic projects. Within the institution-building SWG, subgroups focused on the legal sector, public administration, and local government.

5. UNRWA, *Report of the Commissioner-General of the United Nations Relief and Works Agency for Palestine Refugees in the Near East, 1 June 1993–30 June 1994*, UN General Assembly Official Records, Forty-Ninth Session (A/49/13), table 14. More than two-thirds of these employees are teachers.

6. This led some to charge that the UN agency had come to act like a "profit-seeking" private business.

7. For information on UNSCO, see www.unsco.org.

8. Interviews with U.S. Department of State officials, December 1994 and June 1996.

9. For this reason, for example, the European Union was tacitly excluded from consultations on the timing of the AHLC, CG, and special ministerial meetings in late 1995–1996—the United States, mindful of the symbolism did support convening the ministerial meeting in France. Even at that meeting, elaborate negotiations were required to determine who would chair the meeting (France, but with a "table de présidence" including the European Community, the Italian EU president, the United States, Russia, and Japan) and who would undertake the required premeeting preparation (the World Bank and Norway).

10. François d'Alançon, "The EC Looks to a New Middle East," *Journal of Palestine Studies* 23, no. 2 (winter 1994): 41.

11. Commission of the European Communities, *EC Support for the Middle East Peace Process*, communication from the Commission to the Council and the European Parliament (Brussels, 29 September 1993), 3.

12. In practice, both the World Bank and the United Nations have acted as full members.

13. By early October, the United States and the European Union had agreed on the basic outlines of the AHLC and had also agreed that Norway would hold the gavel at the first meeting of the group in November 1993. The lack of prior U.S. consultation with Norway led the latter to seek a number of changes in the structure of the AHLC, but it eventually found itself bound by the earlier U.S.-EU working document. Although it was initially envisaged that the gavel would rotate (and Canada was asked by the United States at one point to be prepared to assume the AHLC gavel), Saudi Arabia proposed that Norway act as chair, and it hence came to hold the position permanently. "Non-paper: Ad-Hoc Liaison Committee for Assistance to the Palestinian People" and "Coordinating Structure for International Assistance to the Palestinian People" (n.p., n.d.); Rick Hooper, "The Evolution of International Assistance to the Palestinians in the West Bank and Gaza Strip, 1993–96," in *The Economics of Middle East Peace: A Reassessment*, Research in Middle East Economics, vol. 3, ed. Sara Roy (Greenwich, Conn., and London: Middle East Economic Association and JAI Press, 1999).

14. Interview with official, U.S. Department of State, December 1994.

15. Interview with World Bank official, July 1997.

16. European Commission, "The Role of the European Union in the Middle East Peace Process and Its Future Assistance," document IP/98/37 (16 January 1998). Excerpts in *Journal of Palestine Studies* 107 (spring 1998): 148–151.

17. Discussions with donor officials, August 1998, November 1998.

18. "Chair's Summary," AHLC meeting, Frankfurt, 4 February 1999.

19. Gilles Carbonnier, *Conflict, Postwar Rebuilding, and the Economy: A Critical Review of the Literature,* War-Torn Societies Project, Occasional Paper no. 2 (Geneva: UNRISD, 1998), 33–36.

20. Boyce, "Adjustment toward Peace."

21. De Soto and del Castillo, "Obstacles to Peace-Building."

22. World Bank, *Annual Report on the Status of the Trust Fund for Gaza and the West Bank* (30 June 1997), 4.

23. World Bank, *Johan Jürgen Holst Peace Fund: Status Report and Proposals for Future Directions* (20 January 1999).

24. World Bank, *West Bank/Gaza Update* (September 1997), archived at www.palecon.org.

25. Comments by World Bank official, November 1994.

26. Comments by World Bank official, June 1996.

27. Data from World Bank, *West Bank/Gaza Update* (March 1998), archived at www.palecon.org.

28. This section based on interviews with a large number of World Bank officials in June 1995, June 1996, July 1997, and August, September, and October 1998; with U.S. State Department officials, June 1996; and with PECDAR officials, January 1995 and July 1996. See also Barbara Balaj, Ishac Diwan, and Bernard Philippe, "External Assistance to the Palestinians: What Went Wrong?" (unpublished manuscript).

29. According to the World Bank, "the devolution of authority to field managers in the West Bank and Gaza and in Bosnia and Herzegovina has proved critical for the success of these programs and should be considered for other countries where local dynamics are similarly complicated and in flux." World Bank, *Post-Conflict Reconstruction*, 48.

30. "World Bank Establishes Gaza Office," World Bank news release 95/6S MENA, 10 August 1994; Agreement between the Palestine Liberation Organization for the Benefit of the Palestinian Authority and the International Bank for Reconstruction and Development Regarding the Resident Mission in Gaza, 9 July 1995.

31. The World Bank itself later argued that the establishment of a small, closely knit group of senior staff, the reduction of layers of administrative authority (and hence red tape), and the greater autonomy given to individual project/program task managers all served to increase responsiveness and trim operational costs. World Bank, *Post-Conflict Reconstruction*, 9.

32. CPRS, *Prevailing Perceptions on Aid Management,* Research Reports Series no. 9 (Nablus: CPRS, December 1997), 18. The survey questioned thirty-four donor officials (including international organization staff), eighty-two officials from local NGOs, and seventy-four officials from the PA.

33. Interview with IMF official, June 1996; IMF, *Recent Economic Developments, Prospects, and Progress in Institution-Building in the West Bank and Gaza Strip* (Washington, D.C.: IMF, 1997).

34. Interview with official of the Ministry of Economy, July 1996.

35. United Nations, *Supporting the Transition: An Immediate Response of the United Nations to the Interim Period in the West Bank and Gaza Strip* (September 1993).

36. "Secretary General Emphasizes Need to Meet Expectation of Palestinians in Integrated Way, at Interagency Meeting," United Nations press release, 29 June 1994; *Statement by Ambassador Larsen, Special Coordinator in the Occupied Territories,* 29 June 1994.

37. "UNSCO at a Glance," www.arts.mcgill.ca/mepp/unsco/unabout.html.

38. This section is based on more than two dozen interviews and conversations with current and former officials of the UN Secretariat, UNSCO, UNDP, UNRWA, and World Bank in September 1994, December 1994, June 1995, December 1995, February 1996, June–July 1996, May 1997, September 1997, February–March 1998, and July 1998. On the broader difficulties of coordination in the UN system, see Donini, *Policies of Mercy.*

39. United Nations, *Programme of Cooperation in the West Bank and Gaza Strip, 1998–99* (Gaza: UNSCO, 1997), archived at www.arts.mcgill.ca/mepp/unsco/ unfront.html. These agencies included the UN Department for Development Support and Management Services; the Economic Commission for Western Asia; the Food and Agricultural Organization; the International Atomic Energy Agency; the International Civil Aviation Organization; the International Fund for Agricultural Development; the International Labour Organization; the International Maritime Organization; the International Trade Center; the International Telecommunications Union; the UN Conference on Trade and Development; the UN Drug Control Program; UNDP; the UN Environment Program; UNESCO; the UN Population Fund; UNHCR; the UN Center for Human Settlements; UNICEF; the UN Industrial Development Organization; the UN Development Fund for Women; the UN Institute for Training and Research; UNRWA; UNSCO; the Universal Postal Union; the World Food Program; and the World Health Organization.

40. The latter, together with periodic reports by the secretary-general to the UN General Assembly on UN efforts, are available online at www.unsco.org.

41. The approach to the UNSCO compound, "UN Boulevard," is undoubtedly the best-paved and -landscaped road in the Gaza Strip. (The PA, rather than the United Nations, paid for this—albeit probably with donor money.) Opposite the UNSCO gates is one of Gaza's most expensive and elite restaurants, frequented by senior PA personnel, the Gaza elite, and international aid staff.

Similar criticism could also be heard of UNRWA's new Gaza headquarters.

42. See, for example, the summary of donor projects in the West Bank and Gaza prepared by the LACC, *Partners in Peace* (July 1996). Available online at www.unsco.org.

43. Some UNSCO officials date the friction earlier than this, to UNSCO unhappiness at the slow pace of the bank's initial efforts in the territories.

44. Interview, June 1996.

45. *Putting Peace to Work: Strategies and Priorities for the Second Phase of the Development Effort in the West Bank and Gaza Strip* (Gaza: UNSCO–World Bank, 16 September 1995).

46. Although the reappointment reportedly had the acquiescence of Israeli prime minister Barak, the Israeli foreign ministry issued a statement criticizing the expansion of Larsen's mandate.

47. The UNSCO *Quarterly Reports* can be found on the UNSCO Web site at www.arts.mcgill.ca/mepp/unsco/unqr.html. Some in the World Bank felt that UNSCO sometimes exaggerated the data to make its point (and the oft-quoted UNSCO data showing a one-third decline in GNP per capita were subsequently revised to a more modest number when later IMF estimates became available). However, such criticism also reflected the extent to which UNSCO's economic monitoring unit challenged the bank as the primary source of donor and media information on economic conditions and trends.

48. Comments made at Carnegie Endowment meeting in Washington, D.C., on assistance to the West Bank and Gaza, June 1996.

49. Personal communication, November 1998.

50. CPRS, *Prevailing Perceptions on Aid Management*, 11–12.

51. One USAID official described the AHLC as "absolutely, completely, a horrible waste of time and money—a most blatant corruption." Interview, June 1996.

52. At these meetings, "you aren't going to hear [U.S. deputy assistant secretary of state] Toni Verstandig and [U.S. Middle East Peace Process special coordinator] Dennis Ross playing second fiddle [to USAID officials]." Interview with senior USAID official, June 1996.

53. Comments by senior EU aid official, February 1998.

54. Comments by senior UNSCO official, December 1998.

55. Interview with World Bank official, January 1998; discussion with Palestinian official, March 1998.

56. Discussion with two former UNSCO officials, March 1998; comments by UNSCO officials, December 1998.

57. For a broader discussion of "peace conditionality," see James Boyce and Manuel Pastor, "Aid for Peace: Can International Financial Institutions Help Prevent Conflict?" *World Policy Journal* 15, no. 2 (1998); Ball, *Pressing for Peace*.

58. Despite Palestinian urging, donor support for NGOs was *not* covered by the agreement, with the United States arguing that it would be "politically unacceptable to include this element in the package." The United States seemed concerned that many of these NGO activities would be provocative to Israel. U.S. Department of State, comments on draft "Understanding," circa September 1994.

59. The need for "certain basic elements of conditionality" had been noted by the United States in "Issues Regarding Palestinian Assistance," a discussion paper circulated in September 1994.

60. *World Bank/IMF Position Paper on Support for the Palestinian Budget*, circa October 1994.

61. Earlier drafts of the understanding had included references to Israeli actions (and an Israeli signature line), but these were dropped in response to Israeli objections. U.S. comments on draft "Understanding," circa October 1994.

62. Text of Tripartite Action Plan in *Journal of Palestine Studies* 24, no. 4 (summer 1995).

63. Tripartite Action Plan on Revenues, Expenditures and Donor Funding for the Palestinian Authority, January 1996.

64. Secretariat of the AHLC, *Report on the Status of Tripartite Action Plan Provisions*, Oslo (13 May 1998).

65. Letter from Norwegian foreign minister, Knut Vollebaek, to donors, 20 May 1998.

66. *Palestine Report*, 2 October 1998.

67. For a discussion, see Martin Beck, "Can Financial Aid Promote Regional Peace Agreement? The Case of the Arab-Israeli Conflict," *Mediterranean Politics* 2, no. 2 (fall 1997).

68. Patrick Clawson, *EU vs. Israel on Trade: Peace Process Posturing or Commercial Dispute?* Peacewatch 170 (Washington, D.C.: Washington Institute for Near East Policy, June 1998), via *PALDEV Digest* listserv, 28–29 June 1998; *Ha'aretz*, 21 July 1998, via *PALDEV Digest* listserv, 19–20 July 1998. To avert a trade war, Israel proposed relaxing its opposition to an earlier PA-EU trade agreement.

69. *Ha'aretz* (Internet edition), 4 November 1998.

70. *Ha'aretz* (Internet edition), 22 November 1998; *Reuters World Report*, 23 December 1998.

71. Lena Hjelm-Wallen, interviewed in *al-Quds al-'Arabi* (London), 3 April 1998 (via FBIS/WNC).

5. DELIVERING ASSISTANCE

1. Graham Usher, "Arafat Returns—But Not to Dancing," *Middle East International*, 9 July 1994, 3.

2. Nabil Sha'th in *Reuters World Report*, 5 June 1994.

3. Yasir Arafat in *Reuters World Report*, 15 November 1994.

4. *Al-Wasat* (London), 9–15 January 1995, 8–9 (via FBIS/WNC).

5. *Chairman's Summing-Up*, Third Meeting of the Ad-Hoc Liaison Committee, November 1994.

6. MOPIC, *1997 Fourth Quarterly Monitoring Report of Donor Assistance* (31 December 1997), for 1994–95.

7. *Reuters World Report*, 26 October 1995.

8. Personal communication, MOPIC official, March and December 1998.

9. Patrick, "The Check Is in the Mail"; Yamada, "Pledge Gaps in Cambodia: Preliminary Report."

10. World Bank, "Municipal Infrastructure Rehabilitation" (8 September 1996), archived on the Palestinian Development InfoNet (PDIN) at www.arts.mcgill.ca/mepp/pdin/docs/cipmuninfra.html.

11. Nigel Roberts, "The Prospects for the Palestinian Economy" (paper presented to the conference, Resolving the Palestinian Refugee Problem: What Role for the International Community? University of Warwick, United Kingdom, 23–24 March 1998), archived at www.arts.mcgill.ca/mepp/prrn/prwarrob.html.

12. Israel-Palestine Center for Research and Information, *The Legal Structure for Foreign Investment in the West Bank and Gaza Strip*, Commercial Law Report Series no. 1 (October 1994), introduction.

13. UNSCO, *The West Bank and Gaza Strip Private Economy;* UNSCO, *UNSCO Report on Economic and Social Conditions in the West Bank and Gaza Strip* (spring 1998).

14. World Bank, *Industrial Estates and Enabling Environment for Private Sector Development in the West Bank and Gaza* (1995); UNSCO, *The West Bank and Gaza Strip Private Economy.*

15. For a detailed critique, see David Findler, "Foreign Private Investment in Palestine: An Analysis of the Law on the Encouragement of Investment in Palestine," *Fordham International Law Journal* 19, no. 2 (December 1995).

16. UNSCO, *The West Bank and Gaza Strip Private Economy;* Secretariat of the AHLC, *March Report of the Private Sector Development Progress Report* (March 1998).

17. AHLC, *Private Sector Development in the West Bank and Gaza: Status, Problems, Opportunities* (circa May 1998).

18. *ArabicNews.com*, 23 April 1999, at www.arabicnews.com/ansub/daily/day/1999042341.html.

19. These included various microenterprise projects, and the World Bank–designed Financial Sector Development and Palestinian Housing Project. See the project documents archived at PDIN at www.arts.mcgill.ca/mepp/pdindocs/cgnov96/finansec.html and www.arts.mcgill.ca/mepp/pdindocs/cgnov96/microent.html.

20. By July 1997, 159 legal reform activities were active, completed, or pending, involving $72 million in support from seventeen donors and ten UN agencies and programs. UNSCO, *Rule of Law Development in the West Bank and Gaza Strip: Survey and Status of the Development Effort* (July 1997).

21. World Bank, *Project Outline: Gaza Industrial Estate Project* (December 1997).

22. Associated Press, 26 August 1997; discussions with Builders for Peace staff members.

23. Muna Jawhary, *The Palestinian-Israeli Trade Agreements: Searching for Fair Revenue-Sharing* (Jerusalem: MAS, December 1995).

24. AHLC, *Private Sector Development in the West Bank and Gaza.*

25. *Jordan Times* (Amman), 16 September 1996.

26. Norman Kanafani, cited in *Palestine Economic Pulse* 3, no. 4 (July–August 1998): 4. Kanafani also argued that too much of the implementation of the Paris Protocol had passed from the hands of the civilian Joint Economic Committee to the more military-dominated Civil Affairs Committee.

27. For a fuller discussion, see World Bank and MAS, *Development under Adversity?* chap. 6.

28. Comments by senior Israeli diplomat, July 1996.

29. AHLC, *Private Sector Development in the West Bank and Gaza,* 4.

30. Ibid., 5.

31. Local Aid Coordination Committee (LACC), *Co-chairs' Summary* (8 September 1997), archived on the UNSCO Web site at www.arts.mcgill.ca/mepp/unsco/lacc970908.html.

32. Online versions of some of these can be found at the UNSCO Web site, www.arts.mcgill.ca/mepp/unsco/unfront.html.

33. Tripartite Action Plan on Revenues, Expenditures and Donor Funding for the Palestinian Authority.

34. Interview with U.S. Department of State senior official, 13 June 1996; interview with U.S. Department of State official, 10 June 1996; interview with USAID senior official, 11 June 1996. The lack of serious U.S. pressure on Israel over closure was attributed by State Department officials to both the nature of the relationship between the two countries and the unlikelihood that such pressure would succeed.

35. Commerce Secretary William Daley, quoted by Agence France-Presse, 9 December 1998.

36. Statement to journalists by Uri Savir, director-general of the Israeli Foreign Ministry, 12 April 1996, distributed by Israel Information Service, 18 April 1996.

37. *Statement by the Head of the Israeli Delegation, Ambassador Victor Harel,* Consultative Group Meeting for the West Bank and Gaza, 14–15 December 1997; (Israeli) Prime Minister's Office, *The Prime Minister's Report* 2, no. 18 (4 June 1998).

38. CPRS, *Prevailing Perceptions on Aid Management,* 17.

39. Undersecretary of State Stuart Eizenstat, "Israel's Stake in the Palestinian Economic Crisis" (address given at Hebrew University, Jerusalem, 14 June 1998), in *Journal of Palestine Studies* 109 (fall 1998): 158.

40. Peter Hirschberg, "The Grief of Giving," *Jerusalem Report,* 1 May 1997, 29–31.

41. Interviews with PECDAR and World Bank officials.

42. Fayiz Zaydan, head of Palestinian Aviation Authority, interview, in *al-Majallah* (London), 9–15 August 1998 (via FBIS/WNC).

43. *Ha'aretz,* 21 April 1998, via *PALDEV Digest* listserv, 21–22 April 1998.

44. Interview with Israeli Foreign Ministry official, July 1996; interview with senior USAID official, January 1998.

45. "Prime Minister Netanyahu before the Foreign Diplomatic Corps, 22 May 1998," via Israel Information Service, 24 May 1998.

46. See *Ha'aretz,* 22 July 1998, via Israel Information Service, 22 July 1998.

47. *Globes* (Tel Aviv, Internet edition), 27 April 1999, at www.globes.il.

48. CPRS, *Prevailing Perceptions on Aid Management,* 12–13.

49. Ibid., 14–15.

50. Glen Shortcliffe, *Report to UNDP: The Palestinian Authority and Machinery of Government* (30 June 1995).

51. Calculated from MOPIC, *1998 First Quarterly Monitoring Report of Donor Assistance* (31 March 1998). Comparison of MOPIC data with known projects, however, suggests that this may overestimate the amount of technical assistance.

52. Touche-Ross Saba acted as the agent of the World Bank, assuring that the disbursements from the Holst Fund were made against appropriately documented expenditures.

53. Faruq Qaddumi, letter to major donors, 17 October 1994 (emphasis in original).

54. PLO, "The Palestine Emergency Development and Reconstruction Authority" (working paper, September 1993).

55. For further discussion of the evolution of PECDAR and other Palestinian economic institutions, see chapter 4.

56. [Terje Rød Larsen], *Memorandum: Palestinian Economic Council for Development and Reconstruction,* transmitted to AHLC members by Norwegian foreign minister Johan Jørgan Holst, 18 November 1993; PECDAR–World Bank, *Aide Memoire,* 19 April 1994; Presidency of the European Union, "Non-paper: Aid to the West Bank and Gaza," Athens, 11 May 1994. While the European Union was among those expressing the importance of Palestinian "transparency, accountability and efficiency" so as to "[avoid] further delay in channeling the international aid," it also on occasion complained that the United States was being too harsh in this respect, noting that "one should consider whether an encouraging policy rather than a reprimanding one can be proved more productive as far as Palestinian institutions are concerned."

57. *Bylaws of the Palestinian Economic Council for Development and Reconstruction,* 14 May 1994 [in Arabic]; PECDAR, *Handbook of Procedures and Regulations* (approved 11 May 1994, revised 14 June 1994).

58. Interview with UNSCO official, May 1997.

59. Comments by donor official, November 1994.

60. Personal communication with Mahmoud Labadi, director of Aid Coordination and Facilitation Department, PECDAR, 1 June 1998; interview with PECDAR official, August 1998.

61. PECDAR, "Message from the Managing Director," in *Activity Report 1996* (Dahiyet al-Barid: PECDAR, 1996).

62. Interview with senior MOPIC official, January 1998.

63. Interview with senior World Bank official, January 1998.

64. Personal communication with Mahmoud Labadi, 1 June 1998.

65. From 1993 to September 1997, PECDAR-managed or -implemented projects (excluding the Holst Fund) accounted for $304.9 million in donor commitments. The largest contributors were the World Bank ($120 million), Saudi Arabia ($50 million), the AFSED ($36.7 million), the European Union ($31.3 million), Denmark ($20.6 million), and Switzerland ($14 million).

66. *Report of the Special Committee of the Palestinian Legislative Council on the Report of the Head of General Control Office, First Annual Report 1996.*

67. Interview with donor official, July 1998.

68. *PECDAR Info* 2, no. 8 (August 1998): 1.

69. Personal communication with donor official, 2 September 1998.

70. Norway, for example, expressed its concern that "different Palestinian ministries and public agencies continue to present requests to Norway directly, without channelling them through MOPIC, as the coordinating body for all bilateral assistance." *Agreed Minutes from the Annual Review Meeting on Development Cooperation between the PA and Norway*, 16 September 1997.

71. Interview with senior PECDAR official, July 1996.

72. Interview with USAID official, January 1998.

73. For example, suspicions were raised by some about the large number of contracts issued by MOPIC to the consulting firm TEAM and related enterprises, to which Nabil Sha'th and his family have close links.

74. The monopolies reportedly included Dor Energy in the case of oil and fuel, and the Nesher company in the case of cement. Some Palestinian sources also suggest the active collaboration or approval of the Israeli security sources, implying that "Israel bought influence over senior decision makers in the Palestinian hierarchy. . . . almost everyone suspected of corruption in the territories at some point gained tacit support from Israel, and thus the beneficiary became Israel's covert ally. His private interest in maintaining good ties with Israel dovetailed with Israel's national interests." Ora Qoren, "Mother of All Conspiracies?" *Globes* (Internet edition), 30 November 1998.

75. *Ha'aretz*, 4 April 1997. Some estimates (*Palestine Report*, 30 May 1997) suggest that these monopolies earn $200 million or more per year—although these estimates seem high given the total volume of trade.

76. Public Monitoring Department, *First Annual Report 1996* (May 1997); *Statement by the Palestinian Delegation on the Internal Audit Report of 23 May 1997*, presented to the AHLC meeting, 5 June 1997.

77. For example, public land had been sold for $72 million less than its market value to encourage private development; $45.5 million in customs had not been collected on the property of returnees to facilitate their reintegration into the territories; and revenues had not been collected due to economic deterioration and growing poverty in the territories (for example, $44 million in unpaid electrical bills). *Statement by the Palestinian Delegation on the Internal Audit Report of 23 May 1997,* presented to the AHLC, 5 June 1997.

78. *Report of the Special Committee of the Palestinian Legislative Council on the Report of the Head of General Control Office, First Annual Report 1996* [in Arabic].

79. *Palestine Report,* 19 September 1996.

80. Text of the agreement in *Palestine Report,* 2 January 1998.

81. Quoted in David Hirst, "Shameless in Gaza," *Guardian Weekly,* 27 April 1997.

82. CPRS poll results, archived at www.cprs-palestine.org/polls/97/poll30a.html#corrupt and www.cprs-palestine.org/polls/98/poll35b.html.

83. CPRS, *Prevailing Perceptions on Aid Management,* 23. "Misuse of funds" in this survey need not apply solely to corruption, however.

84. Part of this weakness stemmed from inadequate investigatory resources; part of it stemmed from an excessive reliance on hearsay.

85. Interview with IMF official, May 1996.

86. Palestinian Human Rights Monitoring Group, *Why Is the Role of the Tax Authorities Absent?* (20 August 1998).

87. In a November 1997 poll, 61 percent of respondents held that the PA still acted in accordance with public interests. CPRS poll archived at www.cprs-palestine.org/polls/97/poll30a.html#corrupt.

88. European Commission, "The Role of the European Union in the Middle East Peace Process and Its Future Assistance."

89. Rex Brynen, "Neopatrimonial Dimensions of Palestinian Politics," *Journal of Palestine Studies* 25, no. 1 (fall 1995).

90. Aisling Byrne, "Ideology as Science: The Political Economy of Bantustanisation in Palestine," *Middle East International,* 10 April 1998, 20.

91. *Al-Quds al-'Arabi* (London), 25 April 1997, 4 (via FBIS/WNC).

92. Interview with PECDAR official, July 1996.

93. Averages calculated from those evaluating performance as "good" or "very good" in polls conducted by CPRS in September 1996, December 1996, April 1997, June 1997, September 1997, December 1997, and June 1998. Over the same period, support for Fateh was relatively steady at an average of 41 percent, compared to 15 percent for the Islamist opposition and 5 percent for the "nationalist" (leftist) opposition. CPRS poll results archived at www.cprs-palestine.org/polls/97/poll31a.html.

94. Samir Hulayla, interview, *Middle East Report* 186 (January–February 1994): 7–8.

95. Mission of Palestine to the UN, *Palestine and the UN* 3, no. 10 (November 1998): 4.

96. Article 1.3 of PECDAR's original bylaws noted that "The Council shall have its main office in Jerusalem. . . . ," *Bylaws of the Palestinian Economic Council for Development and Reconstruction,* 14 May 1994 [in Arabic].

97. Specifically, Jerusalem projects are disbursed from a separate account. For details, see World Bank, *Palestinian NGO Project: Discussion Paper* (1 April 1997), archived at www.arts.mcgill.ca/mepp/pdin/docs/wbngos2.html.

98. On the proliferation of semiofficial Palestinian establishments—complete with "mug-shots" of the offices concerned—see Peace Watch, *Peace Watch Report: Institutions of the Palestinian Authority in Jerusalem* (14 March 1995).

99. *Yediot Ahronot,* 26 June 1998, via *PALDEV Digest* listserv, 28–29 June 1998.

100. Jerusalem Channel 2 Television, 1800 GMT, 19 October 1995 (via FBIS/WNC).

101. The use of road construction to bolster territorial consolidation and block settlement expansion also accounts for the relatively low degree of donor support for this area (only 22 percent of transportation projects under the 1998–2000 PDP had been funded as of December 1997), which is often seen as politically, rather than developmentally, motivated. Palestinian Authority, *Palestinian Development Plan 1998–2000,* project list and annexes, December 1997, summary table.

102. *Palestine Report,* 8 May 1998.

103. In the case of the European Union, 50 percent of PA officials rated EU performance as "positive" and 12 percent as "negative," and in the case of UNDP, 45 percent rated it "positive" and 12 percent "negative." With regard to USAID, however, only 12 percent rated its performance as "positive," while 43 percent rated it "negative." CPRS, *Prevailing Perceptions on Aid Management,* 18. The fourth institution studied by CPRS—the World Bank—placed between UNDP and USAID in the eyes of PA officials.

104. Interview, February 1997.

105. Indeed, at times UNRWA was forced to "borrow" money from PIP to cover short-term financing gaps in its regular operations.

106. Interview with senior World Bank official, January 1995.

107. Interview with USAID official, December 1994, July 1995, January 1998.

108. Interview with Japanese official, July 1995; interview with MOPIC official, December 1997.

109. World Bank, *The Donor Experience and the Way Ahead,* statement to the Fifth Consultative Group Meeting for the West Bank and Gaza, 14–15 December 1997.

110. In the case of USAID, however, it was too politically sensitive to be formally located in Jerusalem. Consequently, the program is headquartered in Tel Aviv, even if many personnel operate out of Jerusalem.

111. This, of course, is not always the case. The World Bank experienced substantial initial difficulties implementing the TATF because of clashes with the head of

the technical assistance department at PECDAR, finally culminating in high-level intervention with the PA.

112. Calculated from MOPIC, *1997 Third Quarterly Monitoring Report of Donor Assistance.*

113. By August 1997 OPIC had committed around $44 million. Associated Press, 21 August 1997.

114. Interviews, Washington, D.C., July 1995; Builders for Peace, *Building Blocks* 1, no. 4 (October–December 1995).

115. Interview with OPIC official, February 1996.

116. *Reuters World Report*, 11 September 1995.

117. *Statement on Behalf of the European Investment Bank*, Consultative Group Meeting for Gaza/West Bank, 14–15 December 1997.

118. MOPIC, *1998 Third Quarterly Monitoring Report of Donor Assistance.*

119. *Berlingske Tidende* (Copenhagen), 7 March 1996 (via FBIS/WNC).

120. Draft legislation introduced by Senator Alfonse D'Amato and Representative Michael Forbes in June 1995 sought to place greater restrictions and conditions on aid to the Palestinians.

121. PLO Commitments Compliance Act of 1993 (Public Law 101-246), the Middle East Peace Facilitation Acts of 1994 (Public Law 103-246), and the Middle East Peace Facilitation Act of 1995 (Public Law 104-107). The text of the State Department's periodic certifications can be found in the documents section of the *Journal of Palestine Studies.*

122. On the splintering of the pro-Israeli lobby during this period, see Sidney Blumenthal, "The Western Front," *New Yorker,* 5 June 1995.

123. The report was attributed to the British National Criminal Intelligence Service. The British Foreign and Commonwealth Office (FCO), however, flatly denied knowledge of any such estimate, with one FCO official characterizing the $8–10 billion figure as a figment of U.S. domestic politics. Conversation with U.K. FCO official, July 1996.

124. Government Accounting Office (GAO), *Foreign Assistance: PLO's Ability to Help Support Palestinian Authority Is Not Clear*, GAO/NSAID-96-23 (declassified version, November 1995). The report entirely failed to discuss the financial crisis that, immediately before Oslo, had brought about the near collapse of the PLO; it also provided little information on post-1993 donor auditing procedures. It showed little comprehension of the political (and security) dimensions of peacebuilding, stating that "it is not clear why the Palestinian Authority needed to hire 9,000 employees . . . [or] why the Palestinian police force has grown to an 18,000-member force."

125. GAO, *Controls over U.S. Funds Provided for the Benefit of the Palestinian Authority,* GAO/NSAID-96-18 (January 1996).

126. A. M. Rosenthal, "Aid, Congress, and a Mother-in-Law," *New York Times,* 12 June 1995; Benjamin Gilman, "Letter to the Editor," *Washington Post,* 23 September

1996, A18. Gilman also wrote to key donors, requesting their assistance in tracing PLO finances.

127. Representative Jim Saxton, Associated Press, 28 July 1995; Senator Phil Gramm, *Washington Post*, 5 August 1997, A12.

128. *Washington Post*, 1 November 1995, A23; *Jerusalem Post*, 28 May 1997; Amendments to the Foreign Operations FY98 Appropriation Bill (HR 2159), *Congressional Record*, 30 July 1997.

129. *Washington Post*, 12 December 1998, A29.

130. According to *Ha'aretz* (4 December 1994), "Israeli Ambassador Itamar Rabinovich asked the Conference of Presidents of Major American Jewish Organizations to take care not to undermine the functioning of the Palestinian Authority" and stressed the need "to pursue the peace process and let the PLO operate freely." Israeli officials were reportedly annoyed that criticism of the PA by the American-Israeli Public Affairs Committee (AIPAC) would "hamper efforts by the U.S. Administration and Israel to win the approval of the new Congress for the annual aid package to the Palestinians." Also, Jerusalem Channel 2 Television, 1700 GMT, 20 June 1995 (via FBIS/WNC); James Zogby, "The War against the PLO Continues," *Mideast Mirror*, 25 September 1995.

131. Discussions and observations during an interview with a Republican staff member of the House International Relations Committee, June 1996. Senior Netanyahu adviser David Bar-Ilan, in an online chat with ABCNews.com on 4 December 1998, stated that "we fear that money which goes directly to the Palestinian Authority may not be used for the desired purposes . . . corruption in the Palestinian Authority is so rampant that giving it money may be a waste of the donor's efforts. It would be wiser to give the money to projects directly." This statement was promptly circulated by Netanyahu's office in the *Prime Minister's Report*, 7 December 1998.

6. ALLOCATING ASSISTANCE

1. Adel Zaghda and Manal Jamal, *Mortgaging Self-Reliance: Foreign Aid and Development in Palestine,* Phase II Report (Jerusalem: Jerusalem Media and Communications Center, November 1997), 43.

2. MOPIC, *Macroeconomic Framework for Development Planning*, presented to the Consultative Group, 4–5 February 1999.

3. World Bank and UNSCO, *Donor Investment in Palestinian Development, 1994–98: The Promise, the Challenges, and the Achievements* (Jerusalem: World Bank and UNSCO, 1999), 40.

4. For example, Joachim Zaucker, with Andrew Griffel and Peter Gubser, *Toward Middle East Peace and Development: International Assistance to the Palestinians and the Role of NGOs during the Transition to Civil Society* (Washington, D.C.: Inter-Action, December 1995).

5. Martin Beck, "The External Dimension of Authoritarian Rule in Palestine" (paper presented at the annual conference of the Middle East Studies Association, December 1998). Similar arguments have been made by Glenn Robinson, Sara Roy, and others.

6. Nagy Hanna, "What Economic System for Palestine?" (paper presented at the Management of the Palestinian Economy conference, Nablus, 13 December 1995).

7. United Nations, *Programme of Cooperation for the West Bank and Gaza, 1998–99* (Gaza: UNSCO, 1997), 3.

8. Adel Samara, "The World Bank's Policy in the Palestinian Self-Rule Areas: Economic Restructuring and People's Re-education," *News from Within* 11, no. 10 (October 1995): 15.

9. Palestinian Authority (PA), *Presentation to the Fifth Meeting of the Consultative Group [for the] West Bank and Gaza Strip*, Paris, 14–15 December 1997.

10. Survey conducted by Hisham Awartani, Center for Palestine Research and Studies, late 1997.

11. JMCC public opinion survey, *Palestine Report* 25 (April 1997): 8–9.

12. CPRS, *Public Opinion Poll no. 39*, archived at www.cprs-palestine.org/polls/99/poll39b.html.

13. Ibid. Interestingly, these priorities were roughly similar among both West Bankers and Gazans, although the former were more likely to emphasize the importance of water, and the latter more likely to emphasize the importance of health.

14. Calculated from a comparison of EAP targets and actual disbursements, reported in Secretariat of the AHLC, *Matrix of Donors' Assistance to the West Bank and Gaza*. The original EAP can be found in World Bank, *Emergency Assistance Program for the Occupied Territories* (Washington, D.C.: World Bank, April 1994).

15. *Framework Paper for AHLC Ministerial Meeting*, September 1995.

16. PA, *Palestinian Development Plan 1998–2000,* project list and annexes (December 1997).

17. PA, *Palestinian Development Plan 1999–2003* (January 1999), 48.

18. Although MOPIC provides a breakdown of donor commitments and disbursements by "sector" and "category," the latter label mixes channels and types of delivery (for example, "equipment" and "budget support") and purpose (for example, "public investment"). Moreover, not all donor programs appear to be coded correctly. Further adding to the confusion are differences between MOPIC categories and those employed in the PDP, as well as changes in PDP categories from year to year.

19. See figure 6.2 for definitions of "infrastructure," "social services," "productive sectors," and "state building."

20. In figure 6.3, equipment, in-kind, and some other categories are not included, while data on NGO disbursements overlap with the other categories (as NGOs may, for example, offer technical assistance or employment generation).

21. LACC, *Partners in Peace,* 13.

22. Jon Pedersen and Rick Hooper, eds., *Developing Palestinian Society: Socio-economic Trends and Their Implications for Development Strategies* (Oslo: Fafo, 1998), 57. See also World Bank, "Strengthening the Public Sector in the Palestinian Authority—Palestinian Education: A Sector Review," in *West Bank and Gaza Update* (March 1999), accessed at www.palecon.org/update/mar99/education.html.

23. World Bank and UNSCO, *Donor Investment in Palestinian Development, 1994–98,* 27.

24. World Bank, *West Bank and Gaza Update* (March 1999), at www.palecon.org/update/mar99/survey.html.

25. Ibid., at www.palecon.org/update/mar99/education.html.

26. World Bank and UNSCO, *Donor Investment in Palestinian Development, 1994–98,* 16.

27. This discussion draws on the valuable analysis by Brynjar Lia, "Implementing Peace: The Oslo Peace Accord and International Assistance to the Enhancement of Security," Forsvarets Forskningsinstitutt FFI/RAPPORT-98/01711 (Kjellar, Norway: Norwegian Defense Research Establishment).

28. Ambassador Terje Rød Larsen, statement to the Emergency Meeting for the Coordination of Development and Early Deployment of a Palestinian Police Force, 24 March 1994. In fact, at that time only Norway had made a concrete offer (of $2 million) for police costs.

29. Rick Hooper, "The Evolution of International Assistance to the Palestinians in the West Bank and Gaza Strip, 1993–96," in Roy, *Economics of Middle East Peace.*

30. COPP, *Palestinian Police Forces—Equipment,* COPP Donor Matrix 11 (16 May 1994).

31. Statement by the Chair of the Coordinating Committee for International Assistance to the Palestinian Police Force, 7 June 1994.

32. Associated Press, 31 July 1994; Major General Arnstein Överkils, *Visit to the Palestinian Police Forces in Gaza, 2–5 June 1994.*

33. Casualties in the November 1994 confrontation were aggravated by inappropriate riot control equipment and poor command and control. In the first case, donors had been reluctant to provide sidearms and nonlethal crowd control agents for legal reasons or because of potential political costs associated with their use. The result was that the PA police were left to control disturbances equipped largely with AK-47 assault rifles. There was also a delay in providing suitable communications equipment on frequencies approved for Palestinian use.

34. Although it should be noted that Holst Fund transfers to the PA had the implicit effect of freeing up PA financial resources for use elsewhere, including the police.

35. UN General Assembly Resolution 49/21B of 1994, "Financing of the Palestinian Police Force"; "Financing of the Palestinian Police Force: Report of the Secretary-General," 6 April 1995, A/49/885.

36. Graham Usher, "The Politics of Internal Security: The PA's New Intelligence Services," *Journal of Palestine Studies* 25, no. 2 (winter 1996); The Israeli-Palestinian Interim Agreement on the West Bank and Gaza Strip, Annex 1, Protocol Concerning Redeployment and Security Arrangements, Article IV.3.a, archived at www.israel-mfa.gov.il/peace/iaannex1.html#article4; Israeli Foreign Ministry, "PA Police Force Is 60% Larger Than Israel's . . . Oslo Permits 24,000 Police at This Stage . . . PA Deployed 40,000," via Israeli Consulate in Los Angeles, www.israelemb.org/la/politics/pa_pl.htm.

37. One analysis of Palestinian security forces identified the following organizations: the Civil Police (10,000) and Civil Defense (hundreds), responsible for ordinary police and emergency matters; the uniformed paramilitary National Security Force (14,000); Preventive Security (5,000); General Intelligence (3,000); Presidential Security (3,000); Naval Police (1,000); Military Intelligence (hundreds); Military Police (hundreds); and the Special Security Force (hundreds). Gal Luft, *The Palestinian Security Services: Between Police and Army,* Police Focus Series no. 36 (Washington, D.C.: Washington Institute for Near East Policy, November 1998).

38. On 23 March 1999, the Palestinian human rights NGO LAW reported that some twenty persons had died from firearms abuse by security officials since the establishment of the PA.

39. "Israel, the Occupied West Bank and Gaza Strip, and Palestinian Authority Territories," *Human Rights Watch World Report 1999* (December 1998), at www.hrw.org/hrw/worldreport99/mideast/israel.html. See also *Palestine Human Rights Monitor* 5 (September–December 1997), at www.lebnet.com/phrmg/issue5/ph05101.htm.

40. *Middle East Newsline,* 14 May 1998.

41. Wye River Memorandum, 23 October 1998, sections II.B.3 and II.A.1.c.

42. Hanny Megally, executive director, Middle East and North Africa Division, Human Rights Watch, letter to donor governments, 25 November 1998.

43. MOPIC, *1998 First Quarterly Monitoring Report of Donors Assistance*, section 2.2.1. The later figures do not, of course, include the value of covert security assistance.

44. World Bank, *Emergency Assistance Program for the Occupied Territories* (Washington, D.C.: World Bank, 1994), 14–15.

45. Comments by World Bank official, November 1998.

46. Balaj, Diwan, and Philippe, "External Assistance to the Palestinians," 6.

47. Secretariat of the AHLC, *Holst Peace Fund: Status of Funding, Future Needs* (13 May 1998); MOPIC, *Quarterly Monitoring Report of Donor Assistance* (various reports).

48. Interview with World Bank official, April 1997.

49. World Bank, *The Donor Experience and the Way Ahead*, statement to the Fifth Consultative Group Meeting for the West Bank and Gaza, 14–15 December 1997; World Bank, *Holst Peace Fund Status Statement,* 21 November 1997.

50. World Bank, *Post-Conflict Reconstruction*, 36, 38.

51. Data drawn from AHLC, *Report on Fiscal Developments* (various); and UNSCO, *Economic and Social Conditions in the West Bank and Gaza* (winter–spring 1997).

52. James Boyce, "Reconstruction and Democratization: The International Financial Institutions and Post-Conflict Transition" (paper presented at the Latin American Studies Association Annual Congress, Chicago, September 1998).

53. This section is based on work first undertaken by Hisham Awartani for Rex Brynen, Hisham Awartani, and Clare Woodcraft, "Donor Assistance in Palestine" (draft paper prepared for the Pledges of Aid: Multilateral Support for Reconstruction and Transition project, Center on International Cooperation, 8–9 May 1998). For further analysis of employment generation (on which this discussion depends heavily), see Samieh Al-Botmeh and Edward Sayre, *Employment Generation Schemes in the West Bank and Gaza Strip* (Jerusalem: MAS, November 1996); and UNSCO, *Emergency Employment Generation Schemes* (August 1996).

54. Secretariat of the AHLC, *The Employment Generation Program in the West Bank and Gaza* (5 September 1996), 1.

55. Al-Botmeh and Sayre, *Employment Generation Schemes in the West Bank and Gaza Strip*, 24.

56. *The World Bank's Response to the Current Economic Crisis: An Interim Strategy* (April 1996).

57. Secretariat of the AHLC, *Employment Generation Program in the West Bank and Gaza*, 1.

58. MOPIC, *1998 First Quarterly Monitoring Report of Donor Assistance.*

59. World Bank, *Developing the Occupied Territories: An Investment in Peace*, vol. 4, *Agriculture* (Washington, D.C.: World Bank, 1993); World Bank, *Emergency Assistance Program for the Occupied Territories.*

60. Zagha and Jamal, *Mortgaging Self-Reliance*, 29–32.

61. *Palestine Report*, 21 August 1997, 22 October 1997; Graham Usher and Tarek Hassan, "More of the Same," *al-Ahram Weekly*, 13–19 August 1998.

62. These points were made repeatedly in interviews with officials of MOPIC, the Ministry of Local Government, the Ministry of Economy and Trade, and others.

63. In particular, the following discussion is informed by a useful study undertaken by two U.K. consultants, Andrew Bird and Stephen Lister (Mokoro Ltd.), *Planning and Aid Management for Palestine*, July 1997.

64. Bird and Lister, *Planning and Aid Management for Palestine*, 71.

65. Ibid., 68.

66. Interview with UNDP official, July 1997.

67. World Bank and UNDP estimates.

68. Conclusions drawn from Sari Hanafi, "Profile of Donor Assistance to Palestinian NGOs: Survey and Database" (prepared for the Welfare Association, January 1999).

69. NGO funding data is based on MOPIC, *1998 First Quarterly Monitoring Report of Donor Assistance.*

70. Interview, August 1998.

71. Text of the Draft Law Concerning Charitable Societies, Social Bodies and Private Institutions, in *Palestine Report* 1, no. 22 (27 October 1995).

72. UNSCO, *Rule of Law Development in the West Bank and Gaza Strip: Survey of the State of the Development Effort* (May 1999).

73. Suzanne Ruggi, "Regulating NGOs in Palestine," *Middle East International,* 21 August 1998.

74. Interview, June 1996.

75. One study of Islamist clinics in Egypt, for example, found no strong impact on the political views of those using the services. Janine Astrid Clark, "Democratization and Social Islam: A Case Study of the Islamic Health Clinics in Cairo," in *Political Liberalization and Democratization in the Arab World,* vol. 1, *Theoretical Perspectives,* ed. Rex Brynen, Bahgat Korany, and Paul Noble (Boulder, Colo.: Lynne Rienner, 1995).

76. Zaucker, *Toward Middle East Peace and Development.*

77. Anis al-Qaq, undersecretary, MOPIC, interview, *Jerusalem Times,* 25 October 1996.

78. "Funding NGOs," *Palestine Economic Pulse* 3, no. 1 (January–February 1998).

79. Interviews with World Bank officials; World Bank, *Palestinian NGO Project,* December 1997.

80. Survey conducted by Hisham Awartani, CPRS, late 1997.

81. Interview with senior USAID official, June 1996.

82. World Bank, *Donor Experience and the Way Ahead.*

83. www.info.usaid.gov/about/y4naid.html, version of 6 September 1997.

84. Discussion with Western foreign ministry official, November 1994.

85. The discussion of Karameh Towers and Gaza European Hospital is based on that written by Clare Woodcraft for Brynen, Awartani, and Woodcraft, "Donor Assistance in Palestine." See also *Sunday Times* (London), 29 November 1998; *Jordan Times,* 2 December 1998; *Palestine Report,* 26 February 1999; *Globe and Mail* (Toronto), 27 February 1999.

86. Interview with World Bank official, September 1998.

87. *Palestine Economic Pulse* 2, no. 1 (January–February 1998): 2–3; *Middle East International,* 2 October 1998.

88. UNSCO, *The Economy of the West Bank and Gaza Strip* (January 1999), 16.

89. MOPIC, *Macroeconomic Framework for Development Planning* (February 1999).

90. CPRS, *Public Opinion Poll no. 39.*

7. CONCLUSION

1. Text of statements by President Bill Clinton and Secretary of State Madeleine Albright, Conference to Support Peace and Development in the Middle East, Washington, D.C., 30 November 1998, via U.S. Information Agency at www.usia.gov/regional/nea/summit/donconf.htm. Arabic version of Arafat's statement reprinted in *al-Hayah al-Jadidah* (Internet version), 1 December 1998.

2. DAC, *DAC Guidelines on Conflict, Peace, and Development Cooperation;* World Bank, *Post-Conflict Reconstruction;* United Nations Research Institute on Social Development (UNRISD), *Rebuilding after War: A Summary Report of the War-Torn Societies Project, Improving External Assistance to War-Torn Societies: The Bossey Statement,* and *Practical Recommendations for Managers of Multilateral and Bilateral Aid Agencies* (Geneva: UNRISD, 1998). On the obstacles to institutional learning, see Larry Minear, "Learning to Learn" (discussion paper prepared for a seminar on lessons learned in humanitarian coordination, Office for the Coordination of Humanitarian Affairs [OCHA] and the Ministry of Foreign Affairs of Sweden, Stockholm, 3–4 April 1998).

3. On the role of the media, see Larry Minear, Colin Scott, and Thomas G. Weiss, *The News Media, Civil War, and Humanitarian Action* (Boulder, Colo.: Lynne Rienner, 1996), 68–74. On donor conferences, see the reports prepared by Michael Bratton and Chris Lansberg (South Africa) and by Susan Woodward, Zlatko Hurtic, and Amela Sapcanin (Bosnia) for the Pledges of Aid project, Center on International Cooperation, New York University, November 1998.

4. Personal communication with Western foreign ministry official, November 1998; personal communication with MOPIC official, December 1998.

5. *Middle East International,* 14 November 1998, 14.

6. The dinner party was held in February 1998.

7. Personal communication, MOPIC official, December 1998.

8. Nigel Roberts, "The Prospects for the Palestinian Economy" (paper presented to the conference, Resolving the Palestinian Refugee Problem: What Role for the International Donor Community? University of Warwick, United Kingdom, 23–24 March 1998).

9. The use of the term "mosaic" here borrows from the work of UNSCO.

10. World Bank, *West Bank and Gaza Update* (third quarter 1998), 2.

11. UNSCO, *Rule of Law Development in the West Bank and Gaza Strip.*

12. Council on Foreign Relations, *Strengthening Palestinian Public Institutions* (June 1999). Yezid Sayigh and Khalil Shikaki were the principal authors of the report; former French prime minister Michel Rocard was chairman of the task force; and Henry Siegman of the Council on Foreign Relations was project director. The full text of the report can be found at www.foreignrelations.org/public/pubs/palinst-full.html.

13. Boyce, "Reconstruction and Democratization."

14. The Council on Foreign Relations report, while recognizing the importance of the donor role, said little about donor responsibilities in this area. This led one task force member, Lee Hamilton, to append to the report his view that "the report should have included some of the essential next steps of implementation that the Palestinians' international friends and regional colleagues can help facilitate. The value of the report will be greatly enhanced if the international community is able to find the basis for a coherent and coordinated plan to help the Palestinians help themselves."

15. The discussion in this section is based on analysis of more than three dozen polls conducted by the CPRS during 1994–98, archived at www.cprs-palestine.org/polls/index.html.

16. Analysis based on CPRS, *Public Opinion Poll no. 39*.

17. CPRS, *Public Opinion Survey no. 36* (8–11 October 1998), at www.cprs-palestine.org/polls/98/poll36b.html.

18. August survey, Peace Index Project, Tami Steinmetz Center for Peace Research, Tel Aviv University, via *IMRA* (Independent Media Review and Analysis) listserv, 2 September 1998.

19. *Middle East International* (13 November 1998), 14.

20. *New York Times*, 27 April 1999 (Internet edition).

21. Text at europa.eu.int/council/off/conclu/mar99_en.htm#ME.

22. World Bank, *Aid Effectiveness in the West Bank and Gaza,* Ad-Hoc Liaison Committee (15 October 1999), fig. 1.

23. Ibid., fig. 4.

24. Mary B. Anderson, *Do No Harm: Supporting Local Capacities for Peace through Aid* (Cambridge, Mass.: Local Capacities for Peace Project, 1996).

25. John Stackhouse, "How Palestine Became a Foreign-Aid Sinkhole," *Globe and Mail* (Toronto), 27 February 1999.

26. Michael Kelly, "Investing in Arafat," *Washington Post*, 2 December 1998, A29.

Index

Page numbers in italic refer to tables, figures, and boxes.

269

Protocol on Economic Relations. *See*
Paris Protocol
Protocol on Further Transfer of Powers
and Responsibilities, 57
"Protocol Regarding the Establishment
and Operation of the Interna-
tional Airport in the Gaza Strip
During the Interim Period," 70
Public investment, levels of in occupied
territories, 41–42
Public Monitoring Department
(PMD), 140, 142, 145–146
Public Sector Development Progress
Committee, 143
Putting Peace to Work, 101

Qaddumi, Faruq, 133–134
Qaqilya, redeployment of troops
from, 60
Qurai`, Ahmad, 134, 135

Rabin, Yitzhak, 3, 4, 62
Rabinovich, Itamar, 261
Ramallah
Canadian aid office in, 198
land prices in, 117
redeployment of troops from, 60
Rashid, Mohammad, 143
Reagan administration, diplomatic
dialogue with South Africa, 25
Reconstruction
aid coordination in, 11–13
donor financial support for, 11, 206
economic, 220
World Bank involvement in, 14, *15*
See also Peacebuilding
Red Cross, International Committee
of, 81
REDWG. *See* Regional Economic
Development Working Group
(REDWG)
Refugee Working Group (RWG),
54, 198

Refugees, 3
Regime consolidation, aid and,
144–146
Regional Economic Development
Working Group (REDWG),
54, 77, 91, 92
Relief. *See* Humanitarian relief
Roberts, Nigel, 192
Robinson, Glenn, 31
Ross, Denis, 252
Roy, Sara, 49
*Rule of Law Development in the West
Bank and Gaza Strip,* 189,
222–223
Russia
aid implementation in West Bank
and Gaza, *150*
as chair of Madrid conference, 54,
73, 210
as member of AHLC, 92
as member of COPP, 87
Rwanda
per capita aid receipts, *79*
reconstruction financing in, 11, 78

Saba, Joseph, 96
Safieh, Yusef Abu, *137*
Salam, Khalid, 143
Saleh, Abd al-Jawad, *138*
Samaria, Israeli settlements in, 68
Saudi Arabia
donor assistance to Palestine, 83,
84, 85, *150,* 191
as member of AHLC, 92
Save the Children Federation, 182, 183
Sayigh, Yezid, 267
Sayigh, Yusif, 77–78
Sectoral Working Groups (SWGs),
88, 89–90, 105, 106, 174,
176–177, 183, 198
Security arrangements
institutional cooperation on, 177,
178

Rex Brynen is associate professor of political science at McGill University. He currently serves as research coordinator of the Interuniversity Consortium for Arab Studies (Montreal) and as president of the Canadian branch of the Middle East Studies Association (CANMES). His books include *Sanctuary and Survival: The PLO in Lebanon* (1990); *Echoes of the Intifada* (edited, 1991); *The Many Faces of National Security in the Arab World* (coedited, 1993); and the two-volume *Political Liberalization and Democratization in the Arab World* (coedited, 1995, 1998).

In 1994–95, Brynen served as a member of the Political and Security Policy Staff of the Canadian Department of Foreign Affairs and International Trade. He has also been a consultant to the Canadian International Development Agency, the International Development Research Centre, the Office of the United Nations Special Coordinator in the Occupied Territories (UNSCO), and the World Bank. He is the coordinator of *Palestinian Refugee ResearchNet* (www.prrn. org).

United States Institute of Peace

The United States Institute of Peace is an independent, nonpartisan federal institution created by Congress to promote research, education, and training on the peaceful management and resolution of international conflicts. Established in 1984, the Institute meets its congressional mandate through an array of programs, including research grants, fellowships, professional training, education programs from high school through graduate school, conferences and workshops, library services, and publications. The Institute's Board of Directors is appointed by the President of the United States and confirmed by the Senate.

A Very Political Economy

This book is set in Adobe Caslon; the display typefaces are Adobe Caslon semibold and bold. Hasten Design Studio designed the book's cover (the photograph was taken by Rex Brynen), and Mike Chase designed the interior. Pages were made up by Helene Y. Redmond. David Sweet copyedited the text, which was proofread by Karen Stough. The index was prepared by Sonsie Conroy. The book's editor was Nigel Quinney.